ENFORCEMENT AT THE EPA

ENFORCEMENT AT THE EPA
High Stakes and Hard Choices

by Joel A. Mintz

 University of Texas Press, Austin

Portions of Chapters 1, 3, 4, and 5 were originally published in
somewhat different form in Joel Mintz, "Agencies, Congress and
Regulatory Enforcement: A Review of EPA's Hazardous Waste
Enforcement Effort, 1970–1987," *Environmental Law*, 18, no.683
(1988).

∞The paper used in this publication meets the minimum
requirements of American National Standard for Information
Sciences—Permanence of Paper for Printed Library Materials,
ANSI Z39.48-1984.

Library of Congress Cataloging-in-Publication Data

Mintz, Joel A., 1949–
    Enforcement at the EPA : high stakes and hard choices / by
Joel A. Mintz.
        p.   cm.
    Includes bibliographical references (p.   ) and index.
    ISBN 0-292-75187-7 (cloth : alk. paper)
    1. Environmental policy—United States.   2. United States.
Environmental Protection Agency.   I. Title
    GE180.M56   1996
    363.7'56'0973—dc20   95-13922

*This book is dedicated to
my spouse, Meri-Jane Rochelson,
and to the memory of my
friend Doug Farnsworth.*

Contents

Acknowledgments

While researching and drafting this book I amassed an enormous volume of debt. It is a great pleasure to discharge it here.

The 116 professionals who graciously participated in my study gave generously of their time and knowledge (their names are listed, along with other information, in Appendix A). I remain immensely grateful for their candor and wisdom.

Particular thanks are due to Meri-Jane Rochelson, Jim McDonald, Mike Smith, Rich Smith, and Shannon Davies and to Professors John Anderson, Frank Grad, Arthur Murphy, and Subha Narasimhan for reading my manuscript (in one version or another) and advancing valuable suggestions. I owe special thanks as well to five of those I interviewed, Ed Reich, Jonathan Cannon, Tom Gallagher, David Buente, and Dave Ullrich, who spent especially long periods with me sharing their keen insights.

I am thankful for the faculty research grants and reduced teaching schedules provided by Nova-Southeastern University Law Center and for the encouragement and support given by my colleagues on its faculty. I also benefited greatly from the first-rate typing and clerical work of Pat Crossman and the skillful research and proofreading of Doris Raskin, Joe Fried, and Scott Alexander.

This project was improved immensely by the highly professional work of the editorial staff of the University of Texas Press, with whom it has been a pleasure to work. I also wish to mention that some portions of Chapters 1, 3, 4, and 5 were published initially, in somewhat different form, in Mintz, *Agencies, Congress and Regulatory Enforcement, 1970–1987,* 18 *Environmental Law* 683 (1988). The consent of the editors of that journal to the republication of that piece in this volume is acknowledged with my thanks.

Finally, my deepest debt is to my family. Their boundless love and support, at all times and in every way, was absolutely crucial to the completion of this book.

Fort Lauderdale, Florida
June 1994

ENFORCEMENT AT THE EPA

ONE

Introduction

Over the past twenty-five years, federal regulation of pollution has assumed ever-greater importance in the political economy of the United States. By 1990, as hundreds of thousands of entities that are sources of environmental discharge attempted to comply with an increasingly complex regime of governmental requirements, the nation had spent well over $700 billion on environmental cleanup efforts.[1] The same year the U.S. General Accounting Office (GAO) estimated that Americans were spending $86 billion per year, approximately 2 percent of our gross national product, on pollution control and regulation.[2]

A critical actor in this ongoing cleanup effort is the U.S. Environmental Protection Agency (EPA), the governmental body charged by Congress with immense responsibility for implementing more than fourteen statutes respecting environmental quality and the public health.[3] From modest beginnings during the Nixon administration,[4] EPA's workload has increased dramatically to encompass such diverse and complex environmental issues as hazardous waste management, asbestos in schools, acid rain, and the quality of drinking water. Public support for accomplishment of the agency's challenging mission has remained strong, widespread, and consistent.[5]

This book examines a difficult and often neglected part of EPA's responsibilities: the enforcement of federal environmental standards established by Congress in detailed legislation and by the agency itself in regulations that conform with congressional mandates. The book is at once a chronicle of EPA's enforcement history from the agency's beginnings through the Bush administration and an analysis of some important questions regarding EPA's institutional performance and environment that are suggested by more generalized writings on regulatory enforcement, congressional oversight, and EPA implementation of environmental laws.

The practical and theoretical significance of EPA's institutional environment—and of its enforcement activities and structures—has been recognized by scholars, congressional leaders, and executive branch officials alike. As Christopher H. Schroeder has observed,

> When environmental policy moves from legislation to implementation, it enters a complex institutional environment, one shaped by internal and external incentives and pressures. Without a sufficient appreciation of EPA's institutional environment, substantive environmental policy decisions can be deflected, stalled or altered in unintended ways.[6]

Environmental enforcement is clearly a crucial component of EPA's implementation work. Enforcement and compliance monitoring efforts now represent approximately 25 percent of the agency's total budget,[7] and they engage the efforts of approximately 3,200 full-time employees.[8] Furthermore, as Peter Yeager has noted,

> To the public mind, enforcement is the centerpiece of regulation, the visible hand of the state reaching into society to correct wrongs. . . . Both symbolically and practically, enforcement is a capstone, a final indicator of the state's seriousness of purpose and a key determinant of the barrier between compliance and lawlessness.[9]

Enforcement is critical both as a control on firms and individuals who violate environmental standards and as a defense of the legitimacy of the governmental intervention that sustains voluntary compliance.[10] Without it, in the words of Senator Joseph Lieberman, "most of the rest of environmental protection lacks meaning, lacks truth, lacks reality."[11]

The enforcement aspects of EPA's work considered here include the agency's historical evolution, its institutional setting, and its current strengths and shortcomings. In the remainder of this first chapter, I identify a set of questions suggested by the recent writings of other scholars, although not directly examined in them. These questions form the major focus of this study. I also discuss the methodology I used.

Chapter 2 describes the enforcement process at EPA, both generally—in the implementation of such federal statutes as the Clean Air Act, the Clean Water Act, and the Resource Conservation and Recovery Act (commonly known as RCRA)—and as a critical component of a program that has received considerable attention from the Congress, the press, and environmental organizations: the Comprehensive Environmental Response, Compensation and Liability Act (commonly known as CERCLA or Superfund). The description incorporates the insights of students of EPA's programs whose consideration of the agency's enforcement efforts is incidental to the main thrust of their work, in addition to the pertinent observations of those whose work focuses on regulatory enforcement. To create a more detailed portrait of EPA enforcement, these analyses are supplemented by interviews with numerous EPA enforcement officials and my own professional experiences with the agency.

Chapters 3 through 6 recount the institutional history of EPA's enforcement programs. Chapter 3 deals with the agency's initial attempts at enforcement in the early 1970s, as well as the "major source enforcement effort" that was a feature of the Carter administration. Chapter 4 considers the upheavals that beset EPA's enforcement work during the tenure of Anne Gorsuch as EPA administrator at the beginning of the 1980s and the powerful congressional reaction that led to her ouster from the agency. Chapter 5 focuses on EPA's attempts to restart its enforcement programs in the face of persistent criticisms from Capitol Hill during the balance of the Reagan administration. Chapter 6 reviews the key trends in EPA enforcement during the Bush administration.

In Chapter 7 I assess the larger implications of EPA's enforcement performance by addressing salient unanswered questions—identified briefly in this chapter—in light of the agency's contentious enforcement history. I also consider how two aspects of Congress's structure and relationship with EPA—its control of the agency's budget and the decentralization of its oversight activities—have affected EPA's enforcement performance.

Finally, Chapter 8 focuses on two difficult but nonetheless important issues for EPA's enforcement programs: how should "enforcement success" be measured, and what can be done by Congress, environmental organizations, and the agency itself to shore up the weaknesses and inefficiencies that continue to plague the agency's enforcement activities?

Because, as we shall see, EPA's administration of the Superfund Program has been at the vortex of a series of important disputes between the upper echelons of EPA's management and interested members of Congress, the agency's enforcement of RCRA and CERCLA liability standards receives considerable emphasis in this book. That component of EPA's enforcement work is not my sole focus, however, and this study also considers the agency's attempts to enforce the other major regulatory statutes that govern it.

No works of American academics to date have focused primarily on EPA's implementation of its enforcement responsibilities. Studies of regulatory enforcement in the United States and of congressional oversight of regulatory agencies tend to be general in nature, with little or no specific references to EPA. Examinations of EPA—including those that consider its strained relationships with congressional oversight bodies—generally consider the agency's enforcement work only indirectly, or as one small component of a more broad and generalized analysis. A close reading of the pertinent literature suggests several as yet unaddressed questions which careful examination of EPA's enforcement activities can help to resolve.

The first of these questions concerns the style and nature of EPA's enforcement programs as they have evolved to date. Is EPA's enforcement process a "compliance system," in which agency personnel eschew legalistic enforcement tools in favor of a more informal system of bargaining and bluffing, or is EPA enforcement a "deterrence system," in which emphasis is placed on formal legal processes in the hope of punishing wrongdoers and deterring future noncompliance? The answer to this inquiry has implications for the agency's relationship with industrial corporations subject to its regulations, as well as its relationships with Congress, environmental organizations, and other divisions of the executive branch. It may also serve as a basis for comparing the enforcement work of EPA with that of other federal agencies as well as the regulatory activities of state and local governments.

If, as I conclude, EPA's enforcement activities are primarily a deterrence system, a related question arises: is a deterrence system generally appropriate as the basis for EPA's enforcement work? I consider this question as part of an evaluation of the broader implications of EPA's enforcement record.

Another set of inquiries concerns oversight of the agency's enforcement performance by congressional committees, as well as such legislative branch investigators as the GAO and the Office of Technology Assessment (OTA). Has congressional oversight had a significant impact on the nature and direction of EPA's enforcement work? Have congressional overseers contributed to what one observer describes as "regulatory failure" in the enforcement aspects of EPA's implementation of federal environmental laws? Or (as another scholar suggests we should generally expect in such congressional investigations) has Congress's oversight of EPA enforcement "improved policy at the margins"? To what extent have other aspects of Congress's organizational structure and relationship with EPA, including its decentralized subcommittee system and its control of the agency's budget, affected the agency in its enforcement work?

Finally, systematic review of EPA's enforcement activities has raised two other issues that deserve examination. The first of these is a question that EPA's enforcement officials and congressional overseers have debated without resolving: how should the "successfulness" of EPA's enforcement efforts be measured? Second, however enforcement success is defined, are there any changes of approach—by Congress, interested members of the public, or EPA itself—which can materially improve the agency's enforcement work?

Analysis of these issues, in light of the history and development of EPA's enforcement programs, is the central task of this book.

The research for this study included a review of the body of academic literature (a portion of which is adverted to in the second section of this chapter and described in Chapter 7) that directly or peripherally concerns EPA enforcement and its oversight by Congress. In addition, in preparing this book I reviewed EPA enforcement policy documents prepared at the agency between 1971 and 1991, as well as a variety of other EPA files, reports, and records on enforcement activities. I also examined congressional hearing records, newspapers, trade journals, training course materials, and the reports of relevant case studies by congressional committees and subcommittees, industrial associations, private consultants, environmental organizations, nonprofit foundations, the GAO, the Congressional Budget Office, and the OTA.

During the summer of 1984 and much of 1986, as well as the winter of 1991 and the spring of 1992, I interviewed 116 present and former government officials (from EPA, the U.S. Department of Justice [the Justice Department or DOJ], the GAO, and the professional staffs of several congressional committees and subcommittees) to obtain their recollections of the critical trends, developments, and events in EPA enforcement programs.[12] I questioned these same individuals with respect to the various sets of intra-, inter-, and extragovernmental relationships that exist in the federal enforcement field, the management and working milieu of EPA enforcement programs, and their own notions of the ingredients of an effective environmental enforcement effort. I selected the interviewees on the basis of the breadth of their experience in the federal government and the likelihood that they would have been involved in or knowledgeable about EPA hazardous waste enforcement. I sought interviews with present and former officials who had diverse professional backgrounds and perspectives. For the most part, respondents held top or midlevel managerial positions with EPA or were attorneys or scientists and technical experts on the agency's enforcement staff.

Because of the importance of EPA's regional offices in implementing the agency's enforcement program, I conducted interviews with present and former officials in EPA Regions I (Boston), III (Philadelphia), IV (Atlanta), and V (Chicago), as well as in the agency's National Enforcement Investigations Center (NEIC) in Denver, Colorado, and its headquarters office in Washington, D.C. I also held interviews with upper and midlevel managers in the Justice Department's Washington, D.C., headquarters and with counsel to several of the congressional committees and subcommittees responsible for oversight of EPA enforcement activities.

Regardless of their past or present institutional affiliations, I asked respondents a standard set of questions, which was furnished to them in advance whenever possible, along with a brief description of the purposes for and methods in the study.[13] I asked most respondents all of the questions. In a few isolated instances, the respondent completed only portions of the standard interview, due to limitations of time or circumstances or because the interviewee's pertinent views had elsewhere been made part of the public record. I did not omit any items from the standard set of questions—in any interview—because of the actual (or perceived) political preferences of the interviewee.

To avoid losing the complexity of the respondents' perceptions and attitudes, I posed open-ended questions. In addition to the questions included in the standard interview format, I frequently asked spontaneous follow-up questions.

In seven instances, respondents specifically requested that the substance of their interview be off the record in the sense that their remarks not be attributed to them. In a few other conversations, interviewees asked that brief segments of their remarks be afforded similar treatment. These requests have been respected. In all of the other interviews, the respondents raised no objections to being identified as the sources of their remarks.

One methodological issue which arose in the course of my research concerned the relative weight to be given the results of my interviews with present and former government officials, as compared with primary documents written during the period of this study. Although such documents (e.g., EPA enforcement policies and official correspondence) are referred to and occasionally quoted from at pertinent points, I have on balance tended to place more emphasis on the comments gathered from participants in (or governmental observers of) EPA's enforcement efforts. Where these comments contradict one another or contemporary written documents I have noted that fact.

Emphasis on the results of oral interviews stems, in part, from impressions formed during my own professional work with EPA. In particular, I learned firsthand that a great many documents on enforcement policies guidance, and other matters generated by the managers at the agency's headquarters, are drafted with the overriding goal of winning the political support of one or more constituencies. Such constituencies may include other officials within the executive branch, congressional committees and their staffs, environmental organizations, regulated industries, and state and local government officials. Although such primary EPA documents are not devoid of historical significance, relying on them too heavily would be analogous to making judgments about the efforts and products of a private enterprise based solely on its public advertising. In contrast, I believe, the interviews I conducted provide a less distorted picture of the most significant trends, developments, and events in EPA's enforcement history. The results are more in keeping with my goal of presenting the "warp and woof" of the enforcement facet of EPA's work, as well as its relationship with Congress.

Finally, a few words are in order about my own career with EPA. For approximately six years, from July 1975 to June 1981, I held several positions with EPA in its Region V and headquarters offices. I was a staff attorney in the EPA Region V air enforcement program in 1975 and 1976 and a chief attorney in the Region V water enforcement program during 1977 and 1978. In 1979 I served on the staff of the Region V regional administrator as state relations coordinator and policy advisor. I then transferred to EPA's Washington, D.C., headquarters where, in 1980 and early 1981, I participated in enforcement litigation as a senior staff attorney on the agency's Hazardous Waste Enforcement Task Force (HWETF).

I was not employed by EPA during most of the period that is the primary focus of this book. Thus, I was generally not, in any meaningful sense, a "participant observer" of the historical events that this study recounts. The major exception to that is what I have referred to as the "Task Force Phase," the 1979–80 period during which EPA initiated its hazardous waste enforcement work. With respect to that era, I have attempted not to incorporate my personal perceptions unless they were confirmed by several others who were directly involved. I have also attempted to overcome any biases, limitations, and a priori assumptions stemming from my involvement as an EPA attorney by obtaining and closely considering the views of EPA enforcement technical people, regional enforcement attorneys, DOJ managers, and congressional staff counsel with respect to both the periods of my service with the government and my impressions of the general nature of EPA's enforcement process.

Notwithstanding the self-imposed limitations and constraints outlined above, my own EPA enforcement experience was relevant to the preparation of this study. In addition to shaping my perceptions of the functions and historical significance of EPA enforcement policies and records, my background enabled me to prepare a preliminary list of people to interview, a list which changed and grew considerably as my research progressed. Furthermore, I used my EPA experience to frame the standard interview format and provide some working hypotheses about the development and nature of EPA enforcement activities. I altered these hypotheses considerably during the course of my research. I substantially modified my conclusions regarding several matters as I synthesized the differing perceptions of others and the voluminous information in EPA's files.

I have been engaged, challenged, and fascinated by the enforcement activities of EPA for nearly twenty years. This book is an attempt to share what I have learned and to suggest, with respect, some ways in which those who do enforcement work at EPA—and those who oversee, support, and critique that work—might better foster its success.

TWO

"Where the Rubber Hits the Road and Everything Else Hits the Fan"

A Brief Description of EPA's Enforcement Process and the Superfund Program

Enforcement occupies a central place in the administration of regulatory requirements. This is particularly so with regard to federal environmental laws. Laborious, technical, time-consuming, and suffused with tensions, the enforcement process of the U.S. Environmental Protection Agency is, in the words of one skillful, experienced participant, "where the rubber hits the road and everything else hits the fan."[1]

For more than a century, following enactment of the Interstate Commerce Act of 1887, federal administrative regulation of economic activities has become an established fact of American life. In a variety of substantive areas (from aviation to securities to labor relations) Congress has culminated prolonged struggles for reform with the passage of broad legislation aimed at redressing significant public problems. Frequently, however, that culmination is more apparent than real. As students of federal regulation have noted, the first statutes which emerge from agitation for regulatory legislation are often imprecise compromises between social forces that favor regulation and powerful interests that oppose it.[2]

Because regulatory legislation is generally broadly drafted, considerable discretion is often vested in federal administrative agencies. Those agencies are often charged with important responsibilities of establishing specific rules consistent with the general policies and purposes of the regulatory statutes themselves and enforcing those specific rules in administrative and judicial proceedings. According to one knowledgeable observer, "They are like armies of occupation, left in the field to police the rule won by the victorious coalition."[3]

From the perspective of some regulated industries, the enforcement of federal environmental laws represents another, perhaps final, opportunity to effectuate their longstanding policy preferences and views. Part of the reason for this is the sometimes indeterminate nature of environmental regulations. As Marc K. Landy and his co-authors have discovered,

> [R]egulations only reveal their true meaning through the enforcement process. The inevitably ambiguous language of the rules is defined only as decisions are made about what constitutes a violation in specific cases. In that process, arcane technical specifications that spell out what [pollution control] devices are to be installed and how their operation is to be measured often have specific public policy implications. Given the variety of processes and settings that must be dealt with, even rules written in meticulous detail will not eliminate the need for case by case enforcement.[4]

In view of this, firms who are subject to EPA enforcement actions will often attempt to persuade the agency to adopt case-specific interpretations of enforceable EPA regulations that are consistent with their own perceived needs, aims, and regulatory philosophies. At the same time, the enforcement process represents a continuing test of the effectiveness and vitality of the nation's environmental laws. Its outcome determines whether the lofty aims and purposes of federal environmental statutes will ultimately be realized and the public's interest served. In the insightful words of Marver Bernstein,

> The attitude of [an administrative agency] toward its enforcement responsibilities affects its entire regulatory program. Unless it demonstrates a capacity to enforce its regulations, they will be more honored in the breach than in the observance. Those who discover that violations go undetected and unpunished will have little respect for the [agency] and will violate regulations with impunity if it is to their financial or commercial advantage.[5]

In a general sense, the enforcement activities of regulatory agencies can be seen as a sequential series of filtering operations. As Colin Diver has characterized it,

> The initial task is to identify . . . that set of activities involving an apparent violation of the underlying regulatory command. From this set of apparent violations, the enforcement agency must select those appropriate to serve as the basis for a demand for remedial action. The agency further distills this sub-set into a group of offenses warranting the imposition of punitive sanctions.[6]

At EPA, enforcement cases typically go through three phases: inspection and information gathering, administrative case development, and (if the matter has not yet been resolved) formal litigation. In noncriminal cases, the agency has several primary sources of compliance information: self-monitoring, record keeping and reporting by individual sources of pollution, inspections by government personnel, and the specific complaints of concerned citizens.

Most EPA inspections are announced to the pollution source ahead of time to ensure the presence of vital plant personnel. Inspections may be either "for cause," that is, based on a reasonable suspicion that the inspected source is in violation, or else routinely conducted pursuant to a "neutral inspection scheme." Perhaps surprisingly, of the approximately 1,600 individuals who perform EPA inspections, more than 75 percent do so less than 20 percent of the time.[7]

When the agency conducts an investigation on the basis of citizen information, that information may have come from a variety of individuals. Citizen informants often include, for example, disgruntled employees of suspected violators, neighbors, state or local inspectors, environmental citizens organizations, and suspected violators' economic competitors. In potential criminal matters, these sources of information may be replaced—or supplemented—by targeted inspections, conducted under color of search warrant, by EPA criminal investigators and/or special agents of the Federal Bureau of Investigation (FBI), as well as by grand jury proceedings under the auspices of the DOJ.

Once EPA (and/or DOJ) investigators have completed their information gathering, they must determine whether the source in question is in violation of applicable standards and, if so, what type of enforcement response the agency will make. Under most of the relevant federal environmental statutes, EPA has a range of options available to it. It may begin enforcement by issuing a notice of violation to the allegedly violating source, describing the violation and inviting the source to confer informally with agency enforcement personnel.[8] Alternatively, EPA may issue the source an administrative order requiring compliance with applicable requirements and, in some cases, an assessed civil penalty. In addition, EPA is generally authorized to refer enforcement matters to the DOJ for civil action or criminal prosecution. If it deems the circumstances appropriate, the agency may defer to a planned or ongoing enforcement action by state or local environmental officials.

EPA decisions as to which of these various enforcement options to pursue are generally made at the regional level by technically trained personnel working in cooperation with enforcement attorneys. These determinations frequently take account of a number of factors. Regional officials typically consider, among other things, the degree to which the source's discharge or emission exceeds applicable legal requirements, the duration of the violation, the number of previous enforcement actions that have been taken successfully against the same source, any relevant national EPA enforcement policies, the potential deterrence value of the case, the resources available to the agency and DOJ at the time of the decision, EPA's working relationship with interested state and local officials, and the agency's estimation of the enforcement capability of those same officials.[9] These calculations, which are usually made with little public knowledge or participation, have great administrative significance. As Colin Diver has written,

> Persons making these decisions—prosecutors, in the broad sense—occupy a very significant gatekeeping position in the regulatory process. Not only must they ration their own scarce resources of time and energy among competing caseload demands, but they must also ration access to other institutions involved in the adjudication of violations.[10]

One final factor is also of immense importance in the regulatory enforcement work of EPA and other administrative agencies: the clarity and legal enforceability of the written standards and regulations which provide the underpinning for all enforcement actions. Marver Bernstein and other observers have noted that in order to be enforceable, regulations must be understood by persons and firms subject to them. Such standards must set forth clearly what the individual or firm must do in order to comply.[11] This conclusion has particular application to the voluminous set of requirements enforced by EPA, requirements designed to govern the conduct of hundreds of thousands of individuals, firms, and government entities. Regrettably, however, the performance of agency regulation writers has not always been adequate. In a number of instances, imprecise and/or incomprehensible regulatory drafting has precluded the successful initiation and completion of EPA enforcement activity.[12]

In his provocative study of EPA implementation of the Clean Water Act, Peter Yeager has observed: "The [EPA] enforcement process is a deeply textured one. At subsurface levels, it is an uncertain mix of professional ambitions of (usually young) litigators, bureaucratic politics and changing priorities, and virtually constant negotiations with a host of recalcitrants."[13] This complex process creates a number of inherent and all but intractable constraints for the agency's cadre of top and midlevel managers.

At the regional office level, enforcement duties are generally divided among senior career civil servants who head divisions that have responsibility for regulatory matters in one specific environmental medium (air, water, hazardous waste, etc.) as well as regional counsel. These officials report to more than one superior. On the one hand, they are all supervised by relatively autonomous regional administrators, senior officials whose appointments and outlooks are often heavily influenced by state governors and environmental officials. On the other hand, these same regional counsel and division directors are accountable to particular assistant administrators in EPA's headquarters who are appointed to their positions and subsequently confirmed by the U.S. Senate, with different kinds of political support. In view of their divergent power bases, it is not unusual for regional administrators and assistant administrators to disagree on particular matters of enforcement policy. When this occurs, regional division directors and regional counsel are often placed in an uncomfortable and difficult situation for reasons that are self-apparent.

These internal EPA conflicts are not the only constraints that regional managers must face as they carry out enforcement responsibilities. The same officials must maintain effective working relationships with managers and supervisors at the DOJ, an institution which, as we have seen, has primary responsibility for litigation of civil and criminal enforcement matters referred to it by EPA.[14] They must also work cooperatively with state and local agency officials to encourage state and local enforcement actions consistent with agency policies and preferences. At the same time, they must initiate supplementary federal enforcement proceedings when a state or local government has taken an action that the agency deems grossly inadequate.

EPA headquarters executives face a separate set of managerial constraints. Since most EPA enforcement activity is carried out by regional office personnel, the agency's headquarters enforcement officials require the cooperation of regional managers (including regional administrators, regional counsel, and division directors) whose approaches to enforcement may conflict with the preferences of headquarters managers. In addition, headquarters executives must communicate effectively with their counterparts at the DOJ. Moreover, they must be responsive to the demands and criticisms of two frequently opposing institutions: members of Congress (and the staffs of congressional oversight and appropriations committees) and executive branch entities, such as the White House Office of Management and Budget (OMB).

All EPA enforcement managers, whether they sit in headquarters or a regional office, have a multitude of other responsibilities and concerns as well, ranging from hiring, training, overseeing, evaluating, and retaining their staffs to preparing and justifying budget requests, relating to other managers at a peer level, responding to inquiries from investigative entities (such as the EPA Office of Inspector General and the GAO), and keeping abreast of the frequent changes in law, science, and policy that may have an impact on their enforcement work.

Finally, all EPA executives and managers with enforcement responsibilities face one additional constraint: the enforcement process itself is intrinsically and unavoidably difficult to supervise. As Marc K. Landy and his co-authors have observed,

> Because it involves such substantial discretion at the operational level, enforcement is notoriously hard to manage. . . . The great detail involved makes it difficult for bureaucratic superiors, even those with technical training, to know whether the requirements their staff proposes are adequate (or necessary) to meet cleanup objectives. It is equally difficult for them, as supervisors of an ongoing relationship, to know whether initiating coercive measures is defensible or wise. In addition, if enforcement decisions are to be technically appropriate and survive judicial review, engineers and lawyers must work together in their formulation. This creates immediate problems in managing the necessary integration.[15]

In view of these various circumstances and constraints, EPA's enforcement managers face immense challenges. Under conflicting pressures, they must work effectively with a wide range of individuals to accomplish their missions in a timely, defensible way. Given their heavy workloads and the case-by-case nature of enforcement work, they must often rely extensively on the judgment, dedication, and skill of their professional staffs.

At EPA, as at many regulatory agencies and departments, enforcement work involves considerable bargaining. In most instances, bargaining serves the interests and goals of both the agency itself and the regulated enterprises that are subject to enforcement action. From EPA's point of view, the time and energy of its enforcement staff is limited. To accomplish its objectives, it is usually to the agency's advantage to resolve acceptably as many enforcement matters as possible, without resorting to expensive and resource-intensive litigation. Another consideration for agency officials is the bureaucratic wish to retain control over decisions within one's area of responsibility. When compromise is not possible and EPA refers a matter to the DOJ for litigation, some of that control is inevitably relinquished to judges and DOJ attorneys and managers.

From the regulated enterprise's perspective, negotiation and compromise are equally useful. Vicki Masterman, an attorney who represents many private companies in EPA enforcement matters, explains:

> It's an unusual set of circumstances that need to be in place for a company to decide that it makes sense to litigate fully in defense of an [EPA] enforcement action. Even if you think you have a good case, even if you think the equities are in your favor, sometimes you just can't afford the team of lawyers and the years it would take to litigate, especially given the [other] implications it has for your business. Your lenders might require that some additional financial facilities be created to anticipate a loss in litigation. Your SEC [Securities and Exchange Commission] reporting might need to be changed. . . . And that's not to even mention the cloud that hangs over your [manufacturing production] processes if you think you're going to have to change one of [them] entirely.[16]

Although a number of EPA enforcement cases implicate minor, routine violations that are amenable to prompt resolution, in other matters the enforcement process is laborious and time consuming.[17] For all concerned, these more complex cases involve high stakes and hard choices.

For regulated enterprises, the risks of enforcement sanctions—including the possibility of monetary penalties, mandatory pollution control measures that may be expensive to install and maintain, and even, in some criminal cases, jail time for responsible corporate officials—are very great. As Vicki Masterman has observed, "Enforcement [by EPA] is a very real problem for industry. Threats of imprisonment and high penalties strike the deepest chords of fear in corporate environmental managers. . . . From industry's perspective enforcement is key."[18]

Beyond avoiding or minimizing sanctions, regulated industries have an interest in dispelling uncertainties about their future environmental responsibilities and the costs those responsibilities will entail. In many cases, they are also concerned with preserving (or repairing) their public image as responsible corporate citizens and in reassuring lenders, shareholders, and potential investors of their good faith and freedom from impending open-ended liability. At the same time, regulated enterprises must take care that any settlement they enter into with EPA enforcement officials not harm their firm's competitive standing within its industry. Monies expended on pollution control measures and environmental penalties will not be available for investment in productive manufacturing equipment that can increase corporate profits. As they negotiate with regulators, representatives of industrial firms are thus often mindful of individuals within their companies who focus mostly on the bottom line and see little need for or benefit from corporate environmental expenditure.

For EPA's representatives there are difficult choices as well in enforcement negotiations. Any attempt at standardized decision-making by EPA is confounded by the enormous variety of conditions and circumstances that individual cases involve. The agency's enforcement engineers and attorneys frequently face sensitive decisions with respect to the pollution control measures they will accept, the penalties they will assess, the amount of time they will allow a violator to come into compliance, the legal prerogatives and safeguards they will insist upon, and the appropriateness of avoiding, or terminating, negotiations and referring a matter to the Justice Department for civil or criminal action. These judgments are complex and demanding. As one of my own former colleagues at EPA once confided, "You know, we really have to be very reasonable when we're in the enforcement business. The problem is that a lot of times it's just damned difficult figuring out what being reasonable means."[19]

From the agency's point of view, one factor in the successfulness of enforcement staff work is the extent to which enforcement attorneys and engineers work together as a coordinated team. Two senior EPA managers, Dale Bryson and David Ullrich, have discussed this knowledgeably:

> Engineers and attorneys are often of different personality types and they "speak a different language." They have different approaches to problem-solving and perspectives on the issues. They bring very different skills to the enforcement process. . . . [T]he key for the enforcement managers and attorneys and engineers themselves is to overcome their differences and integrate their skills.[20]

In addition to interdisciplinary coordination, successful enforcement staff work also demands persistence, patience, and tact. It requires an ability to communicate with a range of interested individuals and to keep higher-ranking officials (as well as DOJ attorneys) informed and supportive of negotiating strategies and positions. Above all, it requires firm and principled dedication to the public interest.

EPA's administration of CERCLA (commonly known as the Superfund Program) has been immersed in controversy during almost all of that program's twelve-year history. The agency's work in this area (of which enforcement is a central component) has been roundly criticized by congressional investigators, citizens organizations, insurers, scientists, scholars, and representatives of affected private enterprises alike. EPA's approach to the Superfund Program has been critical to the history of EPA's enforcement programs as well as a reason for the agency's often acrimonious relationship with Congress.[21]

CERCLA, which was initially enacted in the lame-duck period of the Carter administration (and subsequently amended in 1986), was intended to bring about the cleanup of inactive hazardous waste disposal sites and to provide a basis for emergency response when hazardous substances are released to the environment. The statute required EPA to expand, and subsequently to revise, a National Contingency Plan, to include, among other things, methods for inventorying, investigating, and evaluating hazardous releases and criteria for determining whether cleanup activities are appropriate and what priority they should receive. Based on this plan, the agency had to prepare a ranked National Priorities List of those inactive hazardous waste disposal facilities that require long-term cleanup measures.[22]

CERCLA provides EPA with broad authority to undertake necessary actions to deal with hazardous substance releases. Consistent with the National Contingency Plan, the agency can conduct immediate, short-term cleanup operations—known as removal actions—as well as longer-term efforts—termed remedial actions—to repair the damage from released hazardous wastes.[23] Initially, the agency can pay for these activities from the proceeds of a trust fund which obtains most of its monies from a surtax against large companies and taxes on petroleum and chemical feed stocks.[24] The costs of these EPA cleanup actions can later be recovered by civil lawsuits, known as cost recovery actions, from what are generally referred to as potentially responsible parties (PRPs), that is, any persons who disposed of, transported, or arranged with a transporter for the treatment or disposal of the hazardous materials in question.[25] The Superfund statute also empowers EPA to issue unilateral administrative orders to PRPs which require abatement actions necessary to protect the public health from "imminent and substantial endangerments" created by hazardous substance releases.[26] Violators of such orders are subject to treble damages.[27] In addition, EPA can ask the Justice Department to initiate a civil action against PRPs to secure necessary abatement measures.[28]

In implementing the agency's legal authorities under Superfund, EPA personnel generally follow a standard set of procedures that evolved over the 1980s and early 1990s. Once the agency becomes aware of the existence of an inactive hazardous waste disposal site, EPA's regional office will dispatch an on-scene coordinator (OSC) to perform an initial investigation (known as a preliminary assessment) at the site. The OSC reviews all existing technical information at the site and prepares a brief report that determines whether any further preremedial response (such as a further investigation or a removal action) is required. If an immediate removal action is recommended to abate a public health emergency, it is usually accomplished promptly, using trust fund monies. If the OSC recommends further investigation of the site, a two-phase site investigation is performed; the magnitude and severity of the hazard posed by the site are evaluated in greater depth, and a decision is made whether (and, if appropriate, where) to include the site on the National Priorities List. After a problematic site has been placed on this list, EPA regional personnel (or their contractors) will generally perform a PRP search, to identify all responsible parties who may be subject to a Superfund enforcement or cost recovery action. The agency will then typically send PRPs notice letters that, among other things, inform them of their potential liability for response costs (as well as of the development of an administrative record), request further information about the site, and release the names and addresses of other PRPs who have also received notice letters.

EPA will also commence preparation of a remedial investigation/ feasibility study, or RI/FS. This document analyzes, in some detail, the extent of the actual or threatened release of the hazardous substances at the site; it also identifies, screens, and evaluates the alternatives proposed to effect a permanent remedy at the site, taking account of cost effectiveness, implementability, and the level of protection afforded the environment. Once this is complete, the agency issues a formal Record of Decision (ROD) that selects the principal remedial actions to be taken at the site.[29]

Before, during, and/or subsequent to the preparation of an RI/FS and a ROD, EPA often participates in time-limited and intensive negotiations with PRPs. From the agency's point of view, these discussions have the goal of securing private PRP funding for all administrative and remedial expenditures at the site in question. EPA may also issue unilateral administrative orders with the same end in view.

When the agency reaches agreement with some or all PRPs, that understanding is usually memorialized in a formal, written Consent Decree, sent to the Justice Department for lodging (and subsequent filing) in an appropriate U.S. district court. If a PRP meets certain statutory criteria, designed to assure that its contribution of hazardous wastes to the Superfund site was only minimal, the agency may enter into a *de minimus* settlement. In such a case, the *de minimus* responsible party is typically released from further liability. In exchange, it must tender a cash out payment of money that exceeds, by a given percentage, that party's volumetric share of the total response costs incurred at the site.

After a ROD has been issued, EPA will then embark on what is known as a remedial design/remedial action (RD/RA). In this phase, the agency will design, construct, and implement the remedy selected in the ROD.[30] Finally, once all necessary response action at the site has been completed, EPA will reevaluate any continuing hazards the site poses and, if appropriate, delete or recategorize it on the National Priorities List.

These then are the procedures most commonly followed by EPA personnel in enforcing federal environmental regulations and in implementing the Superfund program development of EPA's enforcement program.

THREE

Heavy Seas before the Maelstrom

EPA Enforcement in the 1970s

On July 2, 1970, President Richard M. Nixon notified Congress that he planned to reorganize the executive branch to create two new independent agencies: the National Oceanic and Atmospheric Administration (NOAA) and EPA. Months of increasing public concern about the declining quality of the American environment preceded President Nixon's notice.

In January 1969, a dramatic oil well blowout near Santa Barbara, California, coated many miles of beachfront with heavy oil, killing thousands of fish and waterfowl. This and similar incidents focused public attention on the presence and dangers of water and air pollution, problems that had been only peripherally addressed by the federal government before that time. The Earth Day celebrations of April 1970 also dramatized the nation's environmental difficulties—and intensified public pressure to address them.

President Nixon had decided to accept the recommendations of a presidential council on government reorganization (known as the Ash Council after its chairman, Roy Ash) that the NOAA and EPA be established to centralize federal responsibility for antipollution activities.[1] The president's July 2, 1970, message met with wide approval from both Congress and the rapidly growing conservation community. It was followed by an executive order, "Reorganization Plan No. 3," in which EPA was formally created on December 2, 1970. Shortly thereafter, Nixon appointed William D. Ruckelshaus, an assistant attorney general at the DOJ, as the agency's first administrator.

In the enforcement area, the fledgling EPA faced profound challenges. The programs which had been transferred into EPA from other federal departments under "Reorganization Plan No. 3" had little to do with enforcement work. The country's pollution problems were widespread, growing, and uncontrolled. The federal environmental laws in effect at the time contained few enforceable substantive provisions. Environmental enforcement, as limited as it was, had been the exclusive preserve of state and local governments.

At the outset, the leadership of the new agency determined that it was extremely important to establish that EPA was serious about enforcing the relatively few environmental standards which then existed. The agency adopted the phrase "fair but firm" to characterize EPA's enforcement policy. Under this approach, emphasis was placed on "thorough preparation and consideration of all facts pertinent to a case, combined with an unflinching readiness to take whatever enforcement action might be required to deter recalcitrance or foot-dragging and to compel needed abatement efforts."[2]

To convey a tough enforcement message to industrial and municipal sources of pollution, the agency directed many of its initial efforts against large national corporations and big cities. Administrator Ruckelshaus announced EPA's initial enforcement actions, which received extensive media coverage. Under the authority of the Rivers and Harbors Act of 1899 (popularly known as the Refuse Act), enforcement conferences were held at which polluters were required to devise an acceptable cleanup plan within a 180-day period. For example, EPA Region V held Refuse Act conferences in Cleveland, Detroit, Duluth, and other cities to discuss heavily polluted waterways such as Lake Erie, the Cuyahoga River, Lake Michigan, Lake Superior, and the Wisconsin River. These conferences focused on rivers and lakes whose contamination problems EPA and its predecessor agencies had studied. A wide variety of industries (including steel, chemicals, pulp and paper, and others) were targeted for enforcement action with the goal of establishing a strong enforcement presence and a sense of momentum. As part of this effort, the agency attempted to use its limited statutory authority to bring civil and criminal actions under the Refuse Act. In its first two years, EPA took Refuse Act enforcement actions against various FORTUNE 500 corporations. The agency also initiated a handful of enforcement cases under other environmental statutes.[3]

During this initial period, the agency's top managers decided to delegate the responsibility for enforcement cases and strategies to regional administrators and enforcement division directors in EPA's ten regional offices. These offices expanded rapidly. Overall, in its first two years, EPA's enforcement staff grew by nearly five times, to a force of almost 1,500 persons (including water pollution permit personnel).[4] As the offices grew, they received an increasing degree of autonomy in the enforcement field. Although EPA headquarters officials maintained an intense interest in pressing forward with an assertive enforcement approach, they increasingly supported and encouraged regional efforts, rather than directly involving themselves in the enforcement fray.

For many participants in EPA's newly established enforcement program, the first two years were an intensely exciting yet a hectic time. Congress and certain "outspoken and demonstrative" environmental organizations pressured the agency for prompt enforcement results. The agency's activities were carried on in the glare of intense publicity—a fact which "helped immensely" in getting EPA's enforcement effort off the ground.[5] Moreover, the goals of the agency were widely supported by the public. As EPA Enforcement Manager Richard Wilson recalled: "It was a glory day. EPA was a new agency and everyone was for it. You couldn't do anything wrong."[6]

Though many individuals contributed to EPA's inaugural enforcement thrust, two people in particular played critical leadership roles. One was James O. McDonald, the first enforcement division director in EPA Region V. A strong-willed, pragmatic, and inspiring manager with an extraordinary talent for complex negotiations and a bold willingness to seize the initiative, McDonald made a crucial contribution to building a credible EPA enforcement effort. Under McDonald's guidance, EPA Region V took more than 50 percent of the agency's enforcement actions in its first two years, an achievement which earned him EPA's two highest awards, its gold medal for exceptional service and its gold medal for distinguished service.

In addition to McDonald, John Quarles, the agency's first assistant administrator for enforcement and general counsel, played an important part in launching the agency's enforcement program. Then an outspoken and effective advocate of a firm enforcement approach, Quarles won the respect of those who worked for him, as well as the support of the agency's administrator and other government officials.[7]

The agency's first two years were a formative time for its enforcement programs. It devoted energy to hiring new staff and building an enforcement organization in headquarters and the ten regional offices, and it generally succeeded in establishing a reputation as a no-nonsense enforcer of environmental laws. Despite this achievement, the agency's initial enforcement programs were still limited and rudimentary in a number of respects. As noted, EPA began its enforcement push at a time when many of the basic pollution control standards and requirements had not yet been set. Though the agency was willing to enforce, there was not that much law that it could enforce. Moreover, the state of the art of pollution control was relatively primitive. While air and water pollution problems were generally recognized and fairly well measured, the technical solutions to these problems were still months and even years away in some cases. In addition, EPA enforcement faced another formidable barrier during this preliminary phase: resistance to the initiation of federal environmental enforcement activity from state pollution control agencies. Although the states were invited to and did participate in EPA's Refuse Act conferences and other enforcement proceedings, they were often reluctant to support EPA's initial enforcement efforts.

Most state officials bitterly resented the involvement of the EPA's young staff—particularly its growing cadre of attorneys—in what they still viewed as their own domain. A number of state pollution control managers viewed EPA's assertive new enforcement program as unnecessarily stringent and overly aggressive. As the frequent objects of intense proindustry pressures from elected officials at state and local levels, state environmental agencies viewed themselves as defenders of industry's position in early enforcement meetings and openly resisted EPA's enforcement advances.[8] This situation did not halt EPA's budding enforcement program. However, it occasionally posed a "major obstacle" to environmental cleanup during those beginning years.[9]

Finally, this formative period saw the beginning of a trend that was to have profound implications for EPA's enforcement work at later times: detailed and largely critical oversight by congressional committees. In 1971 and 1972, the Subcommittee on Conservation and Natural Resources of the House Committee on Government Operations held a series of hearings that focused on interference by White House officials with pending DOJ enforcement actions under the Refuse Act against alleged discharges of mercury. These hearings succeeded, for many years, in establishing the Justice Department's environmental enforcement activities as off-limits to those who would have preferred to subject them to interest group pressures. Along with oversight investigations of EPA's Clean Air Act implementation by Senator Edmund Muskie's Air and Water Pollution Subcommittee of the Senate Committee on Public Works, the hearings arose in the context of a general upsurge in congressional oversight of the executive branch, as well as open disparagement, by some members of Congress, of early decisions by EPA that proved politically unpopular.[10]

As EPA's enforcement program grew, so did its statutory authority. In 1972 Congress enacted a host of major environmental legislation. The Federal Water Pollution Control Act (FWPCA) of 1972 established a range of measures to "restore and maintain the chemical, physical and biological integrity of the Nation's waters,"[11] including the National Pollutant Discharge Elimination System (NPDES), a massive permit program concerning the discharge of industrial and municipal wastes to surface waters. The Marine Protection, Research and Sanctuaries Act (otherwise known as the Ocean Dumping Act) created new requirements to safeguard marine waters.[12] The Federal Insecticide, Fungicide and Rodenticide Act (FIFRA) was significantly amended to achieve safe use of products.[13] The Clean Air Act, which had been enacted two years earlier, established a panoply of requirements for action to abate various types of air pollution.

Under each of these laws, EPA was entrusted with major responsibilities for both setting and enforcing regulatory standards. Armed with a full complement of legal authorities, the young agency sought to follow up its dramatic entrance into the environmental enforcement field with a continued emphasis on vigorous action.[14] Despite stiffening resistance to environmental regulation in some sectors of the business community, Russell E. Train, who succeeded William Ruckelshaus as EPA administrator in September 1973, determined that the agency would maintain the enforcement momentum it had established in its prestatutory years. Though Train lacked Ruckelshaus's flamboyance, his attitudes toward enforcement were similar.

The 1973 to 1976 period in EPA enforcement was characterized by three general trends. First, the agency continued and further expanded the autonomy accorded to enforcement units in the regional offices. Although headquarters enforcement managers issued policy guidance to the regions (and continued to exhort them to pursue numerous enforcement actions), the day-to-day responsibility for enforcement cases was turned over to regional enforcement officials to an increasing extent. Some EPA officials saw this development as a mixed blessing for the agency's overall enforcement success. Although a number of EPA regional offices, including Regions III and V, were particularly efficient and assertive in their enforcement efforts, others experienced problems in both motivation and the development of enforcement expertise.[15]

Second, the agency's enforcement programs began to experience some of the problems which rapid initial growth often brings to organizations. As David Kee, one of EPA Region V's initial enforcement managers, later recalled, "There was definitely a maturing. We got much bigger. We had some of the problems of a large organization, certainly from a management standpoint. We had to deal with problem employees and a lot of things that weren't so much fun. Also we became more bureaucratic."[16]

Although staff-level enthusiasm for enforcement work remained generally high, the relatively freewheeling, informal style of the agency's earliest days was gradually replaced by a somewhat more formal situation. Enforcement procedures and routines became established, and the enormity of the regulatory tasks that Congress had placed upon EPA became increasingly evident to the agency's career staff.

Third, EPA's enforcement relationship with state pollution control agency personnel slowly but perceptibly improved as the states themselves enacted new environmental laws and reorganized their agencies. Although some states remained highly resistant to federal enforcement efforts, others began to develop an appreciation of the value of vigorous enforcement to improved environmental quality. Spurred in part by the provision of EPA operating grants and federal delegation of primary responsibility for managing the NPDES program within their borders, some states embraced a more aggressive and confrontational approach in the enforcement area as well as a new willingness to cooperate with the agency's regional enforcement staff.[17]

In the air pollution field, EPA began its first program for enforcing the Clean Air Act. As was the case earlier in the water enforcement area, EPA's first air enforcement thrust was largely an attempt to establish a federal "enforcement presence."[18] EPA initiated information-gathering procedures, including written requests for compliance information under section 114 of the act, opacity inspections, and a limited number of stack tests.[19] The agency issued its first formal notices of violation and administrative orders to identified sources of air pollution and began to enforce the limitations on automobile-generated pollution.

At the outset, however, Clean Air Act enforcement was hampered by several problems. One set of obstacles sprang from the first state implementation plans (SIPs), which were hastily drafted by the states and quickly approved by EPA to comply with the strict regulatory deadlines the statute had imposed. Although many states had a good deal of air quality data when the standards were prepared, they often lacked specific knowledge about the sources of pollution and the type and amount of air pollution those sources were emitting. Many of the first SIPs were thus very general in nature and lacked meaningful reference to the particular kinds of industrial facilities they ostensibly controlled.

Once the SIPs became enforceable, EPA devoted a good deal of its staff's time to the determination of how to apply these requirements to the numerous industrial and municipal sources that caused pollution. The agency worked with state and local governments to establish inventories of air pollution emitters. EPA responded to a plethora of information requests from industries that were uncertain whether SIP requirements were meant to be applied to their plants. The agency also reviewed the acceptability of proposed SIP compliance schedules for many individual facilities.[20]

Other problems emerged in the form of sharp disputes between the agency and industrial concerns about the precise types of air pollution control technology that had to be installed at productive facilities and the time by which those controls had to be in place. For electric power plants some state SIPs, for example, established stringent requirements for curbing sulfur dioxide emissions which could only be complied with through the use of expensive and then relatively untried SO_2 scrubber technology. In the steel industry many SIPs called for technology-forcing measures at some air pollutant emission points, including costly controls on pollution from coke batteries. These requirements engendered widespread controversy.[21] Their enforcement consumed a great deal of EPA's time and effort.[22]

Another nettlesome issue which arose during this period was the so-called jobs versus environment question. In several instances, firms which were subject to Clean Air Act requirements began to claim that compliance with those standards would be economically impossible for them to achieve and that strict Clean Air Act enforcement would inevitably result in plant closures and local unemployment. Though most of these claims lacked validity, they proved at times to be a potent weapon for industry in the enforcement context.[23] While relatively few industrial facilities were actually closed as a result of environmental enforcement, EPA spent considerable political energy defending a strong enforcement stance in those relatively few cases where employment claims played a role.[24]

In the water enforcement area EPA ran into problems when it attempted to implement the FWPCA. Throughout much of 1973, an internal debate over a variety of technical and policy issues that the newly enacted statute had left unresolved consumed EPA. Chief among these was the question of the basis for the best practicable technology standards to be included in dischargers' NPDES permits. Although the act seemed to call for EPA to establish industry-specific effluent limitation guidelines before attempting to set enforceable discharge limitations in individual permits, it soon became apparent that the technical work needed to develop such guidelines properly would be difficult and time-consuming. If permit insurance and enforcement were to get under way, the agency would have to find an acceptable substitute for the guidelines as a basis for permit requirements. Toward the end of 1973, EPA decided to press forward with NPDES permits written on the basis of the agency's best engineering judgment as to what constitutes best practicable technology.

This controversial decision opened the door for a massive EPA effort to issue NPDES permits to industries and municipalities that discharged water pollutants.

During the latter part of 1973 and all of 1974, EPA virtually suspended its other water enforcement work and concentrated its staff's energies on processing the permit applications of industrial facilities. In a laudable effort, the agency issued 2,699 NPDES permits to major industrial dischargers, as well as 11,459 permits to so-called minor industrial waste sources, by December 31, 1974.[25] This spate of new permits later gave rise to a wave of requests by dischargers for adjudicatory hearings before administrative law judges. Yet it also prompted many urgently needed water pollution control programs in the private sector and, ultimately, prodded a significant decrease in the discharge of common industrial pollutants such as biological oxygen-demanding (BOD) wastes, suspended solids, oil and grease, phenol, and chromium.

Throughout the 1973 to 1977 period, EPA preferred to proceed on the basis of administrative, as opposed to judicial, enforcement of air and water act violations. In many EPA regions administrative orders were not issued under the Clean Air Act or the FWPCA, as a matter of policy, unless the industrial or municipal party which would be bound by those orders consented in advance to their terms. While this approach prevented EPA from becoming embroiled in litigation, it also created an unanticipated difficulty: in many cases the agency's negotiations with polluters over the terms of administrative orders took months or even years to complete. As some EPA officials saw it, some companies in the regulated community were treating these negotiations as a kind of game that could delay compliance with environmental standards and the expense that compliance would entail.[26]

Cognizant of this, the enforcement divisions of some EPA regional offices moved increasingly toward civil litigation as a means of resolving enforcement cases against regulated parties that were viewed as particularly resistant to lesser enforcement sanctions. This trend was gradual. In fact, it did not occur at all in most EPA regions, and even when it did, the predominant enforcement tool remained the administrative order.[27] Nonetheless, the agency's first, sporadic attempts at judicial enforcement of federal environmental legislation helped to lay the groundwork for the immense litigation program that the agency was soon to undertake.

President Jimmy Carter's inauguration in January 1977 marked the start of a significant shift in the operation of EPA's enforcement programs. The new president had committed himself to a strong federal role in environmental protection during the course of his election campaign. To fulfill that commitment, Carter chose top managers for EPA with environmentalist backgrounds and perspectives.

Douglas Costle, the former director of Connecticut's pollution control agency, became the agency's new administrator. Barbara Blum, who had worked in the president's campaign in Georgia, was appointed its deputy administrator. Marvin Durning, a particularly ardent environmentalist from the state of Washington, became EPA's new assistant administrator for enforcement. Through the efforts of these individuals, the agency's enforcement activities received relatively generous funding in the late 1970s, notwithstanding a general fiscal stringency which affected most of EPA's programs of that time.[28]

One critical change that took place during this period was the initiation of a civil litigation approach to environmental enforcement. Immediately upon assuming office, Marvin Durning perceived the administrative enforcement efforts of the preceding EPA administration as unduly time-consuming and generally ineffective. Determined to redirect the agency's enforcement work, Durning announced the creation of a major source enforcement effort, epitomized by the slogan "file first and negotiate later." Under this strategy, the agency was to identify major violators of the Clean Air Act SIPs and the FWPCA's July 1, 1977, deadline for the achievement of effluent limitations based upon best practicable technology. The agency was then to refer each of these violators to the DOJ, with a recommendation that it institute a civil action against them in an appropriate federal district court for injunctive relief and civil penalties. While any or all of these suits might be resolved subsequent to their being filed, EPA enforcement officials were discouraged from entering into negotiations with any parties subject to enforcement action until after litigation had commenced.

During 1977 and 1978, this strategy was put into effect. In conjunction with the Justice Department, EPA filed a considerable number of civil suits, most of which were ultimately resolved by Consent Decree. Where enforcement litigation had once been the exception at EPA, it now became the rule. The agency's headquarters placed strong pressure on its regional offices to produce litigation referrals. Each region was expected to produce a quota of referrals within a given time period. In contrast, reliance on administrative orders, formerly the mainstay of EPA's enforcement activities, became insignificant.[29]

In tandem with this lawsuit-based approach, the Carter administration's managers introduced a Civil Penalty Policy and a National Penalty Panel to administer it. The Civil Penalty Policy applied to settlement of enforcement actions. Under its terms, state and federal enforcement officials were forbidden to negotiate settlement of the civil penalty aspects of any major air or water enforcement case for less than the amount of money which the defendant had saved by delaying compliance with applicable requirements. The Civil Penalty Policy required that additional penalties apply to alleged violators that exhibited lack of good faith. The policy permitted enforcement personnel involved in case settlement negotiations to discuss and consider a proposed civil penalty offer that was lower than the economic savings amount.[30] However, EPA could not accept such offers unless the National Penalty Panel reviewed and approved the offers.[31]

Another significant innovation was the creation of a Senior Executive Service (SES) of EPA's top management personnel. Under this arrangement, devised by EPA Assistant Administrator William Drayton, the agency's ten regional enforcement directors were required to reapply for their own positions. If rehired, they would be admitted to the SES. In that capacity they would be afforded executive status and have the potential to earn a higher salary. However, they would also be required to agree in advance to be transferred to a similar position in another organizational unit, including a position in another city, if and when the agency's top managers ordered such a change.

Though intended as a means of developing EPA's internal management structure, this policy shift had several unforeseen and unfortunate results. Many of the agency's regional enforcement directors, already unhappy with the new litigation referral system, which undercut the autonomy they had enjoyed, viewed the institution of an SES as a further attempt to undermine their positions. Although most regional enforcement directors did ultimately reapply for and retain their positions with SES status, the experience engendered considerable resentment among the directors, because they considered the SES unnecessary, seriously traumatic, and "hopelessly mishandled." James O. McDonald resigned his position to protest the insensitive and ill-conceived way in which the SES was instituted.[32]

Along with these new policies came significant changes in the allocation of responsibility for environmental enforcement matters. In June 1977 Administrator Costle and Attorney General Griffin Bell entered into a controversial memorandum of understanding, under which the DOJ's attorneys were afforded substantial control over the conduct of environmental enforcement litigation. Costle, a former DOJ attorney, was widely criticized by EPA's regional enforcement divisions for relegating EPA attorneys to a secondary role in the litigation process. The memorandum required the regional divisions to prepare a detailed litigation report to accompany each enforcement matter they referred for civil litigation. This report was to include a summary of the legal theories upon which the proposed action rested and a summary of the evidence that was available to prove the government's case.

Whereas previous litigation reports could be sent directly from EPA's regional offices to the appropriate U.S. attorneys, all litigation reports now had to be sent to the agency's headquarters for staff review. If headquarters enforcement personnel deemed it necessary, this referral package could be returned to the regional office for further development. If and when EPA headquarters gave its approval, however, the matter was then transferred to the DOJ for a second round of review. The DOJ in turn had the authority to seek further information from regional enforcement personnel. Like EPA headquarters, DOJ could reject the regional official's litigation recommendation if it believed the enforcement case in question was flawed or unpersuasive. If and when DOJ approval was secured, however, the matter was referred to the office of the local U.S. attorney for another round of review. Finally, after all of the relevant governmental organizations had given their concurrences, the U.S. attorney filed the proposed enforcement case as a civil action in the appropriate U.S. district court.

These enforcement policies and procedures had a number of consequences, both within EPA's enforcement program and outside it. Within EPA, the Carter administration's bold enforcement approach had profound effects. One of these was a general increase in the influence of EPA headquarters in the agency's enforcement work, accompanied by a proportionate reduction in the near-autonomy that EPA regional enforcement divisions had hitherto enjoyed. No longer mere policy writers and supporters of regionally based enforcement efforts, the headquarters staff was now directly involved in reviewing, and in some cases vetoing, regional recommendations as to specific cases. Beyond that, headquarters officials assumed primary responsibility for certain types of enforcement matters, and concurrence from headquarters became a requirement in a growing number of settlement negotiations.[33] These changes caused great consternation in the agency's regional enforcement offices and resulted in continuing disaffection and protest.

Another consequence of the new procedures was a dramatic expansion of the DOJ's enforcement responsibility. This change brought with it considerable conflict between the agency's regional enforcement staff and DOJ attorneys and managers. While the DOJ's increasing involvement may have lent some litigation expertise and institutional credibility to the government's environmental enforcement effort,[34] it also led to significant discord at the staff level. In a number of instances, EPA regional enforcement attorneys became concerned with the length of time the DOJ took to review litigation referrals. Serious professional disputes also arose over the amount of evidence the government needed to have available before an enforcement suit could be initiated, and some Justice Department attorneys came to be viewed as "nit-picking," "arbitrary," and "high-handed" in their relationships with the agency's regional staff.[35]

Among regulated companies, the agency's "file first" approach was widely viewed as unnecessarily harsh and unduly rigid. Though many suits were resolved and considerable cleanup achieved, industry resentment of EPA's enforcement techniques gradually increased. The jobs versus environment issue, which had first surfaced in the mid-1970s, continued to receive attention in the media in the early Carter years. To an increasing extent, EPA's managers and staff were publicly criticized as ineffective bureaucrats and antibusiness zealots.[36]

The agency's strong enforcement approach also aggravated the disenchantment felt by state officials. Many states resented the agency's attempt to subject them to a uniform policy regarding civil penalties and some flatly refused to abide by its terms. Resistant to further federal encroachment upon their enforcement domain, a number of state officials once again perceived EPA's enforcement managers as insensitive to state concerns and needlessly inflexible in their views.[37] Impervious to these criticisms, however, the agency and DOJ persisted in their assertive civil litigation efforts.

This trend was supplemented by public expressions of support for the application of criminal sanctions to environmental violations. In a February 1978 speech to the American Law Institute–American Bar Association Course of Study on Environmental Law in Washington, D.C., James Moorman, then assistant attorney general for the Justice Department's Division of Land and Natural Resources, announced that his department would prosecute "willful, substantive violations of the pollution control laws of criminal nature." He stated that "for these transgressions, the Department of Justice has begun to invoke grand jury investigations against both corporations and against individuals" and that "the Department of Justice will prosecute criminal conduct in this area." Similarly, in a May 1980 speech to graduating seniors at the University of Michigan, Attorney General Benjamin R. Civiletti emphasized the DOJ's intention to prosecute both individuals and corporations who willfully violate environmental laws.[38]

Despite this enthusiastic rhetoric, however, the Carter administration took few concrete steps to set a criminal environmental enforcement program in motion. Although the creation of a separate
environmental criminal prosecution unit was seriously considered
within the Justice Department during that time, a spirited bureaucratic dispute between the department's Criminal and Lands Divisions as to where such a unit should be housed effectively forestalled
its realization.[39] After much delay, in January 1981 EPA Deputy Administrator Barbara Blum signed a memorandum directing the creation of an EPA Office of Criminal Enforcement and instructing each
of the agency's regional offices to hire two or three professional
criminal investigators, depending upon need.[40]

However, Blum's memo, which called for the new EPA criminal
investigators to report directly to the agency's headquarters Office of
Enforcement, met with strong resistance from regional enforcement
personnel, who sought greater control over the investigators' work.
As a result of this "turf battle" and the weariness of Reagan administration officials, only a handful of criminal investigators were actually hired prior to the middle of 1982. Thus, in contrast to its vigorous and active environmental civil enforcement efforts, criminal
environmental enforcement during the Carter years produced only a
few prosecutions that were "local, sporadic, and in response to disastrous events, rather than a particular enforcement policy."[41]

How should the Carter administration EPA's enforcement efforts
be assessed? In contrast to earlier enforcement regimes at EPA, the
agency's enforcement efforts during the Carter years appear, at first
glance, unerringly consistent, assertive, and effective. However, the
litigation approach that dominated EPA enforcement work during
the Carter administration yielded imperfect results.

Supported by top EPA managers and a talented group of mid-level
officials, the Carter model of enforcement invigorated the agency's
efforts. It eliminated the delays that had characterized some of EPA's
prior administrative enforcement negotiations. It also reinforced and
strengthened the perception, which began in earlier years, that EPA
was serious about enforcing environmental statutes and determined
to take assertive measures to compel compliance and deter inten-
tional violations.

On the other hand, as we have seen, the agency's file first, negotiate later strategy, its Civil Penalty Policy, and its litigation referral procedure had some unfortunate repercussions. Internally, the
agency created a cumbersome and often time-consuming system for
considering and acting upon cases that regional enforcement professionals believed were appropriate matters for litigation. This strategy

gave rise to a relatively high level of rivalry among EPA regional offices, the agency's headquarters, and the DOJ. To some extent, these conflicts diminished the effectiveness of the government's overall enforcement effort. Also, as noted above, the perceived rigidity of the agency's new enforcement initiatives engendered hostility from both regulated industry and state environmental officials. This resentment, and the backlash it created, placed EPA, and to some degree the environmental movement as a whole, under increased political stress as the Carter years continued.

In retrospect, it could be argued that EPA's top managers would have been more successful if their litigious approach to environmental enforcement had been supplemented by a balanced and judicious use of administrative orders and prefiling negotiations with potential defendants. Their approach might also have benefited from a selective laissez-faire attitude toward those EPA regional enforcement divisions that already had strong and assertive enforcement programs in place. That strategy was not adopted, however, and the Carter administration's ambitious enforcement program did not fulfill its potential as a result. Despite this, however, the general enforcement policies of the Carter administration provided the soil in which an ambitious and largely successful hazardous waste enforcement effort was nourished.

In 1977 and 1978, several incidents occurred that served to awaken the American public to dangers posed by the past misdisposal of hazardous wastes. The spotlight of media attention was directed at the "Valley of the Drums" in Brooks, Kentucky, where more than 17,000 corroding drums of toxic and hazardous wastes were strewn about a poorly maintained landfill, contaminating a stream that flowed into the drinking source for a highly populated area. Considerable publicity was also given to the degradation of the James River near Hopewell, Virginia, with ketone, a highly toxic and nondegradable industrial waste, as well as the disastrous chemical contamination problems at the Love Canal in Niagara Falls, New York, which caused 237 families to be permanently evacuated from their homes. Additionally, intensive media coverage was given to the illegal dumping of acutely toxic wastes into a sewage treatment plant in Louisville, Kentucky, an act which forced a lengthy closure of that plant and resulted in the discharge of billions of gallons of raw or poorly treated sewage into the Ohio River.[42]

As public awareness of the hazardous waste problem grew, so too did public pressure for vigorous governmental measures to deal with the situation. Several congressional committees initiated investigations into hazardous waste dumping and EPA's response to it. EPA had not yet proposed any of the hazardous waste regulations it was mandated to promulgate under subtitle C of RCRA. The agency's leaders felt an urgent need to demonstrate, by prompt and effective action, that EPA was concerned about the hazardous waste dump situation and intended to combat it. Under these circumstances, a group of EPA's top managers decided upon a two-pronged strategy for addressing the hazardous waste issue. Persuaded that the agency's legal authority to require cleanup at abandoned hazardous waste sites was fundamentally inadequate, these officials concluded that it would be necessary to ask Congress for a new statute specifically aimed at correcting contamination from inactive dumps.[43] At this time, however, the Carter administration was focused on ways to trim the cost of government operations. There was, in the words of one key participant, "considerable resistance within the administration" to proposing any legislative initiatives in this field.[44] To overcome internal administration resistance, EPA managers decided to increase and, to the extent possible, orchestrate growing public and congressional concern about haphazard waste dumping.

On October 2, 1978, Thomas C. Jorling, EPA's assistant administrator for water and waste management, requested that the agency's regional offices submit their "best professional estimate" of the total number of abandoned hazardous waste sites existing within their regions. Regional officials were also asked to report on the number of sites that might contain "significant quantities" of hazardous wastes. Because no specific criteria were provided for determining which dump sites should be placed in each category, each EPA region used its own methodology to comply with Jorling's request. As a result, the first EPA estimates of the number of hazardous waste sites were highly unreliable.[45] Despite the imprecision and internal confusion resulting from this approach, however, by November 21, 1978, the agency was able to release publicly the results of its "preliminary inventory." In congressional testimony, EPA managers stated that they believed 32,254 sites might contain hazardous wastes and 838 sites contained significant quantities of waste.[46]

The announcement of this information, combined with continuing disclosures regarding incidents of contamination from abandoned waste dumps, set off what one former Justice Department manager later described as a "firestorm of interest."[47] Amidst the continuing public and media demand for firm and immediate action, EPA's managers pressed forward with their plan to propose a new abandoned waste site statute, which they began to refer to as Superfund, in reference to the expanded pool of monies which would be sought for use in a major site cleanup effort.[48] To further bolster its argument that such Superfund legislation was urgently needed, as well as to deflect mounting congressional criticism of the agency's tardiness in promulgating hazardous waste regulations under RCRA, EPA's top leadership put into place the second part of its strategy. With the cooperation of the Department of Justice, EPA's managers took preliminary steps toward establishing a new enforcement campaign to compel known owners and operators of abandoned hazardous waste dumps to remedy endangerments that those dumps created.

On March 28, 1979, Barbara Blum, EPA's deputy administrator, wrote a memorandum to the agency's regional administrators stating that an "aggressive program is needed" in this area. Blum indicated that the agency's top management considered the hazardous waste site issue to be of high priority. She announced that a committee would be formed, under the leadership of Gary Dietrich, EPA's associate deputy administrator for solid waste, and Leslie Carothers, the director of the agency's Region I Enforcement Division. This committee was to "[coordinate] activities related to inactive sites" and to develop a "cohesive, dedicated national effort" with respect to hazardous waste enforcement. Regional administrators were asked to appoint one technical coordinator and one enforcement coordinator "to jointly manage the program activities in your region and to work with Leslie and Gary."[49]

At the end of April 1979, the agency held an imminent hazard workshop in Denver, Colorado. The meeting was attended by the newly appointed regional coordinators as well as over one hundred key staff members from the Department of Justice, EPA headquarters, and the NEIC. At the gathering, during which internal procedures for launching a hazardous waste site enforcement effort were intensively discussed, Barbara Blum reiterated the extremely high priority which EPA's top leadership placed on this program. She promised to seek additional budgetary resources for hazardous waste enforcement and to divert existing agency resources to implement the program. Blum also made a pledge, ultimately fulfilled by EPA and the DOJ enforcement staff, that within one year at least fifty hazardous waste "imminent hazard" actions would be filed in U.S. district courts.[50]

On June 27, 1979, Barbara Blum notified the agency's regional and assistant administrators that a Hazardous Waste Enforcement Task Force (HWETF) was being established at the agency's headquarters. The HWETF was to be chaired at the outset by Jeffrey Miller, EPA's acting assistant administrator for enforcement. The HWETF was responsible for providing "national management" of the enforcement component of the agency's hazardous waste program, which included development of a hazardous waste site reporting and tracking system, establishment of hazardous waste enforcement policies, and increased participation by headquarters staff and the DOJ in developing hazardous waste cases.[51] Within a short time, the task force began a vigorous effort to recruit a small cadre of experienced staff to carry out its responsibilities. A conscious attempt was made to gather EPA's "top enforcement talent,"[52] and task force managers were given a free hand to offer positions to any member of the agency's enforcement staff who they believed would contribute meaningfully to its success.[53] Jeffrey Miller soon chose Douglas MacMillan, a former management division director in EPA Region I who was working with a congressional committee on special assignment, to be Miller's successor as task force director. Lamar Miller, a seasoned chemical engineer who had served briefly as enforcement division director in EPA Region VII, was appointed technical director of the task force. Edward Kurent, previously a headquarters water enforcement attorney and a special assistant to the assistant administrator for enforcement, was chosen task force legal director. A full complement of task force staff members was selected shortly thereafter, and EPA's initial hazardous waste enforcement program began to take shape.

At the time that the hazardous waste task force was formed, EPA had few specific legal standards to enforce under RCRA, a situation largely of the agency's own making. In subtitle C of the act, Congress had required EPA to promulgate specific regulations, within eighteen months, with respect to the active generation, transportation, and disposal of hazardous wastes. The agency had not met this deadline. It thus lacked the regulatory means to redress important aspects of the nation's rapidly reemerging hazardous waste problem.

In the fall of 1979, the Department of Justice created a small headquarters group of attorneys, paralegals, and secretaries under the leadership of Anthony Roisman. This unit, termed the Hazardous Waste Section, was assigned to work with EPA in developing hazardous waste enforcement cases. Because of a paucity of relevant legal authority, this newly created DOJ section and the HWETF decided to rely primarily on section 7003 of RCRA, the so-called imminent hazard provision of that statute, as their primary enforcement tool. It was decided, in the absence of a systematic understanding of hazardous waste site problems and the technology required to resolve them, that the appropriate course was to seek issuance of injunctions that would require the parties responsible for contamination problems at hazardous waste sites to study those problems and to prepare detailed cleanup plans, which EPA would then review and approve. As Lamar Miller remembered it, the task force's basic litigation approach was: "Get the most you can. Don't let anybody tell you that this is the most a judge would give you. Restore [the contaminated groundwater underneath each site] to its original condition."[54]

To bring this new enforcement strategy into effect, the litigation referral system initiated in the early Carter years was modified in several respects. The task force leadership adopted a suggestion by Jane Schulteis and Bill Constantelos, then midlevel managers in EPA Region V, that litigation reports be supplanted by case development plans, which more briefly outlined the evidence available to support the government's case.[55] The task force initiated a series of monthly meetings at the regional offices during which HWETF and DOJ personnel would "encourage, chide and in some cases direct" regional hazardous waste enforcement activities.[56]

As Douglas MacMillan recalled, EPA headquarters managers put enormous pressure on regional officials to produce a steady stream of new enforcement referrals. On several occasions, Deputy Administrator Barbara Blum, a strong supporter of the task force effort who devoted a good deal of time to its implementation, asked her headquarters staff for a series of "regional report cards." These evaluations identified regions whose enforcement efforts were viewed as ineffective by the task force staff. Upon receipt, Blum telephoned regional administrators and other key officials to "really lean on them very directly and bluntly about performance."[57]

The task force also worked to develop a national site tracking system that would identify the universe of abandoned hazardous waste dumps and systematically address the relative damages particular sites posed. Recognizing that their initial information about hazardous waste sites was "totally spotty and anecdotal,"[58] task force members spearheaded an effort to provide a more accurate site inventory. In pursuing this goal, the task force relied in part on data supplied by the Subcommittee on Investigations and Oversight of the House Committee on Interstate and Foreign Commerce, which had conducted a comprehensive survey of inactive waste sites.[59] Using this and other information, the agency developed a preliminary site inventory of 9,600 sites, a listing that later formed the raw material from which the Superfund National Priorities List and the MITRE model were molded.[60]

For those involved in the task force effort, the initiation of a hazardous waste site enforcement program was a time of hard work, excitement, and camaraderie.[61] Enthusiasm abounded and dedication to the task at hand was widespread. As James Bunting, a former task force attorney and manager, remembered the era, "There was a certain sense that you were really being a pioneer."[62] The task force itself was insulated from routine bureaucratic encumbrances which might have slowed its progress.[63] Its efforts were actively and enthusiastically supported by the agency's top managers, including Barbara Blum and Jeffrey Miller, and public interest in the outcome of its work was exceptionally high.[64]

Though shortlived, the HWETF effort resulted in several significant accomplishments. Within a year, the agency and the DOJ had filed fifty-four judicial enforcement actions to compel cleanup of abandoned dumps, a striking achievement in view of the government's still meager knowledge and resources. Furthermore, as task force legal director Edward Kurent later observed, these lawsuits, and the hard-nosed negotiations that they engendered, "gave notice to the general public, to industry, and to the Congress that the agency was on the job, that it had clearly identified the problem and was intent on doing something about it."[65] By its streamlined case referral system, the task force program eased some of the time-consuming red tape burdens that the Carter administration's litigation referral system had generally imposed on EPA regional enforcement officials. Finally, in establishing a national site tracking system and a set of preliminary site assessment procedures, the task force's work laid much groundwork for the ultimate establishment of the Superfund Program.

To be sure, EPA's initial hazardous waste enforcement program had its shortcomings. Because of the relative newness of the hazardous waste site problem, the agency's staff was ignorant of some of the complexities of hazardous waste site contamination and groundwater restoration. In their haste to establish a strong federal presence, EPA and DOJ filed some hazardous waste enforcement actions that later proved difficult to pursue.[66] Moreover, the agency did little planning for the extensive drain on its resources which occurred when the lawsuits it filed in 1979 and 1980 spawned extensive discovery and motion practice in the months and years that followed.[67]

Notwithstanding these difficulties, however, EPA's first attempt at hazardous waste enforcement must be judged an overall success. In little time, and with relatively few resources, it established hazardous waste enforcement as a functioning and important part of the agency's overall enforcement work.

In December 1980, on the eve of President Reagan's inauguration, the leadership of both EPA's HWETF and the DOJ's Hazardous Waste Section anticipated an expansion of the government's hazardous waste enforcement program. The Superfund Act had at last been enacted by a lame duck Congress. In the act EPA had been given the explicit authority to take enforcement action with respect to inactive hazardous waste sites, as well as access to a $1.6 billion trust fund, which promised expanded resources for a redoubled enforcement effort. EPA's RCRA hazardous waste management regulations had at long last reached an enforceable stage. Congress had modestly amended that statute to augment EPA's ability to gather information regarding hazardous waste dumps and to issue administrative orders to redress any danger that they caused.[68]

Despite some misgivings, the top hazardous waste enforcement managers at EPA and the DOJ were guardedly optimistic that the Reagan administration would not attempt to slow the development of an active hazardous waste enforcement program. As former task force director Douglas MacMillan recalled: "Given the political pressure that was building around the issue, I felt that it would be simply suicidal for the new administration to attempt to stand in front of the hazardous waste bulldozer."[69] A number of MacMillan's colleagues agreed with that assessment.[70]

For the individuals who had worked to build EPA's initial hazardous waste enforcement program, the interregnum between the Carter and Reagan administrations was a time of cautious hope. Within a matter of months, that hope turned to anxiety, bitterness, and despair. As Anthony Roisman, the Justice Department's Hazardous Waste Section chief during the task force period, recalled: "To see that potential cut off when the Reagan people came in was incredible, just incredible. We never really recovered from it, I think."[71]

FOUR

Destruction, Confusion, Confrontation, and Disarray

EPA Enforcement and Congressional Oversight in the Gorsuch Era

The arrival of the Reagan administration in January 1981 heralded a dramatic change in the tone, structure, and operation of EPA's enforcement program. The two years that followed would see a sharp decline in the initiation of new enforcement cases, a precipitous drop in career staff morale, and a drastic loss of public credibility for EPA in general. To appreciate the reasons for these trends and the pervasiveness and profundity of their impact, one must first appreciate the manner in which EPA's new top managers were selected by the Reagan administration, the attitudes they held upon taking office, and the specific ways in which they approached EPA's enforcement responsibilities.

The Reagan administration's search for a new set of top EPA managers proceeded at a deliberate pace. Almost all EPA officials who had been political appointees in the Carter administration resigned from their positions before Reagan took office on January 20. Anne McGill Gorsuch,[1] the administration's choice to succeed Douglas Costle as EPA administrator, was not nominated for that position until February 21, 1981, and her formal confirmation was delayed until May 5, 1981. Most of the other Reagan administration appointees to high-level EPA positions were also installed in the mid- or late spring. Rita M. Lavelle, an EPA official whose attitude and activities were ultimately to have an important effect on the administration of the Superfund Program, did not assume the office of assistant administrator for solid waste and emergency response until March 31, 1982, more than fourteen months after the Reagan administration had begun.[2]

The administration's method of choosing EPA's new management team emphasized the selection of individuals with an ideological affinity for the conservative wing of the Republican Party. According to one former high-level EPA civil servant, "The White House personnel office was extremely powerful and it was obsessed with getting those with definite political views, regardless of qualifications, into their place[s]."[3]

Some chosen for high-level management posts had no specific interest in enforcement. William Sullivan, for example, the administration's choice for enforcement counsel and deputy associate administrator for enforcement, stated, "I handled Reagan's stop in Youngstown as a candidate and when they were recruiting they asked for my resume. The EPA was the last agency I wanted to go to, and enforcement was the last job I wanted at the agency."[4] Furthermore, in selecting EPA's leadership, little thought was given to the manner in which those chosen would relate to one another once they assumed office. Anne Gorsuch, the agency's new administrator, had little influence over the selection of EPA's regional administrators and senior headquarters managers, many of whom she had not known before taking office.[5]

The initial attitude of EPA's new leadership toward the agency's enforcement was, like a number of things during this period, controversial. In an interview five years later, Anne Gorsuch indicated that she had favored an effective enforcement program at EPA from the outset of her tenure as administrator.[6] William Sullivan, who led EPA's national enforcement program during the first year of Gorsuch's tenure as administrator, stated that "to think there was a conspiracy to defeat enforcement is crazy."[7]

Conspiracy, in its technical, legal sense, may be too strong a word. Nonetheless, there is *very* considerable evidence that the initial enforcement attitude of a number of the Reagan administration's first set of political appointees was far more negative to environmental enforcement than the remarks of Gorsuch and Sullivan suggest. For example, Sheldon Novick, the regional counsel of EPA Region III at that time, later stated:

[T]here were plainly people in the administration, within EPA, who believed that the EPA itself should be dissolved, that the statutes that it implemented were senseless, and that the federal government had no business in environmental management. Those people, who found enforcement of federal law particularly distasteful, expressed that the EPA should be dismantled, beginning with its enforcement functions. . . . Political appointees at senior levels [other than Anne Gorsuch] began saying things like that.[8]

Novick's recollections with respect to the Reagan administration's first enforcement attitudes find support in an article that appeared in the *Washington Post*. In it James C. Miller III, at that time director of the Vice President's Regulatory Task Force, was quoted as saying, "[T]here is a strong feeling on the part of the White House staff that we ought to be decentralizing regulatory enforcement." The article also indicated that "[f]inal decisions on the roles of OSHA and the Environmental Protection Agency have not yet been made within the Administration . . . but the agencies' enforcement activities will necessarily be cut back, assuming the budget cuts proposed by President Reagan are enacted."[9]

Valdas Adamkus, the regional administrator of Region V, recalled that "when [Gorsuch] came into power, her attitude to enforcement in general was negative; there was no question."[10] Edward Kurent, the agency's water enforcement division director and associate general counsel for waste enforcement during the Gorsuch era, went so far as to suggest that Gorsuch-era political appointees implemented what was "very obviously a deliberate plan to paralyze if not totally dismantle the enforcement program."[11]

Gorsuch subsequently indicated that she and her colleagues had not entered the agency with any negative predisposition toward the career staff.[12] However, a number of EPA's permanent enforcement staff left the agency with an entirely different sense. One headquarters enforcement attorney and manager stated, "They came in with the feeling that the existing career enforcement staff probably weren't the type of employees they would want. They didn't approach them as a professional staff who were competent and who were trying to do their jobs. They came in, I think, with a bias."[13]

Whatever their initial attitudes, motivations, and intentions, it is clear that, toward the beginning of their tenure, EPA's new enforcement leadership made several important changes in EPA's enforcement program and personnel policies. Concerned that the agency's previous enforcement efforts had become unnecessarily litigious and antagonistic,[14] they adopted what became known as a "nonconfrontational" approach to enforcement.[15] The file first, negotiate later attitude of the Carter administration was replaced by the notion that, as one EPA enforcement attorney stated it, "[Y]ou were to talk first and file later only if it was absolutely necessary and only if you could clear it with headquarters."[16]

Informal attempts at encouraging voluntary compliance became the enforcement procedure of choice. At least one EPA regional administrator was directly informed by William Sullivan, the agency's enforcement counsel, that every enforcement case referred to headquarters by his region "will be considered a black mark against you." That individual, who took the view that Sullivan was "one of the level-headed and professional individuals who wanted to do a good job and was only following instructions from others," stated that he considered Sullivan's statement to him the "strongest indication" that federal environmental enforcement was being "dismantled."[17] Additionally, considerable emphasis was placed upon deferring federal enforcement activities in favor of state enforcement.[18]

Beyond these enforcement policies, EPA's new managers carried out a series of reorganizations of the agency's enforcement structure. On June 1, 1981, Anne Gorsuch sent a memorandum to all EPA employees in which she announced that the Office of Enforcement was "abolished" and that its components would be transferred to various media programs (e.g., air, water, and hazardous waste). An Office of Legal and Enforcement Counsel also was established. This office reported directly to the administrator on the activities of the general counsel and in regard to agencywide enforcement.[19]

On September 15, 1981, Gorsuch formally eliminated EPA's regional enforcement divisions. The legal functions of those divisions were transferred to the Offices of Regional Counsel, which reported directly to the Office of General Counsel at EPA headquarters. Members of the technical staff of the regional enforcement divisions were transferred to various media-operating divisions in the regions.[20] Then, in late December 1981, headquarters enforcement *legal* activities were centralized in a new Office of Enforcement Counsel. The headquarters *technical* enforcement staff, however, remained with the various media offices; thus the legal enforcement and technical staffs were permanently divided into separate organizations.[21] A number of these changes were implemented over objections made by some of the agency's senior career enforcement managers, who argued that the reorganizations would have a disruptive and counterproductive effect on the agency's overall enforcement efforts.[22]

In addition to these reorganizations, a number of other trends and developments in the early Reagan days played an important role in EPA's enforcement work. On his first day in office, President Reagan issued a "Memorandum for the Heads of Executive Departments and Agencies," which imposed "a strict freeze on the hiring of federal civilian employees to be applied across the board in the executive branch."[23] This action, described as a "first step towards controlling the growth and size of government and stopping the drain on the economy by the public sector," effectively prohibited EPA's mid-level supervisory management from replacing any staff members that left the agency.

Beyond this, EPA's enforcement program was impaired by budget reductions, as well as rumors of plans to discharge or reduce in force ("rif") the enforcement staff. With the exception of the Superfund

Program, which was supported by dedicated monies, between 1980 and 1983 EPA's budget as a whole declined, in constant 1972 dollars, from $701 million to $515 million, and the number of full-time positions at the agency, excluding Superfund, declined by 26 percent, mostly through attrition.[24] Indeed, as two scholarly observers have concluded, "There is ample evidence that the Reagan administration's adoption of an administrative presidency strategy did result in significantly lower levels of EPA expenditures and in dramatic shifts in internal program priorities away from abatement, compliance, control and enforcement."[25]

Though EPA's enforcement personnel were only minimally affected by rifs during Gorsuch's tenure as administrator, there is evidence that significant cuts in EPA's enforcement force were seriously considered. As Richard Wilson, an EPA career manager, remembered:

> There were certainly people looking at major budget cuts in EPA [enforcement]. In fact, we saw proposed budget cuts from OMB that the only way to accomplish them was to rif. In that sense it was real. . . . What you didn't know from day to day was whether or not they were going to bite the bullet and in fact rif down to those levels or [just] let attrition take its toll.[26]

Ultimately, no major termination of career enforcement staff actually occurred during the Gorsuch era. However, various enforcement programs, elements, and innovations were eliminated as a result of budget reductions, and funding for staff travel and training was significantly cut.[27] Moreover, EPA's enforcement effort was impaired by a relatively high rate of attrition.[28]

Deeply concerned about actual and possible budget cuts and effectively sealed off from the decision-making process, a number of career enforcement managers and staff members began to perceive that ideological and partisan political considerations were playing an increasing role in the evaluation of their professional work.[29] In part this notion resulted from a statement by William Sullivan at a meeting of the entire headquarters enforcement staff in late December 1981. During the month or two before this meeting, several staff attorneys had been hired (at relatively high salaries), notwithstanding the continuing EPA hiring ceilings.[30] As Richard Mays, then a career enforcement manager at EPA, remembered:

> Sullivan made the announcement about the latest reorganization and then following that had a question and answer series. Some member of the staff asked him about the hirings of attorneys and

whether political affiliation had played any role in these hirings. Sullivan's response was that essentially "this was a political world." The Republicans were the administration in power and, all things being equal, he would rather hire a Republican than someone who was not a Republican. The staff didn't like that too much, obviously, because this is a group of people who believe, and I think rightly so, that politics and ideology should have little to do with environmental protection or qualifications in terms of hiring staff.[31]

Other events also contributed to the career staff's sense that the agency's enforcement program was becoming "politicized." Peter Broccoletti, whom Sullivan had selected to be his deputy enforcement counsel, conducted a series of interviews with EPA enforcement attorneys in which at least some of them were asked questions about their memberships in environmental organizations.[32] Broccoletti, whose approach to the career staff was seen as "domineering and intimidating,"[33] allegedly told EPA attorney and manager James Bunting that all of the EPA enforcement attorneys' original job application forms were under political review. Broccoletti subsequently denied this.[34] Nonetheless, Bunting specifically recalled: "People were being evaluated on the basis of what it was they had said there. If someone had listed a Democratic congressman as a reference, then that particular individual . . . was going to be viewed with suspicion."[35]

In addition to politicization, some EPA managers and staff members had the impression that the leadership of the agency had regular contact with representatives of potential candidates for enforcement action outside of the presence of EPA staff members assigned to their cases. As William Hedeman stated, "[B]ehind the scenes, in the Sullivan-Burford era, industry was getting to these individuals quietly and having a major influence on how the enforcement policy took shape."[36]

An extreme but politically significant instance of this arose in EPA's negotiations with representatives of Inmont Corporation concerning a California hazardous waste disposal site. In early September 1981 Thornton "Whit" Field, then special assistant to the administrator for hazardous waste, had a series of conversations with Inmont's attorney regarding Inmont's responsibility for site cleanup which were not reported to the agency's designated negotiators. During one of those conversations, Field revealed EPA's bottom line settlement figure to Inmont, an event which had a critical effect on the outcome of those negotiations.[37]

More generally, during this time some of the regulated parties that were involved in settlement discussions with the EPA's enforcement staff sought meetings with higher-ranking agency officials in the hope that they might receive a more sympathetic hearing.[38] As a result, from one attorney's perspective, "there never was any certainty that the deal you felt you had negotiated aboveboard [and] across the table was going to be something that you could carry through when it came back to headquarters [for approval]."[39] A number of EPA enforcement staff members also developed the perception that the people they reported to—the agency's career enforcement managers—had little influence on setting enforcement policy. Two incidents served to reinforce that notion.

In November 1981 the entire hazardous waste management staff had a meeting in Denver, Colorado. During the course of this meeting, Douglas MacMillan, EPA's highest-ranking career official with specific responsibility for hazardous waste enforcement, made a presentation about the agency's enforcement policy. He indicated that EPA would be using administrative orders to redress RCRA violations. He also stated that when state agencies took RCRA enforcement actions against a regulated party that EPA officials perceived to be inappropriate or inadequate, the agency would, in some instances, be prepared to pursue its own enforcement case against the same party. Shortly thereafter, at the same meeting, Thornton "Whit" Field explicitly rejected the policies that MacMillan had announced. Stating, "I don't buy that and I don't think Anne Gorsuch does either," Field indicated that a formal enforcement approach was "too confrontational for this administration."[40] MacMillan later scarcely remembered this event,[41] but several enforcement staff members perceived Field's statements as a strong signal. His remarks appeared to indicate not only that MacMillan's pronouncement no longer represented the agency's policy but also that the former task force director had been "slapped down very publicly."[42]

Another critical incident occurred seven months later when Rita M. Lavelle, EPA's assistant administrator for solid waste and emergency response, removed Lamar Miller from his position as chief of the technical component of the hazardous waste enforcement program. Miller, whom most staff members viewed as an outspoken advocate of firm enforcement, had been less successful than his counterpart, William Hedeman, in gaining Lavelle's confidence. As one former member of Miller's staff recalled:

They announced the change on a day when he was going into the hospital for some sort of surgery. At the time it was really pretty strange. He wasn't for it. Lavelle said that Lamar was going to head up some sort of a groundwater monitoring branch in OSW [Office of Solid Waste and Emergency Response] which didn't exist at the time and never subsequently materialized. When he came back, they gave him a task on some sort of a "sludge project."[43]

In the minds of a number of EPA's headquarters enforcement staff, Miller's abrupt removal marked an important turning point. Following Miller's removal, one knowledgeable official recalled, the staff "pushed less hard" and negotiated with regulated parties by "taking deals because they were there."[44]

If the authority of the agency's top career enforcement managers had been dramatically undermined, however, it was not at all clear who was actually in charge of EPA enforcement work. Almost from the outset of the Reagan administration, EPA's enforcement program was marked by intense rivalries among the new political appointees. As one seasoned civil servant put it: "In eighteen years in government, I have never seen a group of people as intent on doing one another in as that crowd was."[45]

During the early months of the Reagan administration Anne Gorsuch relied heavily on William Sullivan in enforcement matters to the relative exclusion of Sullivan's superior, associate administrator Frank Shepherd, and Robert Perry, the agency's general counsel. A competition for authority grew among these three attorneys.[46] Within a few months, Shepherd resigned, leaving Sullivan and Perry, two strong-willed individuals, to vie for influence in the enforcement field. In the end, Perry prevailed. He assumed complete control of EPA's legal operation in April 1982. Perry's ascendancy did not end the rivalry within the upper echelons of EPA's enforcement program, however. As Anne Gorsuch told me, there was "almost a constant conflict" between Perry and Rita Lavelle over the strategy to be followed in hazardous waste enforcement cases.[47] There was also considerable disagreement among the agency's regional administrators on a variety of enforcement issues.[48]

With respect to hazardous waste enforcement in particular, the first two years of the Reagan administration saw the institution of several new policies and trends. It is notable, however, that despite the bevy of new policy questions that arose from EPA's initial attempts to implement the Superfund Program, the agency's headquarters provided little written guidance to its regional enforcement personnel.[49] Furthermore, those few Superfund policies that did emerge were sometimes changed with great rapidity.

In general, the Superfund approach that was followed during this period was based on the preference of EPA's top management for strict conservation of the $1.6 billion CERCLA trust fund. This approach was intended to strengthen the argument that the Superfund Act, and the corporate taxes that support it, should not be renewed after the Act's expiration on October 1, 1985.

To implement the Superfund approach, EPA's leadership adopted a strategy that has been described as "lawyers first, shovels later."[50] In fact, this label is misleading. It implies that a tough, litigious approach to Superfund enforcement preceded any use of the CERCLA trust fund for site cleanup activities. In reality, with the exception of hazardous waste enforcement matters that were already pending, EPA's earliest Superfund enforcement effort was anything but litigious. Rather than "lawyers first, shovels later," the slogan "ineffectual negotiation first, shovels never" is a more apt description.

The agency placed heavy emphasis on providing the PRPs at inactive hazardous waste sites with the option of voluntarily cleaning up those sites. The expenditure of trust fund monies for remedial actions at Superfund sites was not permitted unless and until it had been demonstrated, to the satisfaction of the agency's top headquarters officials, that responsible parties at those sites had been identified, that they had been notified of their potential liability for site cleanup expenditures, and that they had voluntarily and intentionally declined to carry out measures on their own.[51]

Other EPA policies and procedures also contributed to a sparing use of the CERCLA trust fund. In March 1982 the agency required states to contribute 10 percent of the cost of RI/FS preparation as a condition to the use of Superfund monies for planning and designing hazardous waste site cleanups. Because most states had limited resources to come up with this 10 percent match, this policy significantly inhibited the use of the Superfund for cleanup activity.[52] In addition, the agency began to interpret the "imminent and substantial endangerment" language of CERCLA section 106 (and RCRA section 7003) as requiring that the agency demonstrate a present public health emergency, as opposed to the mere threat of one, in order to obtain relief.[53] Because of the difficulty of making this showing in many cases, EPA's use of the CERCLA and RCRA imminent hazards sections to redress contamination problems at inactive hazardous waste sites was significantly curtailed.[54]

The agency's leadership placed other restrictions on EPA's use of its emergency or "immediate removal" authority under CERCLA. This was accomplished by the promulgation of a set of regulations, incorporated as part of the agency's National Contingency Plan, which were consistently more restrictive than the statute required.[55]

It was also affected by a policy that forbade EPA's regional offices from expending trust fund monies in excess of $50,000 for removal actions without the personal approval of the agency's assistant administrator for enforcement.[56]

The Reagan administration's first EPA managers centralized decision making in other ways as well. Authority over expenditures, case-specific enforcement strategy, and the wording of documents filed in enforcement litigation was retained in the agency's Office of Solid Waste and Emergency Response and its Office of Enforcement Counsel. Regional officials were given little autonomy in implementing these vital aspects of the Superfund law.[57]

Finally, the Reagan administration's initial approach to RCRA enforcement continued the high level of inattention and inaction that had characterized RCRA enforcement during the Carter years. As one former EPA enforcement official expressed: "[V]irtually nothing was done in terms of writing guidance, making policy decisions or establishing a [sic] RCRA enforcement program."[58] State environmental agencies, which in many cases had "minimal training and too few resources," were delegated total responsibility for RCRA enforcement, with little federal guidance or oversight.[59] The agency's RCRA enforcement program was afforded few resources, and many RCRA hazardous waste management regulations were placed in limbo by the agency's plans to reconsider and revise them extensively.[60]

The cumulative impact of these innovations on EPA's enforcement policies was dramatic and pronounced. The number of new civil enforcement actions forwarded by EPA regional offices to agency headquarters fell by 79 percent in 1981, compared with the previous year, and the agency's civil referrals to the Justice Department fell 69 percent. In the Superfund area, EPA referred no new enforcement cases to the DOJ from January 20, 1981, until April 1, 1982, and only three such cases were filed between the latter date and September 29, 1982. With respect to RCRA civil enforcement actions, EPA filed no cases in 1981 and only three cases during the first nine months of 1982, a sharp contrast to the forty-three RCRA civil cases the agency had initiated during 1980.[61]

In addition to a drop in its workload, EPA's enforcement staff was faced with considerable confusion. As William Sullivan candidly admitted: "The poor regional attorneys were left in a position where they didn't know who the hell they worked for. They couldn't even tell what the procedures were from day to day."[62] Apparently, the continuing reorganizations of the agency's enforcement programs significantly contributed to the enforcement staff's confusion. Some present and former EPA officials saw clear organizational advantages in the demise of EPA's preexisting structure.[63] Nonetheless, a large number of those I spoke with viewed this series of organizational changes as harmful to the enforcement effort. In particular, they believed that the reorganization created barriers to effective communication among the agency's interdisciplinary enforcement staff, giving rise to turf battles and red tape that had not existed previously.[64] In the face of these changes and uncertainties, a number of the agency's mid-level managers became unwilling to make firm policy decisions, fearing that any position they took would be reversed at higher levels.[65]

Not surprisingly, enforcement staff morale declined precipitously in this period, notwithstanding Gorsuch's later recollection that the agency had been "fun" and "jumpin'."[66] As one regional enforcement manager described it: "There was this feeling that the EPA was kind of a ship adrift in the water and that if we wanted to do anything it was time to leave, move on."[67] Staff members "feared for their jobs and for their reputations."[68] In the view of a former headquarters enforcement manager:

> You spent a lot of time figuring out ways to get around obstacles which were internal [to EPA] now, rather than external. You were trying to survive, trying to continue to do your job, while most of your days were spent worrying about whether you would actually have a job, in some cases, or whom you would be working for and whether that person would be a rational human being.[69]

With few exceptions, the agency's political appointees were the objects of intense resentment from the enforcement staff. Their motives were distrusted, their enforcement policies were disliked, and the professional competency of some was questioned. Out of anger and despair, some headquarters enforcement staff members cultivated informal relationships with members of congressional committees, relationships that were to have increasing significance as the Gorsuch years wore on.[70]

In addition to internal disarray, EPA's relationships with various elements outside the agency began to deteriorate. Fearful that budget cuts would result in lost federal grants, a number of state pollution control agency managers also began to mistrust EPA's new approach.[71] In addition, the agency lost considerable credibility with the press.[72]

EPA's weakened enforcement effort also met with increasing disenchantment from some elements of industry. During this period, a number of regulated firms became concerned that the decline in

EPA enforcement was contrary to their interests. They feared that this trend would disadvantage companies that had already expended money to comply with environmental requirements. They were also concerned that weak enforcement would lead to a public backlash in which EPA would be forced to subject industry to Draconian measures.[73]

With respect to the Superfund Program, the staff became involved in what one enforcement scientist and manager referred to as "interminable negotiations" with PRPs.[74] In some instances, it was unclear who had responsibility for various aspects of the Superfund Program.[75] As a result, the site cleanup effort was marked by struggles between those organizational components with responsibility for expending CERCLA trust fund monies and those units charged with enforcing the Superfund Act.[76]

Slowly, almost imperceptibly at first, Congress and the public became concerned about the difficulties emerging in EPA's enforcement efforts. This concern was partly the result of informal analyses by congressional committee staff of enforcement statistics and other information provided by the agency and its staff. It was also affected by the efforts of Save EPA, a committee of former EPA officials headed by William Drayton which had been formed to lobby against the administration's proposals for drastic decreases in EPA's budget.

In the second half of 1981, Congressman John Dingell (D-MI), the politically influential chairman of the Subcommittee on Oversight and Investigations of the House Committee on Energy and Commerce (the Dingell Committee), was supplied with information from EPA documenting the decline in new civil enforcement cases. Additionally, Congressman Dingell took note of the failure of EPA to establish a criminal enforcement program, a step that was first recommended in 1979 by James Moorman, the DOJ's assistant attorney general for lands and natural resources. Additionally, two attorneys on Dingell's subcommittee staff, Richard Frandsen and Mark Raabe, learned informally from members of EPA's career enforcement staff of the confused and demoralized state of the agency's enforcement efforts.[77]

In the fall of 1981 the Dingell Committee held a series of hearings that focused on EPA's need to hire criminal investigators.[78] Although these hearings resulted in a commitment from Gorsuch to initiate a criminal enforcement program, Congressman Dingell and his staff remained privately critical of other aspects of EPA's enforcement work. They began to prepare for additional subcommittee hearings to air their concerns and to press the agency for a more vigorous enforcement approach in the hazardous waste area.

In the meantime, several events took place that served to heighten public awareness of the problems EPA's new enforcement approach had created. During the week of January 25, 1982, *Doonesbury*, the syndicated comic strip by Garry Trudeau, ran a series in which Ted Simpson, a mythical EPA employee, was portrayed as sitting on an office window ledge to protest Gorsuch's purported plans "to dismantle the whole enforcement team." After eliciting a promise from the EPA administrator "to reinstate the enforcement division" and to let the enforcement staff prosecute pollution violators "until such time as the President can gut the laws," Simpson was shown returning from his window ledge only to be told, "I lied. You're fired."[79]

This series of cartoons, which appeared in many newspapers, including the *Washington Post*, increased the visibility of the Reagan administration's EPA enforcement failures. Among other things, it prompted Gorsuch to send a memorandum to all EPA employees on February 5, 1982, in which she denounced "windowsill politics" and "countless press reports and rumors of massive personnel reductions planned for this agency." Gorsuch pledged that "there will be no involuntary separations due to reductions-in-force at the Environmental Protection agency during the remainder of fiscal year 1982" and stated, "I expect to continue the same policy . . . through fiscal year 1983."

Shortly after the Ted Simpson *Doonesbury* cartoons appeared, Russell E. Train, EPA's second administrator, published a guest column in the *Washington Post* in which he sharply criticized the management of EPA and warned of disastrous consequences if proposed budget cuts in the agency's staffing levels were permitted to occur.[80] Because of Train's prominence in the environmental field, his Republican credentials, and his credibility with moderate elements in the business community, his written remarks were seen to significantly weaken the EPA administration's political credibility.

In addition, approximately three weeks later, EPA began a series of actions which, though not directly related to its enforcement program, brought EPA's approach to hazardous waste regulation into sharp focus. On February 25, 1982, the agency formally proposed to reverse rules that had prohibited the burial of hazardous liquids in landfills for a period of at least ninety days on the basis that these prohibitions had been unworkable and unnecessarily costly.[81] This proposal gave rise to vehement protests from environmental organizations, so-called high-tech waste disposal companies, and congressional critics of EPA, including Congressman James Florio (D-NJ), whose Subcommittee on Commerce, Transportation and Tourism held public hearings with respect to the liquids-in-landfills proposals. Within several weeks, EPA withdrew its proposal, establishing instead an interim rule that prohibited the burial in landfills of any container in which liquid toxic chemical wastes are "standing in observable quantities."[82] Although this action quieted the immediate controversy and won guarded praise from some of EPA's leading congressional critics, including Congressman Toby Moffett (D-CT), the chairman of the environmental subcommittee of the House Committee on Government Operations, the entire incident served to further tarnish EPA's reputation with respect to its regulation of hazardous wastes.

Shortly thereafter, the Dingell Committee opened its second set of hearings into the Reagan administration's enforcement approach. Administrator Gorsuch, Enforcement Counsel Sullivan, and other high-ranking EPA officials were called to testify and were subjected to pointed and embarrassing questions with regard to EPA's hazardous waste enforcement program.[83] The agency's site cleanup negotiations with Inmont Corporation were spotlighted, along with the dramatic decrease in its civil enforcement case referrals and the continual reorganization of its enforcement structure.

These hearings were widely publicized. They provided much of the basis for a subcommittee report, ultimately published in December 1982, which contained sharp criticism of EPA's Superfund and RCRA enforcement efforts.[84] In response to the political pressures that the Dingell hearings generated, EPA's leadership continued to institute a series of management and policy changes that they hoped would place the agency's enforcement work in a more favorable light.[85]

In late March 1982 William Sullivan was relieved of his leadership role in EPA enforcement matters. In Sullivan's stead Robert M. Perry, the agency's general counsel, was given expanded responsibility in the enforcement area. Seeking to distance himself from Sullivan's informal "voluntary compliance" approach to environmental enforcement, Perry, with the support of administrator Gorsuch, initiated several measures designed to bolster the agency's faltering efforts. Perry appointed a committee of five experienced career managers to review all aspects of EPA's enforcement program and to suggest improvements.[86] He also appointed Michael Brown, a forceful and dynamic attorney/manager with considerable prior experience in the Consumer Product Safety Commission, to replace Sullivan as enforcement counsel.

In response to congressional criticisms of excessive industry influence on EPA enforcement policies and of the alleged execution of sweetheart deals in particular hazardous waste enforcement cases, Perry instituted a policy prohibiting Superfund enforcement agreements with PRPs unless the government obtained all that it sought in negotiation. This policy effectively forbade settlements in Superfund enforcement matters unless PRP defendants agreed that (1) they would enter into a formal written agreement, usually in the form of a Consent Decree; (2) they would not be formally released from future liability, even if they fully complied with the terms of the agreement; and (3) they would assume all costs of site cleanup. Few PRPs actually agreed to settle on these extremely stringent terms.[87] Perry also began to place pressure on regional enforcement officials to generate large numbers of new enforcement actions.[88] This last initiative resulted in what one former DOJ official described as a "blitzkrieg of referrals" in late September 1982, at the end of the agency's fiscal year.[89]

Beyond this, during this time the agency and the DOJ took small but concrete steps toward the establishment of a permanent criminal enforcement effort. In the summer of 1982 sixteen full-time criminal investigators were hired from a pool of nearly three hundred applicants from other law enforcement agencies. The addition of these individuals—all of whom had served as criminal investigators for a minimum of five years and some of whom had more than twenty years of investigative and supervisory experience—raised to twenty-three the agency's total number of investigators. This was soon followed by the creation of a small environmental crimes unit with the Justice Department's Criminal and Lands Division.[90]

In a political sense, these modifications to EPA's enforcement approach were too little and too late. Most of the administration's critics, both on Capitol Hill and within the agency, remained unpersuaded that EPA's enforcement program had become truly aggressive or effective. On June 15, 1982, Congressmen Dingell and Florio sent Anne Gorsuch an eleven-page, single-spaced letter in which they requested "actual data, rather than unsupported estimates" concerning some 144 indicators of enforcement activity over a three-and-a-half-year period.[91] This letter, which gave rise to an intensive and time-consuming search of EPA's enforcement records and statistics,[92] was supplemented by a second Dingell-Florio letter to Gorsuch on August 31, 1982, in which seventy-three specific requests for additional information were also submitted to the agency.[93]

Other congressmen began to pursue parallel investigations. On September 15, 1982, staff attorneys for the Subcommittee on Investigations and Oversight of the House Committee on Public Works and Transportation, under the chairmanship of Congressman Elliot Levitas (D-GA) (the Levitas Committee), traveled to EPA's Region II office in New York to examine enforcement files pertaining to certain Superfund cases. Upon their arrival, these attorneys learned, to their surprise and distress, that the agency would not permit access to the documents they sought. On the Justice Department's advice, the Reagan administration had decided to rely upon the executive privilege doctrine as a basis for withholding from congressional investigators enforcement files that the agency deemed "enforcement sensitive" in content.[94] There is considerable evidence that this decision was made by the Department of Justice and imposed upon skeptical EPA officials. In a carefully documented report, the House Judiciary Committee concluded that before executive privilege was claimed, the Justice Department was aware of at least nine different incidents which demonstrated that EPA was willing to turn the disputed documents over to Congress.[95]

Notwithstanding its genesis, however, the decision to claim executive privilege proved a fateful one for most of EPA's top managers. On November 22, 1982, after EPA General Counsel Robert Perry had reiterated the Reagan administration's position in correspondence with Congressman Levitas, the House Committee on Public Works and Transportation formally subpoenaed Anne Gorsuch to appear before the Levitas Committee on December 2, 1982, and to bring with her enforcement-related documents regarding some 160 abandoned hazardous waste sites.[96] Gorsuch appeared before the Levitas Committee on December 2, but rather than supply the requested documents, the EPA administrator testified that President Reagan had instructed her to withhold those papers from the House. Later that day, the Levitas Committee voted to hold Gorsuch in contempt of Congress,[97] an action that was reiterated by the full House of Representatives on December 16, 1982, by a vote of 259 to 105.[98]

During the same period that the Levitas Committee encountered resistance to its requests for EPA Superfund documents, the Dingell Committee, which had begun an investigation of the possible allocation of Superfund monies for partisan political advantage, met with similar administration intransigence. On September 17, 1982, Congressman Dingell sent a letter to Anne Gorsuch requesting EPA documents with respect to three Superfund sites. These documents were formally subpoenaed by the Dingell Committee approximately one month later. As she had done in response to the Levitas Committee's subpoena, Gorsuch appeared before the Dingell Committee on December 14, 1982, and expressly refused to provide a number of the subpoenaed documents on the grounds of executive privilege. The Dingell Committee voted to hold Gorsuch in contempt on the same day.[99]

These actions set the stage for a major constitutional confrontation between Congress and the executive branch. On December 16, 1982, the Department of Justice brought suit against the House of Representatives in the U.S. District Court for the District of Columbia. The department sought to enjoin enforcement of the Levitas Committee's subpoena and to have that document declared invalid and unconstitutional. Attorneys for the House promptly moved to dismiss the DOJ's suit, a motion which the district court took under advisement.[100]

In the meantime, the controversy over the documents, the attitudes and record of Anne Gorsuch and other high-ranking EPA officials, and virtually all aspects of the management of EPA since the advent of the Reagan administration became the focus of intense media scrutiny. Believing the "EPA scandal" to be the beginning, at least potentially, of a Watergate-style cover-up, the media provided prominent coverage of the management of the Superfund Program by Anne Gorsuch, Rita Lavelle, and others. This extensive publicity lasted for a period of several months.[101] During that time, EPA's top leadership developed what one civil servant later described as a "bunker mentality."[102] Besieged by the press and Congress, EPA's leaders became isolated from their staffs and increasingly uninvolved in matters not pertaining to the documents controversy.

EPA's enforcement staff was deeply immersed in the executive privilege dispute as well. Enforcement attorneys in EPA's headquarters and its regional offices were asked to respond to Congress's information request by reviewing all of the agency's enforcement files to determine which of the documents contained therein were "enforcement sensitive." This was an extremely time-consuming task, involving the review of thousands of letters, memos, records, and reports.[103] In addition, approximately thirty members of the agency's career enforcement staff were subpoenaed to testify before executive sessions of the Dingell Committee as part of its continuing investigation into Superfund abuses.[104] Many other staff members devoted a good deal of their time to responding to inquiries by the press and individual members of Congress concerning EPA's handling of particular Superfund matters.[105]

On February 3, 1983, U.S. District Judge John Lewis Smith, Jr., granted the House of Representatives' motion to dismiss the DOJ's executive privilege suit. Judge Smith stated, "The difficulties apparent in prosecuting administrator Gorsuch for contempt of Congress should encourage the two branches to settle their differences without further judicial involvement. Compromise and cooperation, rather than confrontation, should be the aim of the parties."[106] With this judicial admonishment, high officials of the Reagan administration decided to enter into serious compromise negotiations with their congressional adversaries. On March 9, 1983, Congressman Dingell and White House Counsel Fred Fielding executed a written agreement under which the Dingell Committee was to be furnished all of the documents it had sought regarding Superfund sites.[107] A similar understanding was reached between the DOJ and the Levitas Committee approximately two weeks later.[108]

As part of the Reagan administration's plan to limit the political damage created by the documents controversy, Anne Gorsuch was compelled to resign as EPA's administrator.[109] She left office on March 9, 1983. Immediately preceding or shortly following that event, some nineteen other top-level EPA officials left their posts, resulting in a nearly complete turnover in the agency's highest leadership.[110]

In other fallout from the congressional investigations, Rita M. Lavelle was indicted by a federal grand jury for providing false testimony to some of the congressional committees that investigated her administration of the Superfund Program. On December 1, 1983, Lavelle was convicted by a jury of most of the felony charges made against her. She was sentenced to six months' confinement, five years' probation (during which time she was required to perform community service), and a $10,000 fine.[111]

By almost any measure, the period from January 1981 until March 1983 was a devastating time for EPA's enforcement work. The number of new civil actions initiated by the EPA fell dramatically during those years. Additionally, the agency's enforcement programs during this period experienced unprecedented levels of disorganization, demoralization, and internal strife. Although there is disagreement about whether the agency's political leadership specifically intended those results, there can be little doubt that it was their actions and omissions that caused them.

It seems inevitable that every incoming administration will place its own political appointees in positions responsible for implementing regulatory requirements. The approach of the EPA's early Reagan administration managers, however, led to an almost complete politicization of the enforcement process. This politicization interfered with the agency's remedial application of hazardous waste statutes and its enforcement of other federal laws, objective tasks requiring persistent professional effort and institutional stability. Beyond this, the EPA managers of the early 1980s failed from the outset to enunciate a clear and defensible approach to EPA's enforcement work. In this respect, their efforts stand in sharp contrast not only to the litigious EPA enforcement strategies of the Carter administration but also to enforcement regimes of the Nixon and Ford administrations, as well as the EPA enforcement programs of the past ten years. Indeed, in the words of four congressmen from the Reagan administration's own party: "[T]he poor performance of the Superfund program [in the 1981–1983 period] resulted from a lack of expertise, inexperience, incompetence and mismanagement" by those responsible for implementing the program.[112]

If the stormy history of EPA's enforcement efforts in the Gorsuch era demonstrates that the political leadership of administrative agencies has a practical ability to inhibit or forestall vigorous enforcement, what can it teach us with respect to Congress's effectiveness in restoring enforcement vitality? Here, the answer appears somewhat more sanguine. In many respects, congressional pressure on EPA's leadership to reverse the failings of the Gorsuch era were effective. Through oversight hearings, extensive requests for information, publicity, and informal attempts at persuasion, Congress appears to have motivated EPA's top management in the summer and fall of 1982 to stem the decline of the agency's hazardous waste enforcement programs. In addition, aggressive congressional oversight activity during the 1983 documents controversy led to the replacement of Gorsuch and her colleagues with new managers who had different enforcement attitudes and management techniques.[113]

In view of these evident congressional successes, it might be surmised that our government has created a check on the enforcement failings of administrative agencies. On that theory, ineffective agency enforcement programs—particularly when they involve regulatory legislation that enjoys broad public support—will invariably be identified by concerned members of Congress and their staffs. These ineffective enforcement efforts will be brought to light at oversight hearings and by other means, and top administrative managers—fearing unwelcome publicity and congressional displeasure—will necessarily be forced to energize and reform their agency's enforcement efforts or face dismissal and political disgrace.

On the surface, this hypothesis has some plausibility. However, upon close examination, it is clear that it fails to grasp some of the larger implications of this phase of EPA's enforcement history. Congress's "victory" in its confrontations with EPA's top managers had a number of critical components, none of which, in retrospect, seems the natural or inevitable result of EPA's enforcement shortcomings. First, the congressional oversight effort was led by an experienced and influential legislator, Congressman John Dingell, who had a reputation for assertive, thorough, and detailed oversight work. No matter how politically self-interested his efforts may have been, without Dingell and the skillful work of his subcommittee staff, the congressional investigation of EPA's enforcement programs would probably not have been as successful as it was.

Second, the dispute between EPA and Congress over the agency's hazardous waste enforcement efforts was marked by a number of costly tactical errors on the part of administration officials. For example, the decision of administration officials in February 1982 to permit the landfill burial of liquid hazardous wastes led to an intense, damaging, and entirely avoidable public controversy, a dispute that lowered the agency's credibility in the hazardous waste area during a critical time. Similarly, the Reagan administration's decision to withhold subpoenaed documents from the Levitas and Dingell Committees converted what had been a simmering dispute over EPA's enforcement record into a major constitutional confrontation. It seems far from inevitable that Congress would have achieved the level of dominance in the area of EPA waste enforcement that it did if the Reagan administration had avoided these damaging errors.

Third, the competition between EPA and Congress with respect to enforcement questions was played out in the spotlight of intense national publicity. This situation, which resulted partly from the constitutional dimensions of the documents dispute and partly from the fact that the dispute appeared to the media to parallel the Watergate scandal of the 1970s, served to raise the political stakes for all concerned. Had the press chosen to pay less attention to the "EPA scandals" of the early Reagan administration (particularly during the autumn of 1982 and the winter of 1983), the March 1983 resignation of the agency's top leadership would not, in retrospect, appear certain and unavoidable.

Rather than demonstrating that it is inevitable that congressional reaction will effectively reverse poor regulatory enforcement performances by federal administrative agencies, EPA's 1981 to 1983 disputes with Congress concerning enforcement appear to yield to a much more modest conclusion. They indicate that, at least in some instances, congressional investigation and oversight of weak administrative agency enforcement have the potential to effectively force a nonenforcing agency into a more vigorous enforcement posture. When the congressional opposition to agency nonenforcement is well publicized, when it is spearheaded by influential and determined legislators, and when it is aimed at administration officials unable to project a politically credible image of moderation and managerial competence, that opposition can create a climate in which ineffectual enforcement practices must be reversed.

FIVE

"Away from the Brink" — But Not Out of the Woods

EPA Enforcement from 1983 to 1989

In July 1988, David Andrews, a private attorney who had served in EPA during the Carter administration wrote:

> There is no question that Bill Ruckelshaus moved the [Environmental Protection] Agency away from the brink of disaster and put it back on the road to recovery. Lee Thomas has kept the agency on that road, but the agency continued to suffer from a perception that it is not fully committed to meet its environmental and public health responsibilities. Therefore there is still some distance to travel before Congress and the public will view EPA as an agency operating with a full commitment to meeting its responsibilities.[1]

Andrews' words aptly described the circumstances of the agency—in its enforcement efforts and otherwise—during the final six years of Ronald Reagan's Presidency. EPA enforcement in the Gorsuch era was characterized by considerable confusion, disorganization, and discontinuity. The agency's relationship with Congress and the press was fraught with discord and confrontation. The number of new enforcement actions initiated by the EPA declined precipitously, and enforcement staff morale was low. The reappointment of William D. Ruckelshaus as EPA's Administrator marked the start of a different approach to the agency's enforcement responsibilities.

Having decided to alter many of the policies and procedures of his unpopular predecessor, Ruckelshaus and his new management team initiated several well-publicized changes. In confirmation hearings before a Senate committee, Ruckelshaus publicly pledged that he would operate his agency "in a fishbowl." He stated, "We will attempt to communicate with everyone, from the environmentalists to those we regulate, and we will do so as early as possible."[2] Ruckelshaus also committed himself to a renewed emphasis on effective enforcement. The hiring ceiling that had been applied to all EPA positions, including enforcement-related jobs, was lifted for the first time in the Reagan administration.[3] There was a gradual increase in the amount of money allocated for enforcement training and travel.[4] In addition, the Superfund enforcement staff was significantly increased, particularly in technical and scientific areas. Beyond this, Ruckelshaus and his colleagues displayed a willingness to consider the recommendations of EPA's career enforcement staff.[5] This new approach to the permanent staff's concerns helped improve morale.[6] In the view of one former enforcement attorney: "The employees were once again viewed as being a valued part of the agency. This improved the situation immeasurably. It instilled new life."[7]

Despite these reforms, in many quarters of the agency skepticism prevailed regarding the new administrator's true intentions with regard to enforcement. That skepticism was deepened by the decision of Alvin Alm, EPA's new deputy administrator, not to recreate EPA's pre-Gorsuch Office of Enforcement and regional enforcement divisions.[8] This decision may well have been based on a genuine belief that further tinkering with the agency's basic enforcement structure would only compound the shortcomings of the prior EPA administration's enforcement approach.[9] Nonetheless, it was viewed by the agency's enforcement staff as an indication that EPA's new top management was less than serious in its commitment to reinvigorate the enforcement campaign.[10]

Concerned with the agency's lack of progress in restoring its enforcement efforts and with the very real possibility of renewed criticism from Capitol Hill, Ruckelshaus decided to dramatize his preference for an effective enforcement program. He chose as his forum an EPA National Compliance and Enforcement Conference in January 1984. Before a large audience of nearly all of the agency's top and midlevel managers with responsibilities in the enforcement field, the administrator announced, "I am nervous about what I perceive to be an apparent lack of action and serious commitment to ensuring that these [environmental] laws and regulations are enforced." Chiding the agency's managers for their poor enforcement performance, Ruckelshaus declared:

> What I was concerned about, frankly, in coming back here was that we had a bunch of tigers in the tank, and the minute we took the lid off the tank and said, "Go get them," the problem might well be an overreaction—that we might start treating people unfairly, just to show everybody how tough we are. Well, I think we opened the tank all right. But on the basis of what I see here the past few months, there may be more pussycats in the tank than tigers.[11]

This speech, delivered with passion and followed by sustained applause, had something of a catalytic effect. Many of EPA's enforcement staffers began to believe that they had finally received the clear signal they had sought. They were, for the first time, persuaded that the agency's new top managers had an interest in building the credible and effective enforcement effort their immediate predecessors had failed to achieve.

That signal was reinforced, in several respects, in the months that followed. As a supplement to Ruckelshaus's speech, the agency's deputy administrator, Alvin Alm, spearheaded a top management effort to pressure EPA's regional offices into meeting their enforcement commitments. Alm's monthly telephone calls and semiannual visits with regional administrators were intended to be a reminder that EPA's top leaders once again viewed enforcement as a priority and that regional managers would be held accountable if their regions did not increase enforcement output.

Beyond this, Ruckelshaus and his staff made efforts to improve the efficacy of EPA's fledgling criminal enforcement program. In July 1983 the agency formally requested that the Department of Justice appoint EPA's small staff of criminal investigators as special deputy U.S. marshals. This request was designed to provide the investigators with legal authority to make arrests, execute search warrants, and carry firearms.[12] Initially, the Justice Department balked at this request. However, the DOJ was soon taken to task by Congress for its intransigence. In a September 1983 oversight hearing before his House Subcommittee on Oversight and Investigations, Congressman John Dingell pointed out that a number of the targets of EPA's criminal investigations had criminal records, operated clandestinely, and carried weapons. Without the authority to carry firearms and execute warrants, EPA's newly hired investigators were placed in a position of disadvantage and, in some instances, personal danger in carrying out their duties.[13] Notwithstanding strong congressional pressure, the Justice Department continued to resist EPA's deputization request. In April 1984, however, the department finally reversed its position. It approved the agency's deputization of its criminal investigators for a trial period, a period which lasted nearly four years.[14]

In the area of civil enforcement, Ruckelshaus and Alm took steps to improve EPA's relationship with the states and to clarify the agency's policy respecting civil penalties. In June 1983, a task force of senior managers was established to develop a set of options outlining state and federal roles in implementing environmental programs. After a brief study, this group recommended that EPA develop an oversight program which recognized that direct program administration and enforcement were primarily state responsibilities, and that the agency foster more trust and mutual respect in EPA/state relationships.[15]

Several months later, EPA issued a policy framework for individual EPA/state enforcement agreements. This document, formally effective in June 1984, set forth the agency's methods for overseeing state enforcement programs. It established a set of criteria to be used for assessing good enforcement program performance and called for semiannual EPA reviews of state enforcement programs, quarterly state reporting on key performance measures, and regular EPA evaluations of state progress in addressing significant violations.[16] While far from a permanent resolution of the agency's often tense relationships with state enforcement officials, this policy, and the individual state-EPA enforcement agreements it spawned, helped to improve intergovernmental communication and to define better the expectations and roles of federal and state enforcement officials.

EPA's evolving civil enforcement policies were further clarified in February 1984 by the issuance of a Uniform Policy on Civil Penalties. This policy required EPA program policies, and regional office enforcement actions, to recover the economic benefit of noncompliance from violators of environmental standards.[17] Although the agency's inconsistent implementation of the policy was to prove an embarrassment in later years, its promulgation was an important step forward in defining EPA's formal approach in a particularly controversial area of enforcement case negotiation.

As a result of its significance in the events that led up to Anne Gorsuch's resignation as administrator, as well as its continuing importance in the minds of many members of Congress and their professional staffs, EPA's implementation of the Superfund Program was afforded a high priority by Ruckelshaus and his colleagues. In this area the new administrator chose to delegate a great deal of authority to Lee M. Thomas, who replaced Rita Lavelle as the agency's assistant administrator for solid waste and emergency response. Thomas, who began his career as an official of the state government of South Carolina in the field of criminal justice, had gone on to become executive deputy director of the Federal Emergency Management Agency (FEMA). In that capacity he had headed the federal government's efforts to provide relief to the residents of Times Beach, Missouri, who had been imperiled by improperly disposed hazardous wastes. An able manager, Thomas quickly impressed his staff with his intelligence and decisiveness. The comments of Michael Kilpatrick, an EPA manager in the Superfund enforcement program, typify the views of many of the agency's career staff: "In my mind, Lee Thomas was the reason why things got back on a smooth track here. The guy just works incredibly hard and is extremely bright. He very quickly learned what the issues were."[18]

Under Thomas's leadership, a number of changes were made in EPA's Superfund approach. The agency's strict limitation of expenditures from the CERCLA trust fund was abruptly ended, replaced by an emphasis on attempting to clean up abandoned hazardous waste site problems as promptly as possible. This was to be accomplished primarily through accelerated use of the trust fund, as well as through renewed Superfund enforcement activities. Thomas increased the use of the CERCLA trust fund to finance preliminary assessments and site investigations and to conduct RI/FSs at dumpsites on the Superfund's National Priorities List.[19] The "lawyers first, shovels later" approach was transformed into "shovels first, lawyers later," a resolve not to allow cleanup activities to be slowed by lengthy enforcement negotiation or litigation.[20]

Lee Thomas also committed himself to the notion that enforcement had significance for the Superfund effort. Although the agency's primary focus in that period was on the cleanup of hazardous waste sites with public funds, Thomas also emphasized the need to initiate more enforcement actions, including administrative orders, Consent Decrees, lawsuits, and cost recovery actions. With the cooperation of a sympathetic Congress, he expanded the agency's Superfund enforcement resources, adding new staff, especially technically trained staff, in EPA's regional offices as well as its headquarters program components.[21] Moreover, Thomas joined with other EPA and DOJ managers in insisting that the Superfund statute be construed to create strict, joint, and several liability for responsible parties in Superfund litigation.[22]

This last stance had significant consequences. Beginning in 1983, the able efforts of attorneys for the Justice Department and EPA resulted in a number of important victories for the federal government in Superfund litigation. In a series of landmark decisions, federal district courts in various parts of the United States upheld the government's strict interpretation of the liability and causation provisions of CERCLA with remarkable uniformity. This trend, which continued through 1985 and beyond, had great influence on the substance of the Superfund Amendment and Reauthorization Act (SARA) that Congress enacted in 1986. The act established a set of ground rules for subsequent EPA negotiations with PRPs in individual Superfund cases that gave the government immense discretion to shape the terms and conditions of settlement agreements.[23]

To implement their push to reinvigorate the Superfund effort, Ruckelshaus, Alm, and Thomas delegated responsibility for day-to-day hazardous waste management to the agency's regional offices.[24] As one veteran regional official stated, "The top EPA headquarters people began to trust the regions again."[25] The stringent concurrence requirement for regional initiation of emergency removal actions was lifted.[26] EPA's regional offices were accorded more autonomy to initiate RI/FSs and to negotiate agreements for studies and cleanup measures by private parties.[27]

Along with augmented regional authority came a gradual increase in written policy guidelines on Superfund issues. Over a period of thirty-six months, the agency issued comprehensive guidance memorandums concerning such critical matters as the specific basis on which EPA could settle Superfund enforcement actions against PRPs, participation of responsible parties in development of RI/FSs, issuance of notice letters to PRPs, use and issuance of administrative orders under CERCLA section 106, and the preparation of Superfund cost recovery actions.[28] In addition, a hazardous waste site planning system was instituted. Under this system, regional offices were required to project their Superfund activities over given time periods and to create tentative management plans for all priority hazardous waste sites.[29]

Taken as a whole, these trends and changes moved EPA's languishing enforcement efforts—both in the Superfund area and outside of it—in the direction of renewal and revitalization. Though relatively brief, William Ruckelshaus's second term as EPA administrator did succeed in pulling the agency's implementation of Superfund and other environmental statutes away from what David Andrews has aptly termed the "brink of disaster."

Nonetheless, the success of the administrator's efforts was constrained and incomplete. Throughout both Ruckelshaus's and Thomas's tenures, EPA's enforcement programs were viewed with intense suspicion by congressional oversight committees, environmental organizations, and certain representatives of the media. This lasting residue of mistrust, and the response to that mistrust by EPA's top managers, played a critical role in determining the substantive content of much of the environmental legislation of the 1980s. It also molded EPA's efforts to carry out Congress's mandates.

A crucial focus of congressional concern during Ruckelshaus's second term was EPA's deficient administration of RCRA. While the Reagan administration's second set of EPA managers paid considerable attention to restoring the agency's Superfund Program, federal RCRA enforcement efforts continued to languish. Stymied by a chronic shortage of resources, particularly among attorneys in the Offices of Regional Counsel,[30] and still the subject of comparatively little top-management attention,[31] EPA's RCRA enforcement effort continued to operate in the shadow of the partially revived Superfund campaign.

This situation did not go unnoticed by EPA's congressional critics. In November 1984 Congress modified RCRA by enacting the Hazardous and Solid Waste Amendments (HSWA), a comprehensive piece of legislation. As two EPA officials noted in a candid law review analysis: "[B]etween 1980 and 1983, Congress perceived EPA as an agency unwilling or unable to fulfill its mandate of environmental protection. Almost every section of the RCRA Amendments might be read as expressing a sense of frustration over the pace and scope of EPA action."[32]

Congressional dissatisfaction with EPA's implementation of RCRA gave rise to vigorous investigations into the agency's enforcement of the HSWA. In December 1984 the Dingell Committee conducted a survey that revealed high levels of noncompliance with the ground-water monitoring and financial assurance requirements of EPA's RCRA regulations.[33] This survey found that, of the 317 hazardous waste facilities with inadequate groundwater monitoring wells, 26 percent had no compliance action taken against them and 26 percent received only an informal enforcement action; that is, a notice or a warning letter. Furthermore, of 188 facilities with no groundwater monitoring wells at all, formal enforcement action had been initiated only at 89 facilities (approximately 40 percent of the total number).[34]

Dingell's survey formed the basis of a hearing by the Dingell Committee on April 29, 1985, during which the agency's RCRA enforcement record was singled out for pointed and embarrassing criticism. As one trade journalist described the proceeding, the EPA officials who testified before the subcommittee were "left grasping at straws as they attempted to defend their apparent inaction in the face of massive noncompliance since the [RCRA] rules took effect in 1981."[35]

Now highly sensitive to the potential consequences of congressional wrath, EPA's managers responded by giving RCRA enforcement a higher priority. Groundwater monitoring and financial assurance requirements, along with RCRA's loss of interim status requirements, began to receive increasing attention from EPA's enforcement staff. The agency launched a loss of interim status (LOIS) initiative against certain land disposal facilities. It targeted facilities that were required to lose their interim status (and thus to close down their operation) if their owners or operators had failed to submit a final permit application and certify compliance with applicable groundwater and financial responsibility requirements. This EPA initiative resulted in the filing of a significant number of civil judicial actions by the Department of Justice and the closure of approximately 1,000 non-complying facilities.[36]

In February 1985 Lee Thomas succeeded William Ruckelshaus as EPA administrator. A former Ruckelshaus assistant who had received his predecessor's political support in his bid to become the agency's top manager, Thomas promptly pledged to continue the reforms that Ruckelshaus, with Thomas's own input and support, had initiated. This was particularly true in the enforcement field. In his first major speech as administrator, Thomas promised a national conference of EPA and state enforcement officials that the agency would pursue a rigorous enforcement effort that would place new emphasis on the pursuit of criminal cases. Specifically, he stated, "[T]here won't be any letup, as long as I'm [EPA] administrator, in any time and attention you heard Bill Ruckelshaus give enforcement last year."[37] In addition, in the agency's annual Operating Guidance for fiscal year 1987, a document intended to guide EPA's development of annual plans, the new administrator listed ensuring "a strong enforcement presence in all of our agency programs" as one of his six highest policy priorities. At a February 1987 senior management forum for EPA executives, Thomas set forth, as one of his "priority themes" for improving agency management, the notion that "[w]e will enforce environmental laws vigorously, consistently, and equitably, to achieve the greatest possible environmental results."[38]

In the summer of 1986 Thomas appointed Thomas L. Adams, Jr., to succeed Courtney Price as assistant administrator for enforcement and compliance monitoring. Adams had previously served for three years as EPA's deputy general counsel for regional coordination. Before that he had been an appellate attorney in the Justice Department's Lands Division and, from 1977 to 1983, assistant director for government relations at Republic Steel Corporation.[39] During Adams's two contentious years as assistant administrator, EPA's general enforcement efforts began to evolve in several new directions. That evolution continued—and in some respects received more emphasis and definition—in the period that followed his tenure.

One important trend was the gradual development of a multimedia enforcement focus. As the volume of EPA enforcement activity once again expanded, career enforcement professionals in several sections of the agency's organizational structure began to realize that EPA's strict segregation of enforcement activities by environmental medium (air, water, hazardous waste, toxic substances, etc.) was inefficient and counterproductive. Ways were needed to integrate the agency's enforcement work at particular industrial facilities and in specific categories of industry and geographical regions in order to provide greater clarity and consistency and to increase EPA's overall leverage in case-by-case enforcement negotiations.

This insight appears to have occurred to several agency officials independently. In EPA's Midwest regional office, Michael G. Smith, a branch chief in the Office of Regional Counsel, recommended a cross-cutting multimedia enforcement strategy for a heavily industrialized portion of northwestern Indiana that won the enthusiastic support of Regional Administrator Valdas Adamkus.[40] At approximately the same time, Thomas Gallagher, the director of EPA's Denver-based national enforcement investigations center who had recently been given responsibility for overseeing the agency's budding criminal enforcement program, began to lobby other agency officials for the initiation of a coordinated approach to enforcement inspections and case development.[41] In EPA headquarters, Senior Enforcement Counsel Richard Mays, with the support and encouragement of F. Henry Habicht III, the Justice Department's assistant attorney general for lands and natural resources, as well as the backing of the agency's office of administration and resources management, drafted a formal multimedia enforcement strategy. That innovative approach was to be implemented at waste disposal facilities subject to RCRA and the Toxic Substances Control Act at which violations of the Clean Air and Clean Water Acts were also found.[42]

Despite these developments, multimedia enforcement, as a meaningful component of EPA's enforcement efforts, played a small role during the mid-1980s. For the most part, as Thomas Gallagher observed, EPA enforcement of that period was divided into "four EPAs: the water, the air, the hazardous waste, and the toxic substances EPA. It was very, very difficult to get a measure of cross-cutting cooperation among all of these."[43] Nonetheless, the sporadic multimedia efforts that developed during the tenure of Lee Thomas and Thomas Adams ultimately gave rise to a more significant attempt to integrate EPA's media-based enforcement programs during the presidency of George Bush.

Another important development during this time was the advent of multicase enforcement initiatives in designated priority areas. For the first time, the agency and the Department of Justice attempted to streamline referral and filing procedures for similar civil judicial actions and to publicize these efforts as a way of enhancing their deterrent effects. Thus, in fiscal year 1985 (i.e., the period between October 1, 1984, and September 30, 1985) the Justice Department filed eleven cases nationwide on EPA's behalf against violators of Clean Air Act building demolition asbestos control requirements. The agency also targeted for civil suit municipal publicly owned sewage treatment plants that had not submitted approvable local pretreatment programs, as required by the Clean Water Act. It issued thirteen administrative complaints to redress violations of Toxic Substances Control Act pre-manufacture notification requirements.[44] Similarly, in March 1986 EPA announced the filing of fifteen lawsuits against municipalities that were in violation of Clean Water Act requirements other than the pretreatment rules. In the same year, the agency and DOJ initiated coordinated civil actions against ten violators of Safe Drinking Water Act underground injection control regulations, eight metal-coating facilities in the Los Angeles basin, and twenty-seven electroplating plants located in the New York City metropolitan area.[45]

Beyond this, the agency placed renewed emphasis on an enforcement technique upon which it had briefly relied in the early 1970s: the debarment of government contractors who are persistent violators of environmental standards by publicly listing them in the *Federal Register*. In 1986 EPA revised its regulations to facilitate contractor listing and established a separate staff in the Office of Enforcement and Compliance monitoring to work with regional personnel in carrying out this program. These efforts yielded at least modest success. Between January 1986 and October 1988 the number of facilities on the agency's Violating Facility List grew from three to seventeen, and the realistic possibility of such listing actions improved EPA's position in negotiating settlement of additional enforcement cases.[46]

EPA's enforcement work during this period was also characterized by increased levels of measured formal activity, a fact that the agency sought to publicize by the periodic release of statistics that lauded its enforcement accomplishments. Thus, in April 1986 EPA reported that fiscal year 1985 had been a record year for the agency with respect to the number of its civil and criminal referrals to the Department of Justice. In addition, it indicated the agency had issued 2,785 administrative orders during the same twelve months, the second highest number of orders issued by EPA since 1981.[47] One year later, an EPA enforcement accomplishments report stated that "in fiscal year 1986, state and federal environmental civil, criminal and administrative enforcement actions continued to be undertaken at record levels . . . the agency referred 342 judicial actions to the Department of Justice, compared to 276 last year. . . . The Criminal Enforcement Program experienced its most successful and productive year since the program commenced by referring an all-time high of forty-five criminal cases to DOJ."[48] In April 1988 the agency indicated that "in fiscal 1987, EPA and the states achieved record levels of environmental enforcement, using the full range of enforcement authorities. The agency referred 304 civil cases to the Department of Justice. . . . The agency established an all-time record for the largest amount of civil penalties imposed in a year . . . over $24 million."[49]

Of particular significance during the concluding portion of the Reagan administration was the growth of criminal environmental enforcement. Under prodding from Congress, this program gradually increased in size and importance, both within the agency and at the Department of Justice. This trend was carefully monitored in the private sector.[50] As one attorney who represents regulated corporations told me: "The willingness of the administration to bring criminal actions against corporate officials has enhanced their interest in supervising their lower-ranking personnel to pay attention to environmental values. Reading in the paper about criminal actions being brought against one's industry or one's company is a great motivator, I would think."[51]

Two other general EPA enforcement trends from the latter part of the Reagan administration are also worthy of mention: a continuing attempt by the agency's Washington, D.C., headquarters, and some EPA regional offices, to promote cooperative enforcement relationships with state and local officials, and the steady decentralization to EPA regional personnel of authority to initiate and settle enforcement cases. Under Thomas and Adams, the agency made an effort to implement its State/EPA Agreement guidance by entering into enforcement agreements with relevant officials in individual states. This effort did succeed in increasing federal-state cooperation in a number of instances and in improving intergovernmental consultation and advance planning concerning certain enforcement cases. At the same time, however, federal-state controversies continued to arise with regard to EPA's occasional practice of overfiling— initiating a separate federal enforcement action when the agency determines that the terms on which a state government has resolved a particular enforcement matter are "grossly deficient" and inadequate.[52] In addition, certain EPA regional offices and states continued to differ with respect to the acceptability of the definitions employed by the states in assessing and reporting on their own enforcement achievements.[53]

While decentralization had been a feature of earlier EPA administrations, it was given new impetus under the leadership of Lee Thomas and Thomas Adams. These managers saw increased regional autonomy as an effective means of streamlining the agency's overall enforcement effort. Despite determined and, at times, bitter resistance from headquarters career professionals and key players on Capitol Hill, Thomas and Adams gradually expanded the independence of regional enforcement officials in the management of particular enforcement cases.[54]

This trend toward regional decentralization was especially pronounced in the Superfund Program. In the spring of 1987 EPA regional offices were delegated the authority to implement a number of important aspects of Superfund, including studies and investigations relating to cost recovery, special notices, demand letters and unilateral administrative orders to PRPs, and both *de minimus* agreements and administrative orders on consent.[55] The following year, regional Superfund authority was further extended in a series of memorandums from Thomas Adams to regional officials. On January 14, 1988, Adams provided the regions with guidance respecting the implementation of an agreement between the agency and the Department of Justice that expanded the categories of civil judicial enforcement cases that were to be referred directly from regional offices to DOJ without the prior concurrence of EPA's headquarters.[56] The following month, Adams formally informed the agency's regional administrators that "a fundamental premise of our efforts is that the Regions have the lead in the agency in case selection, consistent with agency priorities, and in case development and case management."[57] On May 2, 1988, that "premise" was acted upon further in a memorandum that listed only eight, relatively narrow categories of enforcement cases in which the involvement of headquarters staff attorneys was deemed warranted.[58] One month later, Thomas Adams and J. Winston "Win" Porter, EPA's assistant administrator for solid waste and emergency response, jointly issued a memo expanding the authority of regional administrators by waiving the requirement of headquarters concurrence in CERCLA settlements and agreements, pursuant to Superfund sections 106 and 107, where total claims do not exceed $30 million.[59]

The Superfund Program, which continued to receive considerable attention from top EPA managers during the Thomas/Adams years, underwent other changes as well. The most significant of these were a direct or indirect result of SARA. As one EPA (and former Justice Department) official described the period preceding the enactment of this act, "SARA had a very difficult birth process. There were two years of legislative debate leading up to the Superfund Amendments of 1986. The legislation came late and the funding mechanism for Superfund had lapsed. As a result . . . it took some period of time for Superfund to come back to speed. The program suffered accordingly."[60]

Once in place, however, SARA engendered a somewhat more systematic and uniform approach to EPA's implementation of Superfund, particularly in the area of enforcement.[61] The agency increased its reliance on unilateral administrative orders to PRPs[62] and established a standard process for negotiating cleanup agreements, by preestablished deadlines, on specific terms favorable to government negotiators.[63] "Model packages" were also developed for RI/FS's and for the documentation to support successful cost recovery litigation.[64] A planning process was established to monitor regional CERCLA activities and progress.[65] EPA put greater emphasis on private, rather than public, funding of Superfund cleanups.[66] All in all, in the words of one key Justice Department participant of that time, following SARA, "the Superfund process became regularized, at least to the extent that things now moved in some discernible, organized time frame through the system."[67]

With standardization and increased responsibility came additional resources. On February 4, 1985, the Reagan administration asked Congress to increase EPA's operating budget for fiscal year 1986 by 3 percent, including a 45 percent increase in funding for CERCLA activities, as compared with the previous year.[68] Congress, anticipating passage of SARA the following year, raised the agency's appropriation for Superfund enforcement activities from $39 million to $52 million. That funding level rose again over the next two fiscal years—to $100 million in fiscal 1987 and $125 million in fiscal 1988.[69] EPA increased the size of its Superfund enforcement staff during the Reagan administration's final two years from 765 to 1,027 full-time employees, including 103 new attorneys in the agency's Offices of Regional Counsel.[70]

Notwithstanding the salutary trends and events described above, EPA's enforcement programs were beset by a number of significant problems during Lee Thomas's tenure as EPA administrator. Some of these difficulties were internal to the agency's administrative structure, and some were engendered by criticism of EPA from outside. Some were a result of errors and inconsistencies in the approaches of the agency's top managers; others were merely a continuation of troubles that had arisen at earlier phases of EPA's development. Whatever their origins, however, in their totality these problems diminished the genuine progress that characterized EPA's enforcement work in the Thomas years. Because of them, EPA enforcement in the mid to late 1980's cannot be said to have been "out of the woods."

Internally, the agency's enforcement work in this period was marked by prolonged and intensive squabbling for influence and decision-making authority among the various offices within EPA's headquarters that had been given enforcement mandates and responsibilities.[71] The scope and intensity of these disagreements varied with the substantive issues and personalities involved. Nonetheless, in a number of instances internal EPA headquarters disputes had the effect of prolonging the development of agency policies and negotiating positions. As one headquarters manager during that time later stated:

"[EPA] didn't have people [in headquarters] who could give answers quickly. [In matters of case development strategy] you couldn't move from point A to point B without getting everyone in the Western Hemisphere to agree. . . . On any particular issue you might have three or four different [agency] positions, but it was never consistent. . . . It was the worst management nightmare you could think of.[72]

These problems were particularly acute in the Superfund Program, where headquarters policy-making authority was widely distributed. In March 1989 the Environmental Law Institute concluded:

Responsibility for developing and implementing an enforcement strategy for the Superfund Program is diffused, on the national level, among four EPA offices—the office of waste programs enforcement, the office of emergency and remedial response, the office of enforcement and compliance monitoring and the office of general counsel. As a result of this diffusion of responsibility, it is unclear who has ultimate responsibility for a national enforcement strategy. Each office tries to shape the agency's direction, and the agency's position and performance may be weakened in consequence.[73]

In addition to interoffice rivalry, EPA's enforcement programs experienced continuing shortages of resources during the mid- to late 1980s. To many observers, this problem reflected general budget shortfalls that detrimentally affected the agency as a whole.[74] It was particularly acute in the RCRA enforcement program and with respect to full-time EPA criminal investigators. Even in the Superfund Program, however, resource problems persisted in certain areas, notwithstanding the increases in staffing that occurred at this time.[75]

EPA's shortage of enforcement resources contributed to two other persistent and interrelated problems: noncompetitive salary scales for professional staff members and a relatively high level of staff attrition. In October 1987 the GAO reported that the pay for federal attorneys, chemists, and engineers—three key EPA enforcement occupations—trailed the salary levels in the private sector by $7,800 to $41,300, or 25 to 60 percent.[76] This gap, which was merely an extreme version of a general—and continuing—disparity between governmental and private pay scales for professional employees, contributed to persistent turnover among EPA enforcement attorneys and technical personnel. The attrition problem was especially acute among hydrologists, chemists, toxicologists, and attorneys in the agency's growing CERCLA program.[77] However, staff turnover was not limited to Superfund. In fact, as one seasoned congressional observer noted, in *all* of EPA's enforcement programs "[p]eople go there at a relatively young age, relatively inexperienced. Then, just as they get over the learning curve and hit their stride, they get hired away [by employers in the private sector]. This happens to everyone from inspectors to attorneys."[78]

In addition to attrition, EPA enforcement managers faced difficulties in recruiting qualified and experienced staff members from outside the federal government, particularly technical experts with relevant experience in universities or agencies of state government. This was a result of excessively rigid civil service classification standards, which overemphasized the importance of federal agency experience in the rating of job candidates. It was also caused by time-consuming requirements for posting notices of vacant positions and for screening and rating applicants. As one EPA regional office noted in exasperation: "Sometimes the procedural aspects of it get to be overwhelming. Often, by the time you've completed all the required procedures, the [experienced] candidate you really wanted to hire has accepted a position someplace else."[79]

EPA enforcement during the Thomas period was also characterized by significant inconsistencies in the approaches of different regional offices.[80] In part, these discrepancies were a result of differences in the attitudes and preferences of the agency's regional administrators, who were often appointed with the political support of state environmental officials within the regions. As the regulatory historian Alfred A. Marcus has written, after EPA's regional offices were established in the early 1970s,

> The regional administrators perceived issues not only in terms of their own obligation to headquarters, but also in terms of their commitments to the states. In fact, if a regional administrator be-

came aligned with the states' interests, he or she could block decisive agency action by refusing to carry out national policy. Headquarters could do little to appoint a regional administrator to change his or her ways because, once appointed, a regional administrator quickly became entrenched. EPA in Washington could risk firing a regional administrator only if it was willing to alienate his or her local supporters.[81]

Regional enforcement differences were also a result of variations in the enforcement attitudes of state officials. Thus, EPA's own inspector general, in testimony before a subcommittee of the Senate Committee on Environment and Public Works, gave the following candid response to a question posed by Senator Harry Reid (D-NV):

> [EPA oversight of state enforcement programs] varies from region to region and state to state. Some states have, apparently, a stronger commitment on their own to enforcement activities. And so, it is easier for EPA to deal with them because they're more in tune with what EPA wants to accomplish. Others are more difficult . . . . There is a fragile relationship. On the one hand, EPA has got to seek the cooperation of the states, yet on the other hand it's got to beat them over the head if they're not doing a good job. That's a difficult thing to pull off. And we think there are regions who are falling short of being able to pull that off effectively.[82]

Whatever its precise causes, EPA's enforcement efforts in the Thomas years were characterized by regional disparities in the significance, formality, and assertiveness of enforcement activities—a phenomenon which predated Lee Thomas's terms as the agency's administrator and continues to this writing.

Another shortcoming of EPA enforcement in the second half of the Reagan administration was the inadequacy of much of the formal guidance provided by the agency's headquarters to regional enforcement personnel. One regional enforcement supervisor spoke for many when he stated: "The [headquarters] guidance that comes out is not that helpful to [regional] people who practice every day. It's relevant, but it doesn't really wrestle with the hard questions. It's almost obvious. It doesn't get to the fine distinctions you need to make."[83]

In some respects, EPA headquarters' enforcement guidance was too extensive. Its remarkable volume led one headquarters attorney to complain: "We in headquarters develop so many guidances that we cannot keep track of them."[84] On the other hand, the agency's guidance failed to address certain important questions of national enforcement policy, including, most notably, the basis for distinguishing civil and/or administrative enforcement cases from matters in which criminal prosecution would be appropriate.[85] In other instances carefully constructed national enforcement policies, widely acknowledged to be equitable and sound, were ignored or implemented in the breach by regional enforcement officials.[86]

Another set of enforcement problems which the agency has still failed to address adequately concerns the EPA's collection and use of data regarding the compliance status of industrial and municipal sources of pollution. For the most part, the agency's enforcement information support systems were established as media-specific tools for headquarters oversight of regional and state enforcement activities. The systems were designed with little attention to data quality. They also required regional and state compliance personnel to enter a great volume of information into systems that have little operational benefit to them. As a result, according to an outside computer consultant employed by EPA's Office of Information Resources Management:

> Poor quality and timeliness of data plague several of the centralized [EPA enforcement] data bases, limiting their reliability and usefulness even as headquarters tools for oversight and external reporting. . . . Further, just the inability to answer basic questions . . . frequently causes numerous staff to be diverted from their regular duties, and often leads to unnecessary friction among Congress, the agency and various states.[87]

These information management weaknesses posed a particular problem during the agency's initial attempts to institute multimedia enforcement. Incompatibilities of design and content, combined with indifference and resistance from some regional enforcement personnel, severely restricted the utility of EPA's numerous enforcement data systems in cross-media initiatives.[88]

Federal environmental enforcement of the mid- to late 1980s was also inhibited by a recurrence of the institutional rivalry between EPA and the Department of Justice that had unsettled enforcement efforts in the late 1970s. In an article in early 1989 one former Justice Department manager described the situation in these words:

> The environmental enforcement program is further plagued by constant turf fights between the DOJ and EPA over who will actually litigate the cases in court. The tension from these turf battles

is always simmering, and frequently affects the relationship between the DOJ attorney and his EPA counterpart. Unfortunately, such tension is an unnecessary drain of energy that could be better spent on developing and prosecuting enforcement cases.[89]

While discord between the agency and its Justice Department attorneys affected enforcement in all environmental media, it was particularly acute in the growing and resource-intensive Superfund Program. There, the essence of the problem was aptly described in a study by the Environmental Law Institute:

[S]ome EPA and DOJ personnel have expressed dissatisfaction with each other's performance in handling Superfund enforcement cases. Complaints that DOJ delays approval of settlements (sometimes attributed by EPA to bureaucratic delay, sometimes to a line attorney's inability to perceive and resolve supervisors' concerns early in the process) are countered by criticism of EPA's preparation of cases. Some EPA personnel complain that DOJ is risk-averse and unwilling to file certain cases, while DOJ officials express reluctance to file certain inadequately prepared or inappropriate cases because they fear weakening the enforcement program. These tensions inevitably weaken the program.[90]

Other difficulties between EPA and the Department of Justice were caused by resource limitations within the department itself rather than by avoidable frictions in working relationships among professional staff members.[91] One regional enforcement attorney I interviewed stated:

Frankly, [the Department of] Justice is swamped. They're working as hard as they possibly can, but they just don't have the people to do all the work that has to be done. There is a problem just moving paper through DOJ. It's not unusual for it to take six months for a Consent Decree that's been negotiated and signed by the defendants to be entered. Things are really slowing down. They're good attorneys. I have a lot of respect for them. I just wish there were more people there.[92]

During this period, the work of many EPA enforcement personnel also suffered because of a situation that, like interagency rivalry with DOJ, had its roots in the 1970s: extraordinarily inadequate physical working conditions. This problem was not universal within the agency. In fact, the office facilities that housed professional enforcement staffs in many EPA regions were entirely adequate and, in some instances (at least by federal government standards), relatively luxurious. In other EPA regional offices, however, the agency's enforcement staff worked in small, cramped, noisy offices with few windows and battered furniture.

The situation was most extreme in EPA's Waterside Mall headquarters complex. This building, designed in the 1960s as an apartment house complex rather than an office area, is remarkably ill-suited to serve as a government facility. Its narrow, confusingly-arranged corridors, tiny, overcrowded offices, periodic security problems, and general physical isolation from most of the rest of official Washington have long been a source of irritation and resentment among the agency's overworked staff.[93]

This situation was made far worse in the mid-1980s by the emergence of severe indoor air pollution problems that caused serious illnesses for several members of the EPA's headquarters enforcement staff.[94] In fact, the agency did relocate some of its enforcement staff to better quarters in Crystal City, Virginia, at some cost in terms of the physical compactness and efficiency of its headquarters operations, and other steps were also taken to ameliorate the problem. Nonetheless, at this writing, seriously unsatisfactory working conditions continue to prevail in much of the EPA's headquarters complex, and no firm plan is in place to remedy this circumstance on a permanent basis. In the words of one agency official: "It's a real blight on the agency that its people have to labor in conditions like this and feel that they have to jeopardize their long-term physical well-being in order to serve the United States."[95]

In addition to (and in some cases as a result of) these varied internal problems, during the last quarter of Ronald Reagan's first term as president—and the entirety of his second term—EPA's enforcement program experienced recurrent difficulties in its relationship with Congress, the press, and certain national environmental organizations. Notwithstanding the improvements the agency had made in the nature and volume of its enforcement activities, throughout this period the relationship between top EPA officials and Capitol Hill was harsh and adversarial. As one observer has noted, agency officials were called to testify at "frequent, acrimonious oversight hearings."[96] EPA enforcement programs were repeatedly criticized in studies prepared by the GAO and the agency's own inspector general, and many of their criticisms were noted, repeated, or supplemented by journalists or environmental citizens groups.

Some of the mistrust and conflict that characterized EPA-congressional relations in this era were undoubtedly a remnant of the controversies of the Gorsuch years. The stark breakdown of the agency's enforcement efforts between 1981 and 1983 did severe damage to the agency's reputation on Capitol Hill. In retrospect, it seems unlikely that *any* efforts by top EPA managers—no matter how skillful or well intentioned—could have *fully* restored the trust of interested representatives and senators, and their staffs, for the remainder of the Reagan years. Nonetheless, at least some of the continuing tensions that pervaded EPA-congressional relations in the enforcement area, from 1985 through 1988, can be attributed to the agency's own political leaders. Their inability to anticipate and avoid criticism from Capitol Hill or to cultivate informal channels of communication with key congressional staff members undoubtedly exacerbated the difficulties they faced in obtaining Congress's approval and support, as well as that of the public and press.

One incident that took place very early in Thomas Adams's term as assistant administrator for enforcement and compliance monitoring served to focus and intensify congressional suspicions. In September 1986 Adams decided to institute several changes in the management of EPA's headquarters enforcement organization. Among these was the transfer of Frederick P. Stiehl, then the agency's associate enforcement counsel for hazardous waste enforcement, to the position of associate enforcement counsel for pesticides and toxic substances. As Adams later recalled the event, his decision was motivated by a desire to replace Stiehl with a manager who "knew how to make things work politically within the agency." He viewed Stiehl as "worn down" and maintained that the transfer would benefit Stiehl's career.[97] Stiehl, on the other hand, remembered the incident differently. He stated that, rather than being worn down, he had been quite excited at the prospect of grappling with the challenges he anticipated in implementing the soon-to-be-enacted SARA. Stiehl viewed his transfer as "disruptive to the staff" and "the wrong decision, made in the wrong way, at the wrong time."[98]

Whatever its appropriateness, Stiehl's impending reassignment, which became effective on October 12, was promptly made known to Congress by concerned EPA staff members. On October 6, 1986, Representative Dingell wrote a letter to EPA Administrator Lee Thomas questioning the legality of the Stiehl transfer. Describing this personnel action as a matter "of some urgency and concern" which had had "a serious adverse impact on employee morale," Dingell wrote:

> Mr. Stiehl is a career member of the Senior Executive Service (SES) and, as such, is afforded the protection of 5 U.S.C. § 3395(e). The

statute prohibits, in pertinent part, the involuntary reassignment of a career SES appointee within 120 days after the appointment in the agency of the career appointee's most immediate supervisor, who is a non-career appointee and has authority to reassign the career appointee. In this instance the [Thomas] Adams–instigated reassignment of Mr. Stiehl is scheduled to occur approximately 50 days after he [i.e., Adams] became the assistant administrator.[99]

Lee Thomas responded to Dingell in a letter dated December 9, 1986. He asserted that, after carefully reviewing the matter, the agency believed that it had acted in "full compliance with statutory requirements," since Stiehl's transfer had been formally instituted by another EPA official, rather than Thomas Adams.[100]

However legally defensible, the reassignment of Frederick Stiehl harmed the agency's enforcement efforts in two ways. First, the incident occurred when all of the decisions and policies of the newly appointed assistant administrator for enforcement and compliance monitoring were likely to be closely scrutinized. It also came at a time when Stiehl, who had participated in the agency's hazardous waste enforcement efforts from their inception, had an established and cordial working relationship with congressional committee staff members and a reputation among them as a dedicated, no-nonsense enforcement official. Stiehl's abrupt transfer was thus viewed with concern by members of Congress, already skeptical of the EPA's publicly announced commitment to a vigorous enforcement effort. Second, together with the incipient decentralization of enforcement authority to regional officials, Stiehl's reassignment caused anxiety to many of the agency's headquarters Superfund enforcement staff. One trade journal noted that Adams's organizational changes had "sparked fear among some agency staff that a 'less confrontational' style is being developed in the enforcement office, that will result in headquarters becoming less willing to oppose the regions over controversial enforcement actions."[101] Several present and former members of the EPA enforcement staff later confirmed that the Stiehl transfer contributed to a decline in headquarters staff morale, a decline which increased with the passage of time.[102]

Rather than being an isolated incident, Congress's response to Thomas Adams's transfer of Frederick Stiehl set the stage for a chilly—and at times openly hostile—relationship between the agency and Capitol Hill in the enforcement area. Over the next few years, congressional committees and subcommittees conducted frequent, intensive, and often adversarial oversight hearings on such diverse aspects of EPA enforcement as PCB disposal under the Toxic Substances Control Act, the organization of EPA's criminal enforcement program, "sham recycling" of hazardous wastes, implementation of the Superfund Program, hazardous waste site closure, and the enforcement of environmental requirements at federally owned and operated facilities.[103] These investigations were supplemented by a number of reports by the GAO, usually prepared at the request of congressional committees or individual senators or members of the House of Representatives, that found fault with different components of the agency's enforcement program.[104] EPA was also taken to task in reports compiled by its own independent Office of Inspector General.[105]

Of all the external castigation that EPA's enforcement programs received in this period, the most passionate and sustained outcry came in the spring and summer of 1988. Once again the focus was the agency's implementation of the amended Superfund statute. On April 11, 1988, the Subcommittee on Energy, Environment and Natural Resources of the House Committee on Government Operations held a hearing in Crystal City, Texas, at the site of a hazardous waste disposal facility that EPA had earlier placed on its National Priorities List. The opening statement of Representative Mike Synar (D-OK), the subcommittee's chairman, typified the criticism leveled at the agency throughout the hearing:

Two years after the [SARA] Amendments became law, the prospect for swift and permanent cleanup of these hazardous waste sites is not good. We are spending lots of money; we are fattening the pocketbooks of a lot of contractors; and we are also subsidizing the development of lots of thick, detailed technical documents. But . . . somewhere in these lengthy, technical Superfund processes we have lost sight of the ultimate goal, and that is the protection of the environment and public health from hazardous waste.[106]

Similar sentiments were expressed two months later by Representative Dennis Eckart (D-TX) at a hearing of the Dingell Committee:

Is the Superfund Program, in fact, on a course headed for success, or is it struggling for a passing grade? From the information we have gathered in preparation for this hearing, it appears that all is not well, particularly in the pace of remedial activity, the vigor of the enforcement program, and the selection of cleanups that emphasize treatment of the waste and permanent solutions.[107]

While acknowledging some EPA successes, especially with regard to the initiation of preliminary assessments and RI/FSs and the development of a "good, solid" removal program, Eckart decried the agency's inconsistency regarding the remedies chosen at Superfund sites and its inattention to CERCLA cleanup standards and permanent treatment requirements.

These concerns found support in two outside assessments of the remedial aspects of the Superfund Program that were released on the very day Eckart's subcommittee met. The first of these, *Right Train, Wrong Track: Failed Leadership in the Superfund Cleanup Program*, was the seventy-three-page product of a joint effort by the Hazardous Waste Treatment Council and six national environmental organizations.[108] It analyzed and critiqued EPA's Superfund site remedy selection processes by reviewing all seventy-five RODs prepared by the agency in calendar year 1987. The report found that EPA had emphasized capping and containment of hazardous wastes at abandoned dumps to the near exclusion of permanent treatment technologies. It accused the agency of setting cleanup goals unscientifically, ignoring natural resource damage, and exempting Superfund sites from applicable environmental standards. Based on these findings, the authors of *Right Train, Wrong Track* concluded:

> In rewriting Superfund in 1986, Congress provided EPA with the engine and resources to run a program sorely in need of strengthening. While it is difficult to imagine a more specific or better funded statute, the agency has set its program on the wrong course, a course of repetition of past mistakes. Congress has provided the right train, but EPA has chosen the wrong track. Unless agency approach, policy and attitude to the new statute is changed in the immediate future, the agency will derail the statute.[109]

Equally critical—and even more damaging to EPA—was a report by the congressional Office of Technology Assessment (OTA) entitled *Are We Cleaning Up?: 10 Superfund Case Studies*.[110] This study focused on RODs and RI/FSs prepared by EPA regional personnel at ten Superfund sites across the United States. It found that the Superfund Program had been inconsistent in its selection of treatment remedies at similar sites and that permanently effective treatment technologies were being employed too infrequently. The OTA noted that hazardous waste cleanup technology was still a new and fast-changing field and that the agency's Superfund workforce was relatively young and inexperienced. It criticized EPA for failing to use central management controls to further the agency's collective understanding of common site characteristics and common cleanup problems and solutions; and it concluded that, as a result of that shortcoming, the site cleanup decisions made by EPA at the ten sites upon which OTA had focused were "questionable."[111]

These reports, which received prominent coverage in the media, were seen by many in Congress as independent confirmation that their suspicions about poor agency implementation of CERCLA were soundly based. At EPA, on the other hand, they were viewed with consternation. Almost immediately, the agency's top managers initiated a public campaign to discredit the OTA and Hazardous Waste Treatment Council reports and defend EPA's Superfund performance. In a June 18, 1988, interview with the *New York Times*, Win Porter referred to OTA's report as "a limited, superficial study" that drew "global conclusions" from inadequate data. He said the study had been performed by a few officials sitting in Washington "while I have 3000 people out there working hard to make the program a success." He also stated, "I really resent them undermining our credibility with the communities we work with."[112]

Two days later, in remarks to an annual conference of the American Pollution Control Association in Dallas, Texas, Administrator Thomas took a similar tack. He stated that he resented that the OTA had made such broad allegations although it examined only ten sites and had "only minimal contact" with the EPA's Superfund workforce.[113]

At a July 21 seminar sponsored by the Congressional Environmental Study Conference, two other agency officials, Lloyd Guerci and Walter Kovalick, reiterated the agency's defense. Guerci accused the authors of both *Right Train, Wrong Track* and the OTA study, who were present at the conference, of being "deliberately misleading and unfair." He contended that many of the remedies chosen at Superfund sites were an inevitable result of the poor financial condition of both the hazardous waste site PRPs and the government of the state involved. Kovalick emphasized that, in selecting site remedies, the agency had tried to focus on all nine of the remedy selection criteria that Congress had included in the statute. He accused EPA's critics of choosing only one or two of those criteria and insisting that the agency apply them to the exclusion of the other factors.[114]

Whatever impact these countercharges may have had on the agency's Superfund staff, they did little to assuage EPA's congressional critics. In fact, they seem to have heightened the legislators' distrust. The controversy over EPA's enforcement performance in general and the Superfund Program in particular continued to the end of Ronald Reagan's presidency. It provided both a peril and an opportunity for the EPA leadership appointed by his successor.

SIX

Modest Progress and Renewed Suspicion

EPA Enforcement in the
Bush Administration

Environmental protection was a significant issue in the presidential election of 1988. To the surprise of many environmentalists, who expected a continuation of Ronald Reagan's public conservatism on environmental issues, candidate George Bush attacked the environmental record of his Democratic opponent, Michael Dukakis, on the cleanup of Boston Harbor and pledged he would be an "environmental president" promising firm measures to halt the greenhouse effect and stop the destruction of wetland areas. Over the course of Bush's administration, this more pro-environmental attitude resulted in beneficial changes in EPA's enforcement efforts, particularly in the early years. Nonetheless, those efforts continued to be bedeviled by a range of difficulties and, over time, by revived congressional mistrust.

Bush's postelection appointments to high-level positions at the EPA were generally consistent with the conservationist tone of his campaign. He began by choosing the president of the World Wildlife Fund and the Conservation Foundation, William K. Reilly, to be the agency's new administrator. Reilly had served as a senior staff member of the Council on Environmental Quality in the early 1970s and was considered a protégé of former EPA Administrator Russell Train. F. Henry "Hank" Habicht II, who had been assistant attorney general for lands and natural resources at the Department of Justice during the Reagan years, was selected as deputy administrator. Both choices were generally well received by environmental advocates and were confirmed by the Senate without significant dissension.

However, the establishment of a new top management team at EPA had little immediate impact on the controversy that had surrounded EPA enforcement in general—and the Superfund Program in particular—at the close of the Reagan administration. In the spring of 1989, two further detailed and critical assessments of the agency's implementation of CERCLA were publicly released. Although the first of these, a 210-page report by the Environmental Law Institute (ELI) entitled *Toward a More Effective Superfund Enforcement Program* (the ELI Report), had been prepared by its authors at the request of EPA itself, which had been asked by the Appropriations Committees of both houses of Congress to commission a study of CERCLA enforcement, the report's conclusions were far from complimentary to the agency's Superfund enforcement program.[1]

The ELI Report found a number of flaws in the existing Superfund Program that, in its opinion, prevented the program from achieving "effective enforcement," which was defined as a regular, prompt, and efficient inducement for private responsible parties to clean up Superfund sites completely and at their own expense. The agency was criticized for failing to communicate a national enforcement strategy to regional personnel, for declining to recognize or rely upon the potential power of its statutory enforcement authorities, for conducting ineffective PRP searches, and for perpetuating a duplicative and inefficient organizational structure at the headquarters level. Its institutional arrangements for measuring performance and allocating resources were also seen as obstacles to efficient enforcement.[2] In a critical passage of the ELI Report, the agency's leaders were exhorted to provide clear and consistent support for Superfund enforcement:

> A sense of urgency and commitment should accompany the pronouncements of agency leaders in order to promote support for program goals and foster cooperation between managers, especially between those at headquarters and those in the regions. Clearly stated missions build strong cultures and strong cultures drive and control the program.[3]

Further doubts about EPA's approach to Superfund implementation were expressed in a 214-page critique issued in May 1989 by Senators Frank R. Lautenberg (D-NJ) and David Durenberger (R-MN), the chairman and ranking minority member of the Subcommittee on Superfund, Ocean and Water Protection of the Senate Committee on Environment and Public Works.[4] The Lautenberg-Durenberger Report, which was drafted by professional staff members Seth Mones and Jimmie Powell, summarized many of the criticisms of the EPA's post-1986 Superfund Program that had been raised at five public hearings the subcommittee had held during 1987. It noted inconsistencies in regional approaches to cleanup remedies and in the screening of sites for inclusion on the National Priorities List, delays in the accomplishment of various cleanup steps, "failure to oversee and prevent state noncompliance with EPA requirements, and conflicts of interest by the Agency's Superfund contractors." Like the ELI Report, Lautenberg and Durenberger's study found that the agency had underutilized its full range of enforcement tools by being unwilling to enhance its negotiating posture through initiation of enforcement actions, such as unilateral administrative orders, during negotiations. "In fact," Lautenberg and Durenberger concluded, "EPA has allowed negotiations to continue beyond the time period the Agency itself deems acceptable."[5]

Some of the Lautenberg-Durenberger Report's harshest criticisms concerned the agency's proposed deferral policy—the suggestion, by some EPA officials, that Superfund sites not be placed or maintained on the National Priorities List if they could be addressed by PRPs or other federal or state programs:

> Deferral of sites with rankings sufficient for inclusion on the Superfund cleanup list could deprive these sites of the many comprehensive requirements and authorities applied at other Superfund sites. . . . EPA's attempt to limit the size of the Superfund list through a deferral policy threatens to be an exception capable of swallowing a good portion of the law.[6]

These alarms did not go unheeded by the agency's new set of top managers. At his January 1989 confirmation hearing before the Senate Committee on Environment and Public Works, William Reilly committed himself to an assertive EPA enforcement effort. He told the assembled senators:

> I want to stress before this committee that I understand and accept as my duty, first and foremost, to implement the environmental laws of this land as Congress has written them. . . . [E]nforcement must be inspired by a sense of vigor and urgency, for the aim of the enterprise is no less than the protection of human health, of life, and of the natural order that sustains civilization. So I pledge to take aggressive and timely enforcement action, whenever it is warranted, to safeguard public health or environmental quality.[7]

Deputy administrator Habicht made similar statements in testimony before Congress.[8]

Aware that the criticisms that were being made were principally directed at policies and approaches established by their predecessors in office, Reilly and Habicht viewed the situation as an opportunity to streamline the Superfund Program and establish the sincerity of their pledge to invigorate the EPA's enforcement efforts.

In one of his first acts as administrator, Reilly directed a task group of EPA managers and professionals to undertake "as thorough a review of the [Superfund] program as could be completed in about ninety days."[9] This review, conducted under the supervision of Lewis Crampton, a special assistant to the administrator who later became the agency's associate administrator for external affairs, was intended to respond to EPA's outside critics and acknowledge the need for improvement.[10] The report it produced, which came to be known as the Ninety Day Study, contained detailed recommendations concerning the agency's implementation of CERCLA, a number of which "crystallized" ideas that had been discussed within the agency in the closing years of the Reagan administration.[11]

The Ninety Day Study began with the candid admission that

> In the often contentious debate that has developed over Superfund policy, EPA has operated without its most valuable asset, the benefit of the doubt. Though the program has picked up speed, Superfund continues to fall short of public expectations. Whether fairly or not, debate centers around the program's flaws, both real and perceived—at all levels from national policy to local site management.[12]

To help restore public confidence, the Ninety Day Study recommended a number of measures that promoted consistency in the selection of Superfund site cleanup remedies. The report also suggested specific steps for accelerating and improving remedial actions, bringing innovative techniques to bear on pollution at Superfund sites, giving interested citizens a greater role in the Superfund Program, improving CERCLA management and administrative support, and communicating program results to the public.

In the enforcement area, the Ninety Day Study adopted many of the suggestions that had been made in the ELI Report. It recommended that EPA increase its use of unilateral administrative orders, take prompt enforcement measures against viable and recalcitrant nonsettling PRPs, and conduct response actions at all sites that have viable PRPs before using the trust fund, except in emergencies. The study also urged the agency to maximize regional office flexibility in shifting funds among sites, improve its documentation and recovery of removal action costs, improve its coordination with the Justice Department, and undertake a formal study of the organization of the Superfund Program to evaluate whether a reorganization among headquarters offices is appropriate.

The Ninety Day Study was publicly released, with Administrator

Reilly's endorsement, on June 13, 1989. In its preface, Administrator Reilly endorsed all of the report's recommendations. Two days later, at a hearing before a subcommittee of the Senate Committee on Environment and Public Works, Reilly responded to a question from Senator Lautenberg by stating that he would refrain from implementing the agency's proposed deferral policy, unless and until it was specifically reauthorized by Congress.[13] He also pledged a large increase in the budgetary resources the agency would request from Congress to implement the Ninety Day Study's suggestions.[14]

On Capitol Hill these developments were seen as salutary and encouraging. In the minds of interested members of Congress and their staffs, the new administration's approach effectively disassociated Reilly and Habicht from the unpopular policies of their predecessors.[15] While not uniformly endorsed, it substantially succeeded in boosting the agency's credibility while generating what Lewis Crampton referred to as a "rhetorical cease-fire" with Congress and other critics.[16]

Fortunately for the agency's new leadership, this budding improvement in EPA-congressional relations in the enforcement area was accompanied and strengthened by the appointment of a forceful assistant administrator for enforcement and compliance monitoring with established contacts and credibility on Capitol Hill. James M. Strock's nomination was announced on August 4, 1989, and he was confirmed soon afterward with little opposition. Strock had been a special assistant to the EPA administrator from 1983 to 1985. For the following two years, Strock had been a member of the staff of the Senate Committee on Environment and Public Works. Then, after a two-year stint as a senior associate with a Washington, D.C., law firm, he served from 1988 to 1989 as general counsel and acting director of the U.S. Office of Personnel Management.[17]

Strock's background as a Senate committee staff member proved helpful to him in improving the frequency and tone of communications between the agency and its congressional overseers. In contrast with the approach of his predecessor, Thomas Adams, Strock devoted a good deal of his time to holding informal dialogues with interested congressional committee staff members. Those meetings, together with his existing reputation on Capitol Hill as an advocate of strong and effective EPA enforcement, helped restore the faith of at least some congressional observers in the agency's commitment to a vigorous enforcement effort.[18]

Internally, Strock saw a need to overcome the fragmentation of enforcement authority at the EPA headquarters level by extending the responsibility and influence of the office he headed. In that endeavor, he won the support of Administrator Reilly and Reilly's deputy, Hank Habicht.

On April 18, 1990, the agency's Office of Enforcement and Compliance Monitoring was formally reorganized and retitled the Office of Enforcement. A new multimedia Office of Federal Facilities Enforcement was created within this new entity. It included both the former Office of Solid Waste and Emergency Response Federal Facilities Hazardous Waste Compliance Office and the Office of Federal Activities that had previously been a part of the Office of Enforcement and Compliance Monitoring. The jurisdiction of the Pesticides and Toxic Substances Enforcement Division was expanded to cover enforcement actions under the community right-to-know provisions of CERCLA Title III. As a way of encouraging a stronger emphasis on RCRA enforcement, the former headquarters Hazardous Waste Enforcement Division was divided into two new units: a Superfund Enforcement Division and an RCRA Enforcement Division. The latter was headed by Kathie Stein, an aggressive attorney who had been recruited from the staff of the Environmental Defense Fund. In addition, regional counsel, whose offices handled all legal aspects of the enforcement work of EPA regional offices, began to report to the assistant administrator for enforcement, rather than to the agency's general counsel. Regional administrators and deputy administrators were required to be rated periodically by the EPA's administrator and his deputy as to their job performance on enforcement activities.[19]

These organizational changes were accomplished despite the vigorous opposition of certain regional counsel. These officials viewed the administrators of their regions as their primary clients. They viewed Strock's proposed reorganization—and his proenforcement position generally—as a potential threat to those clients' interests. In addition, the Office of Solid Waste and Emergency Response objected to losing control over some aspects of federal facilities enforcement. Other headquarters and regional officials also resisted various components of Strock's reorganization plan. As one headquarters enforcement attorney bluntly assessed it,

> Strock pushed hard for a stronger role for the office of [enforcement] vis-à-vis other [headquarters] offices within the agency and vis-à-vis the regions. I think he has pissed some regional people off. I *know* he's pissed some program office people off. . . . But I think there's been more of a trend to make this office more powerful and more important.[20]

In the civil enforcement area, Strock established a new set of priorities. With the firm and active support of deputy administrator Habicht, he stressed the development of a regional screening process to judge the strategic value of individual enforcement cases, coupled with a renewed emphasis on multimedia enforcement. As Strock envisioned it, the case-screening process should be designed to "aid the decision whether a single-media or multimedia response is warranted and what form of authority should be used to address the violation." The process "should involve coordination among the Program directors, Regional counsels and criminal enforcement agents to assure that the best remedy is selected for a particular case."[21]

With regard to multimedia enforcement, Strock endorsed the development of special enforcement initiatives that would more fully concentrate enforcement efforts and resources toward "resolving specific environmental compliance problems that might fall through the cracks of the traditional statute-specific, media-specific enforcement process."[22] These initiatives would include geographic-based approaches, in which one or more EPA programs would identify all polluting facilities in a given ecosystem (such as Chesapeake Bay) and then inspect those facilities to determine their compliance status and take any enforcement actions necessary to redress noncompliance. Multimedia initiatives would also include compliance-based approaches, in which the agency would identify patterns of noncompliance by particular corporations or their subsidiaries within and across media. Several EPA programs and/or regions would then cooperate in a coordinated enforcement response to resolve noncompliance across all relevant environmental media.[23]

Strock's advocacy of this multimedia approach was endorsed in an important memorandum, dated February 19, 1991, from Deputy Administrator Hank Habicht to the agency's top managers. Noting that on September 25, 1990, Administrator Reilly had established an overall goal of "twenty-five percent enforcement with multi-media efforts," Habicht stated that that goal "is part of the overall 'integrated' direction in which we are trying to move the agency." He directed each EPA regional office to prepare an "end of the year report" on its efforts to achieve the administrator's 25 percent multimedia enforcement goal and on how successful these efforts had been. He also asked each region to draft a short transition plan that "maps out the base program, program-specific and multi-media targeting and enforcement initiatives, and other multi-media enforcement initiatives." He directed the Office of Enforcement to create an agency work group of headquarters and regional enforcement officials to develop recommendations for multimedia enforcement and "maintain an awareness of the progress of the regions and share results."[24]

This directive coincided with an attempt to establish, within the agency's Office of Enforcement, an integrated method for obtaining cross-media information. The general concept was that an automated system would be employed to compile a list of the different identification numbers used in the agency's major enforcement data bases to refer to particular regulated facilities. That information would then be employed to access data on regulated facilities.[25]

In addition to multimedia activities, Strock's approach also emphasized better communication of EPA's goals and achievements. In an article published in August 1990 he explained his preferences in that area in this way:

> To get its enforcement message across to Congress, the media, the public and the regulated community, EPA plans to develop better explanatory measures of enforcement improvement—beyond "the numbers" when possible—and to communicate such information accurately, clearly and concisely. Because no single measure, taken alone, can provide an accurate "thumbs up" or "thumbs down" assessment of the enforcement program, the Agency is working to develop a series of useful indicators of environmental improvement from enforcement. Such indicators will range from disseminating compliance rates within targeted industries or sectors, to expanding the deterrent impact of large penalties through public announcements, to promoting pollution prevention activities included in settlement agreements.[26]

Strock's new enforcement agenda contained several other items, such as assisting state agencies to develop their own cross-media targeting and case-screening capability, developing a comprehensive enforcement training capability with an emphasis on multimedia casework, reviewing existing permits and regulations with a view to enhancing their precision and enforceability, and developing the right mix of EPA administrative, civil, and criminal enforcement cases.[27] In the criminal area he favored more resources, improved training of investigators, and the fostering of a team approach among special agents, enforcement attorneys, and technical staff. He also saw a need to attribute proper emphasis to large, resource-intensive criminal prosecutions in the agency's management tracking and budget systems.[28]

One of James M. Strock's most innovative EPA enforcement projects was actually completed after his tenure as assistant administrator was over. At Strock's request, six work groups of experienced EPA enforcement professionals prepared a set of reports that analyzed the effectiveness of the agency's enforcement programs and offered detailed recommendations for improving the enforcement process. This effort, which came to be known as the Enforcement in the 1990's Project, was based on five guiding principles that closely reflected the enforcement philosophy Strock had developed in informal consultation with interested members of Congress and their staffs:

1) Agency/state relationships represent the key to more effective enforcement activity in the future.
2) In targeting enforcement cases, EPA's management system should be sufficiently flexible to encourage multi-media cases.
3) As a means of measurement, and as a medium of communication to the public, the counting of cases, referrals, convictions, penalties and the like, which constitutes "an established and important part" of the enforcement process, should be supplemented by "alternative measurements" which reflect "tangible improvements in environmental quality."
4) Environmental regulations should be developed in such a way that their enforceability is assured from the outset.
5) Positive behavior modifications in the regulated community, and more effective enforcement, can be promoted by the use of innovative approaches, different incentives, and leveraging actions.[29]

The project resulted in a balanced and thoughtful report, finally released in October 1991, that addressed critical areas of EPA enforcement policy.

With the active support of the agency's two highest officials, Strock's strong-willed pursuit of his enforcement priorities appears to have had some beneficial impact. In February 1990 the agency's *Enforcement Accomplishments Report for Fiscal Year 1989* touted "record or near-record levels in virtually every category of enforcement activity."[30] During the first year of the Bush administration, EPA made 364 civil judicial referrals to the Department of Justice and more than 4,000 administrative actions. Superfund settlements and judicial enforcement actions increased significantly, as did the value of civil penalties assessed against violators of environmental laws.[31]

While the significance of these numerical indicators can be over-stated, they do serve as at least a crude indication of success for the agency's civil enforcement efforts in this period.

EPA's renewed emphasis on criminal enforcement also bore fruit in the early Bush years. This approach received consistent public and private support from Deputy Administrator Habicht. In testimony before a Senate subcommittee Habicht described criminal enforce-ment as "critically important." He stated that one of its most impor-tant results is "to encourage companies and executives to put sys-tems in place . . . so that they know what's going on, and they know they can't look the other way and think everything will be all right."[32]

Justice Department environmental enforcement statistics for fis-cal year 1989 showed a 70 percent increase in the number of pleas and convictions obtained, an 80 percent rise in the value of assessed criminal fines, and a 35 percent increase in jail time imposed on con-victed environmental offenders compared with the previous fiscal year.[33] The same set of records reflected further increases the follow-ing year. On November 15, 1990, the Department of Justice an-nounced it had brought a "record number" of environmental prose-cutions in fiscal year 1990. The 134 indictments returned in that period against alleged violators of federal environmental statutes represented a 33 percent increase over the preceding twelve-month period.[34]

The environmental criminal enforcement efforts of EPA and DOJ received an additional boost from the enactment in October 1990 of the Pollution Prosecution Act of 1990. Introduced by Senator Joseph Lieberman (D-CN), the legislation called for a 400 percent increase in the number of EPA criminal investigators, as well as the addition of 50 new civil investigators for the Superfund Program.[35] Congress subsequently appropriated the funds necessary to augment the agen-cy's staff of criminal investigators. However, it declined to provide monies for additional civil investigators.

Another advance during this period was the issuance of a more stringent civil penalty policy for RCRA violations that called for the assessment of substantially increased forfeitures. The new policy es-tablished a matrix with three penalty classifications based upon the seriousness of the violations in question. It required EPA regional of-fices to provide documentation to support the penalties they as-sessed against RCRA violators and to justify any assessments that were inconsistent with policy guidelines.[36] The agency continued—and intensified—its reliance on state enforcement efforts in this period, a trend that improved EPA's institutional relationship with some, but not all, state environmental agencies. It also made incremental progress in enforcing environmental standards against certain federal agencies and facilities,[37] although such progress was uneven.[38]

Despite these gains, however, significant problems continued to plague EPA enforcement in the early years of the Bush administration. Although, as mentioned previously, the organizational structure of the agency's enforcement efforts underwent a formal reorganization in the spring of 1990, those changes failed to overcome a continuing fragmentation of enforcement authority within EPA headquarters. Recognizing this, Jim Strock sought, ultimately without success, to strengthen further the responsibilities of the office he headed. In a closed December 5, 1990, meeting with William Reilly and Hank Habicht, Strock requested that the administrator approve a plan to move technical enforcement personnel from all other EPA headquarters offices (with the exception of the Office of Solid Waste and Emergency Response) into the Office of Enforcement. This plan, which was outlined in a briefing book presented to the administrator, was intended to create a more rational chain of command for enforcement policy decisions. It contemplated no changes in the prevailing organizational arrangements within EPA's ten regional offices. Reilly and Habicht made no commitment to Strock at the December 5 meeting. They thanked him for raising the question of the workability of the agency's organizational arrangement and promised to give his proposal further consideration. Anticipating this response, however, Strock emerged from the meeting guardedly pleased about the prospects for his reorganization plan.[39]

Strock's cautious optimism was soon to prove unfounded. On January 11, 1991, *Inside EPA*, an environmental trade journal, published a front-page article describing Strock's proposal and noting the substance of his recent meeting with Reilly and Habicht.[40] The article, which was based on information that had apparently been leaked by an individual with access to the briefing materials Strock had presented to the administrator, contained language certain to catch the attention of any affected EPA official:

> Several EPA staff say that the plan is a power play by Strock, motivated more by his wish to command additional resources and policy authority than by environmental need. . . . An EPA staffer warns that by expanding his power over EPA enforcement decisions, Strock would be able to drive policy and priorities for every office. "He is becoming everyone's boss," laments one EPA staffer.[41]

Publication of this article ignited a brief but bitter dispute. Caught by surprise, other EPA assistant administrators and their allies promptly made very plain their fervent opposition to Strock's reorganization proposal. Arguing that the plan would undermine their ability to establish priorities within their own areas of competence and that it would disrupt recent advances in the agency's enforcement work, these individuals prevailed upon the administrator and his deputy to reject any further enforcement reorganization.[42]

Soon after these events, Strock resigned as EPA's assistant administrator for enforcement to assume the newly created position of secretary of the California Environmental Protection agency.[43] After a six-month interregnum, during which Deputy Assistant Administrator Edward Reich served as acting assistant administrator, Strock was permanently replaced by Herbert Tate, a former prosecutor for Essex County, New Jersey, with close ties to New Jersey's former governor Thomas Kean.[44] Although the question of EPA's ineffectual enforcement structure was subsequently reviewed by the GAO,[45] no further changes were made to that organizational arrangement during the remainder of George Bush's term as president, a situation that hampered the efficiency of EPA's enforcement work. Moreover, despite the enthusiasm of the agency's top managers for a multimedia approach to EPA enforcement, this worthwhile effort ran into two significant difficulties: inadequate information management capability and internal resistance from single medium–oriented enforcement personnel.

In 1989 the agency's Office of Enforcement began to develop an integrated method for obtaining cross-media information from the data bases of the fourteen separate national information systems EPA had previously created to support its enforcement work. The new method, known as the Integrated Data for Enforcement Analysis (IDEA) system, was dependent upon another automated system, the Facility Index System (FINDS), whose primary aim was to compile lists of the different identification numbers the agency's major data bases use to refer to particular regulated facilities and to access data, with respect to individual facilities, in nine of the pertinent data bases. Unfortunately, these systems were poorly designed and deployed without sufficient field testing. As a result, they were far from user friendly. In some instances, IDEA and FINDS required EPA enforcement personnel to refer to manuals that took up to six feet of shelf space in order to formulate inquiries and interpret results. They reflected other deficiencies as well, including incomplete listings of the names different EPA programs employed to refer to particular industrial facilities, facilities that lacked any FINDS identification number, and multiple FINDS identification numbers for the same facilities. Furthermore, to compound these problems, the agency failed to budget for proper redesign of the software.[46]

In view of these difficulties, a review by the GAO concluded:

EPA's efforts to bring together data from different environmental programs to accomplish its cross-media enforcement mission and correct its material internal control weaknesses are jeopardized by systems development deficiencies, insufficient maintenance plans and inadequate data quality. The cross-media enforcement system does not provide all the capabilities users need to assess environmental risks, target and prioritize enforcement actions, develop enforcement cases or plan strategically on a cross-media basis at the state and regional levels. As a result, EPA cannot assure that it can identify the most important cross-media enforcement priorities.[47]

EPA's fledgling multimedia enforcement program was also plagued by a paucity of cooperation from officials at both the headquarters and regional levels whose primary responsibilities concerned only one environmental medium. As one headquarters enforcement attorney described it:

One of the problems you get into when you start trying to get the lawyers multimedia is that you get some resistance from their clients, the program offices, who are much less willing to look at things from a multimedia perspective and are not really happy about having their lawyers working on several different areas as well as their area. That's something that's going to have to be worked out.[48]

Although these difficulties were not enough to thwart the multimedia enforcement effort entirely, they did meaningfully limit its effectiveness in certain EPA regions.[49]

In implementing RCRA, EPA and its state agency counterparts largely ignored certain important categories of violations. As one agency study frankly admitted:

Substantially increased compliance and enforcement presence is needed for [hazardous waste] generators and non-notifiers [i.e., those who have failed to notify the EPA that they are managing a regulated hazardous waste site.] . . . Because generators and non-notifiers have consistently been a low priority, only about one third of all generators have had even one RCRA inspection, and pro-active efforts to deter non-notifier activity have been limited.[50]

Additionally, in many instances EPA and the states failed to take "timely and appropriate" enforcement actions regarding other RCRA infractions.[51]

Beyond this, EPA's enforcement work in all areas continued to suffer from a shortage of personnel,[52] as well as other chronic problems that predated William Reilly's tenure as EPA administrator. Those long-standing problems included inconsistencies in the enforcement approaches of EPA regional offices, difficulties in recruiting qualified staff as a result of inappropriate civil service limitations, inadequate headquarters guidance, poor working conditions in certain agency facilities, and periodic frictions between EPA personnel and the Department of Justice.

Although the relationship between EPA and its congressional overseers concerning enforcement issues improved significantly at the beginning of the Bush administration, that trend did not continue indefinitely. While not as strident or sustained as it was during the Reagan years, criticism of the agency's enforcement efforts by members of Congress and the GAO did increase in intensity over time, especially in the period following the departure of Jim Strock as assistant administrator for enforcement.

As in previous years, a major focus of congressional investigators was EPA's administration of the Superfund Program. In December 1990 the Dingell Committee held a hearing with regard to oversight of Superfund contractors by the agency's Office of Inspector General. Six months later the committee issued a report concluding that EPA's Office of Inspector General was plagued by "serious leadership deficiencies" that prevented it from "effectively [pursuing] waste, fraud and abuse by the Environmental Protection Agency's major contractors." The committee cited what it characterized as "a number of disturbing problems" relating to failures by the inspector general's Office of Investigations. It recommended that the agency "develop and implement a comprehensive plan to investigate potential fraud in the Superfund Program."[53]

From Superfund contractor abuses, the attention of Congressman Dingell, as well as Senator Lautenberg and other interested congressional overseers, turned to the pace and consistency of cleanup activities at Superfund sites. On June 19, 1991, in an effort to respond to growing congressional concerns, Administrator Reilly directed the agency's Office of Solid Waste and Emergency Response to investigate EPA's options for accelerating the rate of CERCLA remedial actions and determine whether the Superfund Program was using realistic assumptions to evaluate and manage environmental risks. Reilly also appointed an agency task force to study EPA's Superfund contracting system.[54] One month later, Don Clay, the agency's assistant administrator for solid waste and emergency response, sent the administrator a detailed set of recommendations which came to be known as the Thirty Day Study.[55] His suggestions were ultimately adopted by Reilly and publicly released on October 2, 1991, two days before an important oversight hearing had been scheduled by the Levitas Committee.[56] Among other things, Clay suggested that EPA's CERCLA remedial investigation and remedy selection process be standardized through the development of a "technology-based approach to remedies," guidelines for certain contaminated soils and groundwater contaminants, and regulations that designate particular cleanup technologies as appropriate for specific categories of sites. He also urged that the agency issue a national policy requiring PRPs to begin remedial design work prior to the entry of Consent Decrees requiring them to do so and that it resolve various intra- and interagency disputes which delay site cleanups.[57]

Clay's Thirty Day Study was supplemented by an EPA Alternative Remedial Contracting Study that was also approved by the administrator and made public on October 2. The report found that managerial and administrative expenditures by Superfund contractors were, in many instances, excessive. It recommended stepped-up EPA audits of contractor bills and charges, as well as other measures.[58]

To implement the recommendations contained in these two studies, the administrator appointed Richard Guimond, EPA's deputy assistant administrator for solid waste and emergency response, to oversee Superfund procurements and budgeting and assure uniformity among cleanup decisions. Guimond was assigned a national staff of twenty troubleshooters to assist him with these tasks.

Appropriate as they were, these actions by EPA failed to mollify the agency's overseers on Capitol Hill. On October 4, 1991, Senator Lautenberg told a House subcommittee hearing that the agency had made little progress in implementing the reforms it had promised two years earlier when it issued the Ninety Day Study. He opined that EPA had been treating the Superfund Program like an "unwanted stepchild" and dismissed the agency's Thirty Day and Alternative Remedial Contracting Studies by stating: "The disturbing thing . . . is that it hasn't already been done. . . . It's time to stop issuing reports and start implementing the law."[59]

Congressman Dingell took a similar stance. In a prepared statement he indicated that the Alternative Remedial Contracting Study showed only that "EPA has a firm grasp of the obvious." In Dingell's view, the report was "merely acknowledging what everyone else has known for months. . . . [M]any of the EPA's proposals embrace recommendations contained in a July 1991 subcommittee report, in GAO reports dating back to 1988, and in a forthcoming GAO report requested by this subcommittee."[60]

While Congress's criticisms of EPA's Superfund efforts received much attention, other aspects of the agency's enforcement performance were also given negative reviews by congressional investigators, including, most significantly, the GAO. In a series of reports, GAO cast doubt on the efficacy of EPA's compliance and enforcement programs in such diverse areas as inland oil spills, Clean Water Act pretreatment standards, air pollution control, and NPDES permits.[61] In addition, in a study released on June 17, 1991, that was widely read by interested members of Congress and their staffs, GAO castigated the agency and its state counterparts for failing to follow EPA's penalty policy, which requires assessment of civil forfeitures at least as great as the amount by which a company has benefited by not complying with applicable environmental standards.[62] GAO's report, which owed much to earlier studies on the same topic that had been performed by EPA's Office of Inspector General, found that in nearly two out of three penalty cases concluded in fiscal year 1990 (by EPA's air, water, hazardous waste, and toxic substances enforcement programs), there was no evidence that the economic benefit of violators' noncompliance had been calculated or assessed. Moreover, it concluded, notwithstanding the applicability of State/EPA Agreements, state and local enforcement authorities adhered to the agency's Civil Penalty Policy in an even smaller percentage of cases than did the agency's own regional officials.[63]

These continuing congressional investigations were carried out against the backdrop of intensifying rivalry, within the Bush administration itself, over questions of environmental policy. On a host of issues—including EPA's implementation of the Clean Air Act's permit program, the definition of wetlands for purposes of the Clean Water Act, and the administration's approach to international treaties on global warming and biodiversity—EPA Administrator Reilly clashed with the Council on Competitiveness, headed by Vice President Dan Quayle, which advocated the relaxation of environmental requirements as a means of reviving the flagging national economy. These disagreements resulted in several painful and significant defeats for Reilly during the spring and summer of 1992.[64]

These events and the national publicity they gave rise to contributed to a public perception that, contrary to some of its earliest positions, the Bush administration had tilted against environmental protection. This view, which was at least partially reinforced by congressional criticism of EPA's enforcement activities, led to a further questioning of the administration's goals and intentions. Within the agency, the morale of the enforcement staff again declined.[65] Among EPA's congressional overseers, the closing months of George Bush's presidency were a time of renewed suspicion and mistrust.

SEVEN

Lessons Learned

Congressional Oversight
of EPA's Enforcement Approach
in Broader Perspective

What, then, are the larger lessons of EPA's enforcement history? What does the agency's past performance in this critical aspect of its responsibilities contribute to our broader understanding of regulatory enforcement in general and congressional oversight of governmental agencies and EPA in particular?

In the past few years, the writings of American scholars have reflected a modest but growing interest in both congressional oversight of federal agency activities and the general nature of the enforcement process in regulatory bureaucracies. In addition, a handful of academics, writing from differing perspectives and on varying themes, have assessed EPA's performance of its statutory mandates and broader societal responsibilities.[1]

The largely neglected study of regulatory enforcement as an aspect of agency behavior was given new impetus by the publication in 1984 of *Enforcing Regulation*, a collection of essays edited by Keith Hawkins and John M. Thomas.[2] In their introduction to this provocative volume, the editors make a distinction between two vastly different approaches to regulatory enforcement by governmental agencies: the "compliance system" and the "deterrence system." In a compliance system, they write, the primary concern of agency personnel is with satisfying the broad aspirations of applicable regulatory statutes by preventing violations and remedying underlying problems. Enforcement officials rely heavily, if not exclusively, on "privately practiced, low-visibility bargaining and bluffing." Formal legalistic enforcement tools are resorted to with extreme reluctance in a compliance system. Instead, emphasis is placed on the development and maintenance of an amicable social relationship between regulatory personnel and regulated entities—a relationship presumed beneficial for the discovery of future problems and the effective detection of violators. A deterrence system of regulatory enforcement, in contrast, is much more an arm's length process whose essential purpose is to detect offenses and punish violators. The enforcement style is generally "accusatory and adversarial," and formal legal processes are routinely relied upon for the resolution of enforcement disputes. In a deterrence system, the major preoccupation of agency officials is with punishing wrongdoers, both as a means of doing justice in individual cases and as a way of deterring future violations of regulatory standards.[3]

This formulation raises an empirical question: should the enforcement process that prevails at EPA be seen as a compliance system or a deterrence system? The better view seems to be that the agency's enforcement activities as they have developed over time constitute a deterrence system of regulatory enforcement. With the brief exception of the Gorsuch era of the early 1980s, both the EPA's written enforcement policies and its actual practices have consistently emphasized the initiation of *formal* enforcement actions against violators of federal environmental standards. Those formal actions have ranged from notices of violation and administrative orders to civil judicial actions and, more recently, criminal prosecutions.

The formal, legalistic nature of EPA's enforcement efforts is reflected in the agency's system for measuring and publicizing enforcement success. It is also evident in the EPA's sizeable legal staff, the high volume of cases it regularly refers to the Justice Department for civil action or criminal prosecution, the monetary value of the civil and administrative penalties it has assessed against violators, and the large body of enforcement policies, guidance documents, and studies it has issued that require or urge the use of formal enforcement methods.

One clear example of the agency's preference for a formal approach to enforcement can be found in its recent *RCRA Implementation Study*. In discussing the compliance and enforcement aspects of the implementation of RCRA, the study included a sort of declaration of principles that comes very close to defining a deterrence system: "An effective enforcement program must detect violations, compel their correction, ensure that compliance is achieved in a timely manner, and deter other violations. The RCRA enforcement program will obtain substantial involuntary compliance only if the regulated community perceives that there is a greater risk and cost in violating a requirement than in complying with it."[4]

It should be acknowledged that these formal measures, practices, and policies do not represent every aspect of EPA's enforcement approach. For various reasons the written policies and guidances drafted at the agency's headquarters have not always been followed by enforcement officials in regional offices or state agencies. This is particularly true with respect to state officials, many of whom have traditionally favored informal enforcement activities and resisted the imposition of monetary penalties on environmental violators.[5] The commitment of at least some EPA inspectors to a formal legalistic approach to enforcement has been questioned by some agency attorneys.[6]

Notwithstanding these circumstances, however, it seems most accurate to describe EPA's enforcement practices as constituting, in the main, a deterrence system. Though the agency's enforcement approach may lack uniformity, its legalistic nature is historically rooted and deeply ingrained.

In view of this, the next issue that arises is normative: is EPA's deterrence approach to its enforcement responsibility appropriate? Would the agency be better served by a less formalized approach that emphasizes the development of constructive working relationships with regulated entities? In "The 'Criminology of the Corporation' and Regulatory Enforcement Strategies," Robert A. Kagan and John T. Scholz have advocated a very different paradigm of regulatory enforcement.[7]

Kagan and Scholz describe three differing images of the business corporation in the context of regulatory enforcement. In the first image, business firms are "amoral calculators" who will carefully and competently assess opportunities and risks. They will intentionally disobey regulatory standards when the probability that they will be caught, along with the fine they are likely to receive, is small in comparison to the profits they will receive by noncompliance. Under a second paradigm, regulated companies are "political citizens" who will normally comply with applicable requirements or orders they regard as unreasonable or arbitrary. The third category includes business firms that are generally in compliance with regulatory limitations unless they experience organizational problems that result from failing to keep abreast of legal requirements or oversee their subordinates effectively.

The authors contend that each of these images suggests a somewhat different regulatory enforcement strategy. Amoral calculators require an aggressive and formalistic inspection regime, combined with a formalized deterrence system of compliance of the type described by Hawkins and Thomas. However, where the political citizen theory holds, agencies should persuade political citizens of the rationality of the agencies' regulations and should be flexible in adapting the law to accommodate legitimate business problems which strict enforcement might create. Moreover, in circumstances where regulatory noncompliance is a result of organizational failure and incompetence, agencies should serve as consultants, analyzing information gaps and organizational weaknesses in regulated firms and educating businesspeople about technologies and management systems that should ensure future compliance.

In Kagan and Scholz's view, each of the three theories of corporate behavior they describe "seems to capture an important aspect of reality." Thus, they contend, rather than taking the "counterproductive" approach of relying on any single theory of noncompliance,

> Regulators should be alert to the possibility that violations may derive from amoral calculation, principled disagreement or incompetence. Inspectors should be prepared to shift from strict policeman, to politician, to consultant and back again according to their analysis of the particular case.[8]

Appealing as this proposal may be in the abstract, as it applies to EPA's situation it is flawed in several respects. First, Kagan and Scholz's recommendation appears to increase the likelihood that equally situated sources of pollution could receive inconsistent treatment from regulatory officials: a difficult-to-eliminate problem under even the best of circumstances. EPA regulates hundreds of thousands of facilities under nine major federal statutes. Its enforcement activities involve thousands of attorneys, inspectors, and engineers in the agency's ten regional offices as well as its headquarters. Moreover, the reason that violations occur at particular sources of pollution at particular times is often difficult for EPA officials to evaluate. Thus, if agency officials must decide on a case-by-case basis if every violation they become aware of is a result of an amoral calculation, a principled disagreement, or an organizational failure and then adjust their regulatory responses accordingly, the likelihood that the same circumstances will receive disparate EPA responses will undoubtedly be high.

This problem is likely to be compounded by another inconvenient circumstance: evaluation of the root causes of noncompliance is outside the present responsibilities, experience, and expertise of EPA enforcement officials. Moreover, attrition among enforcement attorneys and technical personnel has historically been a significant problem at the agency. Many EPA enforcement professionals have only been at their jobs a short time. Thus, it would be difficult for EPA to rely consistently on its staff to determine why motivated sources of pollution have violated environmental requirements in particular instances.

Beyond these factors is another concern: federal environmental regulation has some attributes that distinguish it from other types of regulatory regimes. In comparison to many agencies, which focus on particular industries or locations, EPA's jurisdiction is immense. Its regulations affect dozens of industries as well as thousands of state and local governments and numerous federally owned facilities. The costs of complying with EPA requirements are frequently high; in at least some private industries, they can have a marked impact on the profitability of regulated firms. In many instances, what Kagan and Scholz refer to as the "pressures for responsible behavior" exerted on business corporations by the market, trade associations, insurance companies, labor unions, and others are less persistent or significant in the context of environmental protection than in other regulatory fields. In combination, these circumstances appear to create a greater likelihood that violations of environmental standards will be motivated more by what Kagan and Scholz describe as "amoral calculation," a situation in which a deterrence system of enforcement is unquestionably appropriate, than in other areas of regulation.

Finally, in their own writing, Kagan and Scholz have identified significant practical difficulties with the two alternatives they mention to strict, legalistic enforcement. As they note, there is no "bright line" that separates reasonable from unreasonable regulatory requirements. Thus, it is often particularly difficult in situations of noncompliance for regulatory personnel to distinguish principled noncompliance from calculated self-interest. Furthermore, a "consultative approach" by agency personnel could encourage complacency among regulated parties and create a public perception of capture or corruption. Moreover, as Kagan and Scholz recognize, alternatives to a deterrence system of enforcement face formidable political obstacles:

> Legislatures, prodded by . . . environmental groups . . . often refuse to grant regulatory officials discretion. Even when they do, funding is not generous, which makes it difficult for most agencies to recruit, train and retain inspectors sophisticated enough to serve as competent consultants *and* as tough-minded sifters of justified from unjustified excuses *and* as stern sanction-appliers when necessary.[9]

In contrast with Kagan and Scholz's proposal, a legally rooted deterrence system of enforcement as practiced by EPA, albeit imperfectly, over most of the agency's history seems reasonably well suited to the challenges and realities of environmental regulation at the federal level. Such a system prevents the inevitability of difficult case-by-case judgments regarding the motivating causes of environmental violations by relatively inexperienced staff members. It recognizes the necessity of principled and equitable arm's length contacts with the vast number of pollution sources regulated by the agency. It tacitly acknowledges that many regulated parties feel compelled by competitive pressures to make amoral calculations as to whether they should come into compliance with applicable standards. It also tends to decrease the probability of a public perception that EPA makes its enforcement decisions on the basis of favoritism, corruption, or other inappropriate factors.

These benefits notwithstanding, a deterrence system of federal environmental enforcement, even if it is carried out with absolute uniformity and professionalism, is not a perfect resolution of EPA's problems in responding to noncompliance by regulated parties with environmental statutes and regulations. As Martin A. Spitzer has observed:

> [E]nvironmental compliance is a different matter than compliance with traffic laws; many people do not know what to comply with or how. Small and medium businesses—the bulk of the regulated universe—often do not know what they are supposed to do. Many firms, particularly the smaller ones, are ill-equipped to learn the rules.[10]

In response to this problem, EPA would do well to expand its outreach to the regulated community as a *supplement* to its enforcement activities. Agency personnel can work with trade associations and other groups, including university-based assistance programs, to transfer information regarding firms' compliance with applicable requirements. They can hold conferences, print brochures, and establish regulatory "hot lines" to the same end. Regrettably, EPA has thus far not chosen to make much use of these proactive techniques. Despite their promising potential for reducing noncompliance that results from organizational failure, EPA has done little to promote voluntary compliance beyond promoting deterrence by traditional formal enforcement techniques. As one EPA official has frankly acknowledged: "Promotion activities have traditionally been underfunded [by EPA and the states] and [are seen as] the most expendable activity in a compliance and enforcement program."[11]

Another pertinent set of inquiries concerns a different topic: the effects of congressional oversight on EPA's enforcement performance. To what extent have Congress's investigations of EPA activities had an impact on the agency's policies and practices?

Steven Shimberg, the minority staff director and chief counsel of the Senate Committee on Environment and Public Works, contends that Congress's influence on EPA has been minimal:

> With respect to the hundreds or thousands of relatively minor decisions confronting EPA, congressional oversight, or the mere threat of oversight, can be used to alter behavior and change decisions. With respect to the major policy decisions, however—decisions that shape federal environmental policy—traditional forms of congressional oversight have little effect. Behavior may be altered but rarely are decisions altered solely as a result of congressional oversight. When a major policy question is working its way through the system (first within EPA and then within the executive branch as a whole), the voices heard from Congress in the name of "oversight" are treated just like those from any other interest group.[12]

This observation stands in stark contrast to the conclusion reached by Joel D. Aberbach in his analysis of the politics of congressional oversight. After examining the relationship between congressional investigators and executive branch officials in some detail, Aberbach concludes that

> Congressional oversight has a significant effect on agency behavior. . . . Congress plays an active role both in writing the laws that establish the skeleton and muscle and in setting the budgets that give the lifeblood to administrative agencies. When Congress shows an interest, agencies ignore it at their peril.[13]

Who is correct? Do congressional investigations affect agency policy decisions significantly or marginally? While not dispositive of the question, the record of congressional oversight of EPA enforcement activities tends to support Aberbach's perception far more than it does Shimberg's. In a number of instances, important EPA decisions regarding the approach the agency should take in carrying out its enforcement responsibilities have been shaped more or less directly by congressional oversight and concern.

One good example of this, which we considered in Chapter 5, is the agency's renewed emphasis on enforcement (both generally and in the Superfund context specifically) in the period that followed Anne Gorsuch's departure as EPA administrator in 1983. Having forced Gorsuch's resignation, Congress continued to press the EPA for improvements in its enforcement programs. The agency's attempt to intensify its enforcement efforts, to emphasize civil penalties based on the economic benefits attained by violators through noncompliance, and to elevate the importance of enforcement in the CERCLA program can all be traced to Congress's influence.

Similarly, EPA's 1985 decision to launch a loss of interim status (LOIS) initiative—to enforce various requirements of RCRA against land disposal facilities—was a result of intensive pressure on the agency for stronger action in this area by the Dingell Committee. Additionally, the "enforcement first" approach to EPA's administration of CERCLA, adopted by William Reilly in the Ninety-Day Study of 1989, was part of an attempt by the agency's then new leaders to satisfy persistent congressional critics by taking a new direction in that closely watched field.

Beyond these direct effects on EPA enforcement policies, congressional oversight has also influenced EPA decision making indirectly in other critical respects. Thus, for example, Congress's sustained insistence on active and vigorous enforcement activity has encouraged the agency to emphasize the *volume* of its formal enforcement actions (including its annual count of civil judicial referrals, administrative orders, criminal prosecutions, civil penalties, etc.) in measuring and evaluating its enforcement successes. Congressional interest has motivated EPA officials to expand the scope of EPA's criminal enforcement work, and congressional inquiries have periodically placed demands on the time and energy of the agency's top managers, as well as its professional enforcement staff.

In view of these pervasive and highly significant influences of congressional investigations on EPA enforcement work, the next logical question is, Has it all been helpful? Taking Congress's oversight of the agency's enforcement programs as a whole, has it contributed to a more effective and credible effort in this area or, as some have contended, is it one important cause of a generalized regulatory failure?

One thoughtful, productive scholar, Richard Lazarus, has been largely negative in his assessment of Congress's oversight of EPA. He believes that Congress's consistently adversarial tone has unduly harmed the agency's reputation, chilled innovative decision making, placed excessive demands on EPA resources, skewed the agency's priorities, and damaged the morale and self-esteem of its employees.[14]

Lazarus's analysis conflicts with the conclusion of Joel Aberbach. Though his work does not concentrate on EPA specifically, Aberbach is far more optimistic than Lazarus concerning the impacts of congressional oversight. He defends the overall performance of the federal legislature in these terms: "It seems fair to say that oversight addresses problems and checks, or even corrects, many errors affecting at least the more organized and articulate members of the polity. As a result, congressional oversight probably improves policy at the margins."[15] Once again, the history of EPA's relationship with Capitol Hill in the enforcement area is largely supportive of Aberbach's conclusion. While some of Lazarus's criticism of congressional oversight of EPA is undoubtedly well taken, a careful review of Congress's performance in overseeing the agency's enforcement efforts reveals more success than failure. Although not free of mistakes, Congress has, in the main, pushed EPA's enforcement policies in directions that improved their efficacy and benefited the public at large.

At the outset, it is important to note that much of Lazarus's thesis is premised on the notion that EPA's history has been characterized by what he refers to as "a destructive pattern of regulatory failure." As Lazarus sees it, the competing efforts of the OMB, on the one hand, and EPA's congressional critics, on the other, combined with frequent judicial rejection of important EPA regulations have given rise to a "pathological cycle" in which "agency distrust has begotten failure, breeding further distrust and further failure." This seems an overstatement. While EPA's situation has been regularly enveloped in conflict, in part for the very reasons that Lazarus describes, his assessment of the agency's overall efficacy seems unduly gloomy and overdrawn.

Other observers have taken a different position. In a thoughtful evaluation of the agency's work in 1986, for example, Steven A. Cohen opined:

> The U.S. Environmental Protection agency has made a significant positive contribution to the protection of environmental quality in the United States. . . . My argument is simply that, given its mission and resources, and the political bureaucratic arena in which it operates, the EPA's performance can be termed a success, albeit a qualified one.[16]

To the same effect is the writing of Dean E. Mann, who stated respecting the agency's work, "That environmentally protective policies were adopted and implemented with modest effectiveness is obvious."[17]

Moreover, even the GAO, whose persistent criticisms of EPA's work I have earlier noted, has expressed a more favorable view of the agency's achievements than has Richard Lazarus. In a detailed and lucid analysis of EPA's management of environmental programs, the GAO stated: "EPA has accomplished much to protect human health and the environment since its creation in 1970. It has put in place a comprehensive regulatory structure and has made notable progress in identifying and combatting many of the major causes of pollution."[18]

When one turns to EPA's overall enforcement record, Lazarus's undiluted negativism seems all the more misplaced. Although significantly flawed in a number of respects, the agency's enforcement programs have also enjoyed some notable successes. As Kevin Gaynor observed in 1989: "In fact, [EPA's] civil enforcement of many environmental programs is arguably quite good and may be the best kept secret."[19] Over time, the agency has gradually increased both the volume of its enforcement case work and the total amount of the penalties it has assessed against environmental violators. Additionally, the agency's criminal enforcement program, which has also expanded, has had a significant impact on the behavior of regulated corporate officers. In the words of one private environmental attorney: "The fact that there is a serious threat of criminal enforcement out there for serious violations has certainly gotten people's attention in the private sector. It has had a vast impact."[20] Other private lawyers and consultants in the environmental field have expressed a similar view.[21]

In his examination of congressional scrutiny of EPA, Lazarus takes the position that Congress's actions have "chilled decision making and innovation within the EPA" and denied the agency needed flexibility to respond to "the uncertain contours of environmental problems."[22] Whatever validity this conclusion may have with respect to the EPA's rule-making activities, it seems of little relevance in the enforcement arena. EPA's management and staff have devised some innovative approaches in several areas of the agency's enforcement work, as illustrated by EPA's multimedia enforcement efforts and its thematic enforcement initiatives. In addition, as described earlier, EPA's RCRA LOIS enforcement initiative and Superfund enforcement first policy were bold changes in agency practices that were stimulated, rather than inhibited, by congressional interest.

Equally difficult to credit is Lazarus's claim that congressional oversight has made unreasonable demands on EPA resources that have "significantly reduced" the agency's capabilities.[23] Though several of the present and former agency enforcement officials I spoke with did identify this as a problem,[24] the overwhelming majority of the individuals whom I interviewed in that category did *not* mention this concern. Indeed, a number of those who talked with me saw positive value in Congress's oversight of EPA, especially during the Gorsuch period.[25]

In noting this, however, I do not wish to suggest that the resource demands placed on EPA by congressional investigations are either minimal or unimportant. Nor do I contend that Congress's method of overseeing the agency is efficient and nonduplicative. EPA's budget is not presently designed to take account of the agency's work in responding to congressional oversight, a fact which contributes to a chronic underestimation of EPA's workload. This situation should be remedied. Furthermore, as Lazarus persuasively demonstrates, EPA is potentially subject to intense and adversarial oversight from an immense number of committees and subcommittees with overlapping concerns and, at times, conflicting agendas. Given this, Lazarus's suggestions that Congress reduce the number of committees and subcommittees with jurisdiction over the agency and that it take steps to improve oversight coordination among existing committees seem well worth considering.[26]

Another objection that Lazarus raises regarding congressional oversight of EPA relates to EPA's policy priorities. He contends that extensive congressional investigations "skew" EPA's agenda as it responds to the multiple requests and complaints of individual committee and subcommittee chairs with oversight leverage.[27] At least as it relates to EPA's enforcement policies, this concern seems exaggerated. In responding to Lazarus, Steven Shimberg aptly noted: "While oversight does affect EPA's priorities, this is not necessarily a bad thing. EPA must be responsive to public concerns. If the agency cannot garner public support for its priorities, those priorities *should* be 'skewed' by Congressional oversight."[28]

Shimberg's point is borne out by the experience of Congress's oversight of EPA in enforcement matters. Although Congress has indeed had considerable influence, both directly and indirectly, over the shape and thrust of the agency's enforcement programs, that influence has, for the most part, been constructive. Administrative agency autonomy is, in many instances, efficient and worthwhile. However, it should not be seen as an end in itself. To the extent that EPA's congressional overseers have succeeded in guiding the agency in the direction of improved effectiveness and societal benefit, it seems inappropriate to condemn their efforts.

Finally, Lazarus identifies two additional difficulties with Congress's scrutiny of EPA: it damages EPA's reputation among the public at large and it harms the self-esteem of agency professionals. Of those two concerns, the first seems far more valid than the second. Lazarus believes that "the intensity and negative quality of Congressional oversight of EPA has done much to create and perpetuate the view that EPA is incompetent, negligent and even corrupt." He argues that this negative public image, which has been mostly unjustified in his opinion, has eroded judicial, as well as public, confidence in the agency's decisions and undermined EPA's ability to implement federal statutes.[29]

Lazarus's point has some merit. As the EPA enforcement/oversight experience reveals, Congress's investigations of EPA's work have been almost unrelievedly critical in both tone and substance. In many respects this is quite understandable. From its initial investigations of EPA and Justice Department implementation of the Clean Air and Refuse Acts in the early 1970s, through its first examinations of EPA's lackluster response to uncontrolled hazardous waste dumping, its confrontations with Anne Gorsuch and her colleagues, its inquiries into the inadequacies of EPA's enforcement of RCRA, and its investigations of Superfund administration in the late 1980s and early 1990s, Congress's critiques of the agency's activities have often been based on genuine and serious problems. A number of these problems were later corrected by executive branch officials in ways that improved significantly the quality of governmental administration.

That achievement notwithstanding, congressional oversight in its cumulative impact indeed may have diminished excessively EPA's overall public reputation. As noted previously, a number of objective observers—from well-regarded scholars to the GAO—have found much to praise in the agency's overall performance. Most oversight hearings and reports on EPA do not reflect this. If public confidence and respect are prerequisites for enhanced EPA effectiveness, then the agency's congressional critics should tailor their rhetoric accordingly.

Regrettably, such an approach creates problems. When congressional investigators find fundamental flaws in an administrative agency's practices and policies, it is entirely appropriate for them to bring those shortcomings to public attention. Attempts to present a full portrait of the agency's overall performance may, in the event, mute the investigators' message and thus diminish the likelihood of their success in coaxing needed reforms. Moreover, as several scholars have noted, oversight proceedings which present and dramatize only the negative aspects of agency performance often have obvious political advantages for their sponsors, advantages that many elected officials will be loathe to forgo.[30]

Despite this, it seems reasonable to urge members of Congress and their staffs to be aware of the unintended as well as the contemplated consequences of their oversight of administrative agencies.[31] When the activities of EPA and other agencies merit praise, congressional overseers should openly give it. Rather than undercutting its efforts, such candor would, in the long view, only serve to reinforce Congress's credibility. It would also provide the public with a balanced and undistorted picture of how some of its most important governmental institutions are performing.

With respect to the impact of congressional oversight on the self-esteem of EPA employees, however, Lazarus appears to miss the mark. He writes: "Another victim of oversight has been agency morale, since the barrage of [congressional] criticism has inevitably affected employee self-esteem. . . . This has made it more difficult for EPA to recruit the most qualified agency personnel and may also be a cause of high agency turnover."[32] Among the numerous present and former EPA enforcement officials I interviewed, *not one* shared this perception.

To be sure, some EPA employees were highly critical of congressional oversight of the agency. For example, one former EPA headquarters official told me that "the number of oversight hearings, in toto, was excessive."[33] Another agency employee referred to congressional oversight committee staff members as "arrogant, snobbish and very tough to deal with" and stated: "[At] times, their job was to grandstand and make political hay out of what they could and annoy working stiffs like myself."[34]

The majority of EPA officials I interviewed were generally, although not uniformly, positive in their view of Congress's investigations of the agency's enforcement work.[35] Most significantly, none of the officials I spoke with identified congressional criticism as a significant source of diminished agency morale, a barrier to effective personnel recruitment, or a contributing cause of generalized turnover among EPA's professional staff. In view of this arguably subjective but nonetheless telling evidence, that facet of Lazarus's argument seems misinformed. At the same time, my interviews with EPA personnel did not support Steven Shimberg's claim, in response to Lazarus, that more often than not EPA's staff feels "betrayed from within."

The EPA enforcement/congressional oversight experience raises one final issue: to what extent have other aspects of Congress's work, including the decentralized nature of its lawmaking process and the manner in which it allocates resources to EPA, affected the efficacy of the agency's administration of federal environmental statutes? Lazarus has addressed this question as well.

As Lazarus sees it, the oversight responsibilities of congressional committees and subcommittees are divided in such a way that each committee and subcommittee tends to examine environmental problems through its own "narrow jurisdictional lens." The result of this "excessive fragmentation," in Lazarus's opinion, is "different laws and even different provisions of the same laws working at cross purposes."[36] In some respects, this observation is certainly correct. There are, indeed, a number of ways in which federal environmental statutes are duplicative and conflicting.[37] Moreover, overlapping demands from congressional investigators can, at least sometimes, strain the scarce resources of EPA's management and staff.

At the same time, the *enforcement* provisions of the legislation implemented by the agency have not, in general, posed a serious barrier to EPA's work. As Jeffrey G. Miller concluded in his thorough discussion of EPA's statutory enforcement authorities and their interpretation in the courts: "While the [EPA's] enforcement tools . . . could be sharpened and augmented in some respects, EPA generally has sufficient enforcement authority to mount credible and effective enforcement programs, if it has the will to do so."[38]

With respect to the resources made available to EPA by Congress, Lazarus has concluded that "Increases in EPA's budget have lagged far behind increases in the agency's statutory responsibilities."[39] In this regard, his discussion is entirely accurate and is fully confirmed by EPA's enforcement programs.

Budgetary shortfalls have long characterized EPA's situation. As early as 1980, John Quarles, the agency's former deputy administrator, observed: "In the nine years of EPA's existence, its manpower has roughly doubled while its program responsibilities have been multiplied by a factor of twenty . . . Today, it cannot perform its workload."[40] Inadequate as it may have been in 1980, this situation clearly worsened during the 1980s. In an analysis presented to the Senate Committee on Environment and Public Works in March 1991, Richard L. Hembra, director of environmental protection issues of the GAO's Resources, Community and Economic Development Division, testified that for over a decade EPA's budget had been "essentially capped" despite a considerable growth in its responsibilities. In Hembra's words:

In constant (1982) dollars, EPA's operating budget, which covers all its programs except for the Superfund cleanup program and construction grants for sewage treatment plants, went from $1.7 billion in 1979 down to $1.0 billion in 1983 and rose back up to $1.7 billion again in 1991.

Yet during this same period, EPA's responsibilities grew enormously. The 1984 amendments to the Resource Conservation and Recovery Act, for example, known as the Hazardous and Solid Waste Amendments, significantly broadened EPA's responsibilities for regulating the generation, treatment, storage and disposal of hazardous waste. The amendments also directed EPA to issue regulations for underground storage tanks. In 1986, the Safe Drinking Water Act was amended, requiring EPA to regulate 83 specific drinking water contaminants. In the same year, the Asbestos Hazardous Emergency Response Act was passed, requiring EPA to set standards for responding to the presence of asbestos in school buildings, and to study the problems of asbestos in other public buildings. The 1980's also saw significant new responsibilities for the EPA under amendments to the Clean Water Act, the Federal Insecticide, Fungicide and Rodenticide Act, and Superfund legislation (in Title III, the Emergency Planning and Community-Right-to-Know Act).[41]

As described in Chapter 5, the general inadequacy of EPA's budgetary resources was clearly reflected in a paucity of resources for the agency's enforcement activities. This situation had negative impacts on EPA's enforcement performance in a number of crucial respects. In particular, personnel shortages have impaired the agency's ability to bring non-Superfund civil actions,[42] including but not limited to RCRA suits;[43] they have also made it more difficult for both EPA and the DOJ to expand their dockets of environmental criminal prosecutions[44] and to negotiate as effectively as they otherwise might in *all* enforcement cases.[45]

Beyond this, budgetary problems have made it more difficult for EPA to handle information requests under the Freedom of Information Act, to maintain accurate records of enforcement activities, to influence state enforcement appropriately, and to identify PRPs in Superfund cases.[46] These difficulties are also an important cause of what is widely perceived to be inadequate clerical and secretarial support for the agency's enforcement staff, a situation which often leads to inefficient use of the scarce time of professional enforcement personnel.[47]

Why has EPA been chronically underfunded? Part of the answer lies in the opaque and intensely competitive process by which Congress allocates monies to all federal agencies and departments. After protracted, complex, and contentious discussions within EPA and the executive branch as a whole, the president usually presents a budget request to Congress in January or February of each year.[48] That request includes proposals for EPA as well as for all other components of the federal government. Following this, the Budget Committees of both houses of Congress pass budget resolutions that contain advisory recommendations with respect to different budget functions, as well as binding limits on domestic discretionary spending. The House and Senate Appropriations Committees then allocate domestic discretionary funds among thirteen subcommittees, each of which has jurisdiction over particular federal agencies or departments. At that point, each subcommittee becomes responsible for preparing a bill which divides its particular allocation among the various agencies that fall within its jurisdiction. At this stage, the subcommittee chairs frequently give priority to the preferences of members of their subcommittee, as well as members of the Appropriations Committee as a whole. The views of representatives of interest groups are also considered, and there are continuing discussions among subcommittee staff members and representatives of the agencies and departments whose budget requests are being considered.[49]

In EPA's situation, most critical decisions with respect to the agency's funding are made by the House and Senate Appropriations Committee Subcommittees on HUD, VA and Independent Agencies. These panels have remarkably broad and diverse budgetary responsibilities. In addition to EPA, their jurisdiction includes, among some twenty-four other agencies and entities, the Consumer Products Safety Commission, the National Science Foundation, the Department of Veterans Affairs, the Department of Housing and Urban Development, and the Selective Service System. The competition among those various agencies and departments for the limited allocation available to the same subcommittee is remarkably intensive.

While EPA does have supporters among individual members of Congress, as well as lobbyists representing a coalition of interests that range from state and local governments to national environmental organizations, the agency is chronically disadvantaged in this process by several factors. First of all, in the tangle of powerful agencies and interests that regularly vie for HUD, VA and Independent Agencies Subcommittee funding, EPA's needs are easily overlooked. Despite its size and relative importance to the environmental and economic life of the nation, EPA is perennially cast in the role of small fish in an extraordinarily big subcommittee pond.

Second, unlike several of its more formidable competitors, such as the Department of Veterans Affairs and the National Aeronautics and Space Administration, EPA does not have a single, unified, and well-organized constituency in support of its budget requests. Instead, members of Congress with an interest in EPA issues range from strong supporters of environmental protection to bitter opponents of specific agency programs or activities. This hampers EPA in its efforts to compete with agencies and departments whose work does not engender controversy.[50]

Third, in the House of Representatives there is no single committee whose responsibility it is to authorize substantive legislation for EPA to administer. Instead, as we have observed, EPA is overseen by a multiplicity of standing committees with varying and sometimes directly competing interests. This situation denies the agency a unified institutional base of support within the House itself in the rough and tumble of budgetary competition.[51]

Another unfortunate outcome of this diffuse situation, as well as of the overall budgetary stringency of the late 1980s and early 1990s, has been a tendency for individual members of Congress to lobby for appropriations which are, at the same time, narrow in scope and clearly identified in budget legislation. This procedure, known as "earmarking," has increased in recent years with respect to EPA's budget.[52] Several typical examples of this practice can be found in the bill reported by the Subcommittee on HUD, VA and Independent Agencies of the Senate Appropriations Committee for fiscal year 1992. With regard to EPA abatement, control, and compliance, this bill included appropriations of "$1,000,000 for the Lake Onondago management conference" and "$500,000 for lake water quality activities by the State of New Jersey, including such activities at Lake Hopatcong, Swartswood Lake and Musconetgong Lake, and other lakes the state deems appropriate."[53]

How might Congress's appropriation process be reformed to allow EPA a greater chance of receiving the budgetary allocation it needs to function effectively? Several changes would be helpful. First, the jurisdictions of the various subcommittees of the House and Senate Appropriations Committees could be restructured to create a separate subcommittee for environmental protection. While this subcommittee would still need to compete with other appropriations subcommittees with respect to the relative size of its pot of money, such a rearrangement would minimize, at least at the subcommittee level, the need for EPA to compete against a large number of agencies and departments that enjoy united and potent political backing. Second, the committee structure in the House of Representatives could be modified to create a single committee with the exclusive authority to authorize legislation pertaining to pollution control. This would create a core of support and sympathy for adequate EPA funding. It would also decrease the burden that widely decentralized oversight places on EPA resources. Finally, committee memberships in both the House and the Senate could be altered so that there is an overlap between the members of committees that draft the statutes EPA must implement (and oversee its performance) and the committee members that have control over the agency's budget. This reform, too, would make it more likely that appropriations subcommittee members would be familiar with the agency's needs and supportive of its budgetary requests.[54]

Even if all of these changes were accomplished, however, EPA would still face formidable barriers to obtaining all the funding it needs. Since the mid-1980s, the Congress has operated in an atmosphere of extreme budgetary restraint as it has grappled with the problem of an ever-expanding federal deficit. This difficulty, a legacy of the political decisions and indecisions of the 1980s and early 1990s, paints a grim backdrop against which the budgetary dramas of the next several years must be played out.

Nonetheless, in considering future funding levels for EPA, one can hope that the Congress will take account of the true dimensions of the agency's expanded workload, the urgency of its budgetary needs, and the larger cost to society if federal environmental legislation is not implemented effectively. If the Congress fails to do this, it seems certain that many of our environmental laws, so proudly heralded at the time of their enactment, will be administered haltingly—and only partially enforced.

EIGHT

The Future of Environmental Enforcement

Over the course of EPA's history, changes in presidential administrations have generally given rise to significant alterations in the
agency's approach to its enforcement responsibilities. The Carter administration innovated a civil litigation–oriented major source enforcement effort; and it later created a special task force to initiate
enforcement cases concerning hazardous waste disposal. In its earliest months, the Reagan administration made a series of dramatic
changes which, in their cumulative impact, drastically curtailed
EPA's enforcement efforts and cast into doubt the agency's credibility
and good faith. The Bush administration responded to congressional
and environmentalist criticism of the Superfund Program by empha-
sizing its enforcement component and effecting other reforms. It also
made other modest but significant improvements in the agency's
general enforcement approach.

As noted in the epilogue, the initial years of the Clinton administration have seen further fluctuations in the enforcement activities
as EPA's latest set of top managers have begun to grapple with a number of the issues and themes that have preoccupied their predecessors, in varying contexts and to differing extents, during the agency's
first two decades. In this chapter, I explore a subset of these issues.
In particular, I consider how EPA can best go about evaluating the
effectiveness and efficiency of its enforcement efforts. I also discuss
how EPA's officials—as well as the agency's congressional overseers
and interested environmental organizations—can take affirmative
steps to effect improvements in EPA's enforcement work.

EPA's present system for evaluating the successfulness of its enforcement work is based on a set of numerical indicators. EPA officials keep a record of the number of administrative orders, civil referrals, and criminal referrals issued or made by the agency over the
course of a fiscal year, as well as the total amounts of administrative
and civil penalties it has assessed against environmental violators.
These figures, which play a role in EPA's internal allocation of re-

sources, are then made available to the Congress and interested members of the public. This system, which has been widely referred to as "bean counting," has been subject to extensive and sometimes heated criticism, both from within the agency and from outside it. The views of Kevin Gaynor, a former Justice Department prosecutor now in private practice, are similar to those of other skeptics:

> Despite Agency efforts to establish priorities, there is little accounting for quality. Thus, an action brought against a small company for a minor reporting violation under the Clean Air Act counts as much as a complex air case brought against a major stationary source that requires a far more significant commitment of Agency resources. In the fourth quarter of every fiscal year, the Department of Justice is deluged with [civil enforcement case] referrals as each region tries to meet its referral goals. Unfortunately, a number of these cases are dogs, and are being referred only to obtain a bean.[1]

This assessment has much merit. Though numerical indicators are not without significance, they are, at best, a crude yardstick that will only measure whether or not *some* kind of enforcement work is taking place. The reporting of raw numbers of enforcement actions gives no indication of the severity and complexity of the violations addressed, the extent to which those subject to enforcement action have committed previous offenses, the promptness with which the agency has initiated or completed action, the number and severity of violations that have *not* been addressed, and the extent to which the actions taken have deterred further violations. Moreover, in many instances, exclusive reliance on enforcement action totals as a measure of EPA's effectiveness does indeed encourage regional officials to pursue minor, easily resolved matters, regardless of their larger significance, as a means of demonstrating a high volume of enforcement activity.

If the agency's traditional method of assessing enforcement success is less than adequate, however, what should replace it?[2] What alternatives exist to EPA's present tendency to report only on the total numbers of enforcement actions taken (and monetary penalties assessed), and what are the relative advantages and disadvantages of those alternatives?[3] These questions do not have simple answers.

One provocative suggestion has been advanced in testimony before Congress by Joan Z. Bernstein, a former EPA general counsel who is now vice president and general counsel of Chemical Waste Management, Inc.:

The Agency's enforcement success should be measured by real, beneficial impact on the environment. . . . I feel that the Agency has succumbed, to a certain degree, to a kind of myopia which measures enforcement success primarily in terms of raw numbers of cases brought and penalties assessed, rather than measurable cleanup of the environment and prevention of further pollution. A new emphasis on enforcement cases addressing real contamination of our environment, rather than on technical or paperwork violations—while perhaps requiring somewhat more effort to pursue—is much needed.[4]

As a long-term goal, Bernstein's prescription is difficult to question. The federal statutes that EPA administers are, after all, intended to protect the environment. To the extent that the agency's enforcement efforts are demonstrably effective in furthering that end, it seems logical and sound to conclude that they are a success.

Unfortunately, attempts to translate this proposal into a practicable system for measuring enforcement effectiveness seem, at least in the short run, unlikely to succeed. There are several reasons for this. First, as one technically trained EPA regional official told me, "It is now just too hard to go out into the environment and collect data [on the environmental impacts of particular enforcement actions]."[5] Changes in environmental conditions may result from a host of factors, from shifts in weather patterns to alterations in the volume of manufacturing activity in a given area, which are caused solely by variations in market conditions. Thus, it is hard to associate particular environmental results with the outcomes of specific enforcement actions. This problem is compounded by the fact that significant amounts of time frequently pass between a source's achievement of compliance with regulatory requirements and any manifestation of environmental improvements. Moreover, the data presently kept by federal, state, and local officials on environmental conditions are not generally recorded or reported in relation to emissions or discharges by identified pollution sources.[6] Finally, many environmental requirements enforced by EPA and its state and local counterparts are intended to *prevent* environmental problems, rather than to ameliorate already existing ones. In the area of RCRA enforcement, for example, William Muno has pointed out:

[B]ecause of the program's heavy emphasis on prevention, no news is good news. So what's the [environmental] indicator [to assess enforcement success by]—the fact that the company had a contingency plan, a waste analysis plan and a training plan? It's pretty hard to measure the environmental impact of that.[7]

In light of these considerations, environmental indicators as a principal measure of the successfulness of EPA enforcement efforts are unreliable.

Another possible barometer of enforcement effectiveness is the level of compliance achieved by industries subject to environmental regulations. This approach could provide a rough indication of the extent to which enforcement efforts have deterred violations. It also has the advantage of encouraging the agency to supplement its enforcement program with attempts to educate (particularly small) sources about their legal obligations—a useful approach too often rejected by EPA personnel.

However, reliance on compliance rates as a gauge of enforcement successfulness has several distinct shortcomings, particularly when it is to the exclusion of other measures. First, compliance rates are hard to assess with accuracy. Because of a chronic shortage of resources, it is difficult for EPA—or state and local—personnel to conduct on-site inspections at more than a fraction of the sources that are subject to environmental standards.[8] While the results of source self-monitoring may fill some gaps in the agency's understanding of overall compliance levels, self-monitoring and record keeping are currently required with respect to only some environmental requirements, and the results of source self-monitoring which are required may be unreliable in certain instances. Thus, industrial compliance rates are generally now based on "guesstimates" by government officials, rough approximations that are, at best, indirectly supported by partial and incomplete data. To the extent compliance rates are used as an indicator of enforcement performance, EPA officials would have an incentive to report levels of compliance that are as high as they feel is defensible. There would be little objective basis for independent evaluation of the validity of their figures.

Second, compliance rates alone provide no information as to the size or environmental significance of those pollution sources that are in violation. If a small number of sources discharge a disproportionate share of the environmental pollution in a given area, even an accurate indication that a high percentage of the sources in that area are in compliance may mask serious and continuing environmental problems.

Third, even if they do reflect genuine environmental improvement, high compliance levels may have many causes. They may reflect voluntary compliance that is a result of "good corporate citizenship," a situation that cannot necessarily be correlated with the deterrent threat of a credible enforcement program. Higher compliance rates may also indicate that environmental standards are unduly lax and, for that reason, extremely simple and convenient for regulated firms to comply with.

Fourth, relatively low rates of industrial compliance do not necessarily reflect a failure of enforcement efforts. Such figures may simply indicate that EPA (and state and local) officials are doing a particularly good job of detecting regulatory violations and that the agency has promptly initiated appropriate enforcement actions in a meaningful number of cases which have not yet been brought to a conclusion.

Alternatively, EPA's enforcement effectiveness may be measured by the promptness with which EPA initiates action against known violators and the length of time it takes for noncomplying sources to come into compliance after enforcement actions have been begun. This information may well be useful. It may provide a very approximate indication of the extent to which agency enforcement personnel are following up on violations that are discovered by EPA inspectors. Unreasonable delay by the agency at this stage may diminish the credibility—and deterrent impact—of its entire enforcement program. These data may also show whether EPA's enforcement staff is pursuing individual cases in a diligent, persistent, and skillful way *after* they have been formally initiated.

Overreliance on this type of information, however, has its disadvantages. First, numerical data regarding the promptness of the agency's enforcement responses provide no indication of whether EPA has taken *appropriate* enforcement actions, in light of the seriousness of the violations, as well as the good or bad faith and the recidivism (if any) of the violators involved. In fact, the use of such measurements may unduly encourage the agency's staff to resolve enforcement matters through simple administrative orders, rather than through more time-consuming civil or criminal litigation, even when the latter would be a more sound, deterrent, and equitable approach. Second, indications of the timeliness of EPA's enforcement responses provide no information as to whether the agency has inadvertently or intentionally failed to inspect sources which are significantly contributing to environmental degradation. Third, delays in a source's achievement of compliance, subsequent to initiation of an appropriate enforcement action, may not truly reflect lax or inappropriate efforts by EPA's enforcement staff. Such delays may be the result of attorney understaffing at the Department of Justice, which represents the agency in civil enforcement litigation. They may stem from crowded judicial dockets or from skillful and persistent foot dragging by a recalcitrant source which even the most skillful enforcement attorneys and engineers could do little to avert. They could be a result of the need for careful, persistent investigation which is often prerequisite to the successful prosecution of a criminal environmental case.

In view of all this, it is apparent that no single enforcement measure can provide a fair and balanced picture of the efficiency and effectiveness of EPA enforcement programs. How then should the agency revise its outmoded system for evaluating enforcement success? Though reasonable observers can surely differ, my own sense is that the EPA would do best to supplement its current emphasis on compiling totals of the enforcement actions it has initiated (and the penalties it has assessed) by gathering and reporting on a variety of other enforcement information. Specifically, in addition to the records it now keeps, EPA (and its state and local counterparts) should keep regular accurate data on the total number of pollution sources subject to regulation, the number and percentage of pollution sources inspected in particular industries and geographical areas, and the overall rates of compliance in those same industries and areas. Moreover, with respect to compliance rates, the agency (and state and local officials) should indicate any assumptions that have been made with respect to sources that have not been inspected by government personnel and the reasons behind those assumptions. In keeping these data, it would also be helpful for EPA to keep separate records of the number of follow-up inspections it takes at noncomplying sources that have entered into Consent Decrees or other enforceable agreements in resolution of enforcement cases, as well as the number, nature, and timing of any follow-up actions taken to redress noncompliance with such agreements.

Beyond this, the agency should keep track of the rates of recidivism among known violating sources, the amount of time that expires between EPA identification of violations and the initiation of enforcement actions, and the decrease in pollution discharges and emissions that the agency anticipates as a result of enforceable agreements that resolve enforcement cases. This last set of data, which the agency should be able to compute through the use of emission factor calculations and other types of engineering estimates, will provide at least a crude indication of the environmental benefits of EPA enforcement work. As agency resources permit, it would also be useful for EPA to experiment with ways of adjusting its methods for collecting data on environmental quality in order to measure any and all environmental improvements which can specifically be attributed to environmental compliance achieved as a result of enforcement orders or agreements.

As noted previously, most of these measures, when examined in isolation, are far from adequate indications of the adequacy of EPA enforcement programs. Nonetheless, when they are taken together, these diverse sets of data will, I submit, provide a reasonably complete and balanced profile of the strengths and weaknesses of the agency's enforcement work.

I do not wish to suggest, however, that the enhanced data gathering I recommend will provide any infallible yardstick of EPA enforcement effectiveness. It might be fruitful for EPA regional (as well as state and local) officials to supplement the various data I have referred to with anecdotal information regarding the nature and outcome of significant enforcement cases brought within given time periods. Other kinds of information may also be helpful to demonstrate the appropriateness of the enforcement responses that were taken (and the sanctions that were imposed) by EPA personnel in representative samplings of enforcement cases.

It should be noted that the kinds of expanded record keeping and reporting I have recommended do have one ineluctable drawback: they will require that additional resources, specifically and consistently earmarked for the keeping and presentation of enforcement data, be made available to EPA and state and local officials. As one EPA manager told me: "Record-keeping functions are consistently underestimated in the agency's budget process."[9] In the press of other enforcement work, the completion of enforcement statistics is often given a low priority by overworked EPA regional employees, as well as by individuals with enforcement responsibilities in state and local environmental agencies. This situation is exacerbated by the fact that enforcement record keeping is an intrinsically tedious, unglamorous task; moreover, much of the centralized data EPA regional personnel and state and local officials have been asked to compile provide little direct benefit to them in the operation and management of their front-line enforcement efforts.[10]

For increased record keeping to provide a truly useful basis for examining the strengths and shortcomings of EPA enforcement work, it must receive greater attention—and a far greater share of allocated resources—from top agency managers and congressional overseers alike. To the extent that this does not occur, EPA is destined to continue its reliance on a set of numbers that provides a distorted and incomplete picture of its enforcement achievements.

The process of enforcement at EPA is complex, dynamic, and difficult to manage. Any attempt to redirect its inner workings must come to terms with formidable and deeply rooted constraints. Despite this fact, however, the agency's enforcement programs are not immutable. If they have the will to do so, a determined and skillful team of high-level EPA managers can institute measures that will take advantage of the agency's existing strengths and, at least at the margins, reduce or eliminate its shortcomings.

The professional capability and dedication of EPA's employees is one of the agency's most valuable assets.[11] Regrettably, EPA's managers have historically done a poor job of managing its talented and committed workforce. Staff career development and training have been considered low priority matters, and agency employees encounter numerous obstacles when they seek functional or geographical mobility. EPA's top managers would do well to address these problems in the months ahead.[12]

One logical focus of EPA enforcement reform is the relationship between the agency's headquarters managers and the enforcement personnel in EPA regional offices. The authority that headquarters enforcement executives have over the enforcement work performed at a regional level is shared with the agency's ten regional administrators, a semi-autonomous group of political appointees who frequently rely on state and local officials for protection and support. To the extent it exists, EPA headquarters' "control" over regional enforcement programs is usually accomplished through centralized budgetary allocations, formal headquarters appraisals of the performances of regional officials, and voluminous written enforcement policies and guidance which are, in many cases, too devoid of specifics to be of practical benefit in day-to-day enforcement case development.

This arrangement is not inevitable. Although EPA enforcement work is, to some extent, intrinsically decentralized and case specific, intensified headquarters management of discrete and carefully chosen facets of EPA's regional enforcement programs seems both feasible and appropriate. For one thing, the agency's central managers can insist that both EPA regional enforcement personnel and state and local officials consistently adhere to established EPA civil penalty policies and that they document their efforts to do so in every settled case. Additionally, EPA headquarters managers can devote the resources and attention that are needed to improve the agency's chaotic enforcement information management systems, as well as its still incipient and promising multimedia efforts. Beyond this, enforcement officials in EPA's headquarters must grapple with the long-standing problem of material inconsistencies in attitude and approach in the enforcement efforts of different regional offices. In view of the historical autonomy of the agency's regional administrators, this seems likely to prove a thorny task.

One solution worth considering is for the agency's headquarters officials to delegate enforcement authority to regional offices on a region-by-region basis, rather than making such delegations to all regional personnel simultaneously, as has been traditional. In addition, headquarters officials could insist upon periodic region-by-region reconsideration of enforcement delegations that have been made in the past. This procedure would enable headquarters enforcement personnel to conduct regular audits of regional enforcement performances in different areas and, if circumstances warrant, to withhold enforcement redelegations in particular regions unless and until conformity with national policies is achieved. If this approach is coordinated with formal headquarters performance appraisals of EPA regional officials, as well as with the agency's internal budget process, it could provide headquarters managers with the leverage they need to establish a measure of accountability in EPA regional enforcement programs.

For such an arrangement to succeed, it is imperative for EPA's headquarters enforcement staff to have sufficient experience, judgment, and skill to evaluate ongoing regional enforcement work and, when appropriate, to take over regional responsibilities on a temporary basis until such time as regional officials are deemed willing and able to resume them appropriately. Although some EPA headquarters staff members may well have the necessary qualifications to take on these delicate, demanding tasks, it is by no means certain that those individuals are now *collectively* prepared to do so. This issue should receive careful and serious scrutiny, *in advance*, by EPA's top management. To the extent that the agency's headquarters staff is not found qualified to perform the tasks they would have to be assigned, consideration of the mix of incentives and inducements needed to recruit an acceptably skilled and experienced headquarters staff would certainly be appropriate.

Finally, in light of the agency's often stormy history of adversarial relationships with Congress, EPA's top leaders would be well advised to cultivate a smooth working partnership with interested lawmakers on Capitol Hill. Rather than wait for tensions to mount, they would do well to take the initiative in developing a dialogue with senators and members of the House of Representatives who have, in the past, been critical of the agency's performance.[13] They should also give high priority to meeting on a regular, informal basis with the members of congressional committee staffs that have jurisdiction over environmental matters. Without necessarily surrendering their executive prerogatives, they should be open to considering recommendations received from the legislative branch regarding matters of policy and enforcement practice.

These recommendations for EPA executives and officials will not succeed in removing all of the obstacles that the agency's enforcement programs have faced over time. As I have repeatedly shown, the U.S. Environmental Protection Agency is not, in significant ways, the master of its own fate. Its management and staff are, in good measure, dependent on the understanding and support of Congress and the public as they carry out their challenging and vital enforcement responsibilities. Given this, some suggestions are also in order as to how our national legislature, as well as organizations of environmentally concerned citizens, can act to nurture the functioning of a firm, fair, and effective EPA enforcement program.

In many respects congressional oversight of the agency's enforcement work has been a success. While not free of difficulties, this oversight has, on a number of occasions, effectively identified significant inadequacies in EPA's enforcement approaches and then prodded the agency to remedy those shortcomings. At the same time, certain chronic problems—difficulties that have plagued EPA enforcement programs through several administrations—have received relatively scant congressional attention. Thus, although Congress has focused on inaction, timidity, and inconsistency in the agency's enforcement of particular statutes (often in the context of particular enforcement cases), it has largely ignored such persistent questions as turnover among professional enforcement employees, the nature and quality of EPA's management of its workforce, the adequacy of working conditions for the agency's enforcement staff, and the extent to which civil service personnel rules pose impediments to the recruitment of skilled EPA employees. While these matters may be dismissed as mundane or insignificant, they go to the very heart of the agency's long-term ability to sustain an effective enforcement effort. EPA's congressional overseers must broaden their focus so that issues of this sort are periodically and systematically reviewed.

In addition, members of Congress and their staffs would do well to be cognizant of the duplication that too often characterizes their oversight of EPA. Unfortunately, this inefficiency often stems from deeply rooted political circumstances. Nonetheless, it would be generally helpful for the House of Representatives to restructure its committee system to minimize the number of committees and subcommittees that have jurisdiction over particular substantive components of EPA's work. It would also be of benefit if separate sub-committees on the House and Senate Appropriations Committees were created to consider *only* EPA budget matters, and if the members of those subcommittees were also assigned to panels with EPA oversight jurisdiction. Beyond this, the Congress needs to give full and serious consideration to cutting back the number of presidentially appointed/Senate-confirmed positions at EPA. In particular, the agency's ten regional administrators should be designated as SES career-reserved positions. This step would go far toward eliminating a situation in which these powerful officials are beholden to political supporters in state governments—and sometimes unresponsive to the agency's national leadership.[14]

In addition to Congress, environmental organizations can also take several meaningful steps to foster EPA's enforcement activities. Although such organizations have enjoyed numerous successes (lobbying Congress for the enactment of environmental legislation and initiating litigation to challenge EPA regulations), their inattention to the enforcement aspects of EPA work and the politics of EPA budget requests has been unfortunate. As one environmental attorney candidly told me: "The environmental community has not been as good at [watchdogging EPA enforcement activities] as we should be . . . The community has been somewhat remiss at full time keeping tabs on what the EPA Office of Enforcement is doing."[15]

The explanations for this vary. Some of the environmentalist lawyers I interviewed mentioned a paucity of staff resources[16] or a perception, on the part of environmental organizations, that engaging in such work is inappropriate.[17] Another told me, "It is not extremely glamorous to watchdog EPA enforcement although it is very important. It's hard for [environmental organizations] to raise money for that."[18] Whatever their reasons, by largely ignoring the enforcement practices of EPA officials, environmental organizations have missed outstanding opportunities to further the public's interest in environmental protection. In fact, more active involvement on their part would have several advantages. It would provide them with a greater opportunity to assess independently the enforcement attitudes and capabilities of agency personnel and to identify any glaring deficiencies and weaknesses.[19] It would give them a stronger base of information from which to decide how and where to bring independent enforcement actions under the citizen suit provisions of environmental statutes. It would allow them to identify what they view as successful governmental enforcement efforts and to advocate replication of those approaches elsewhere. It would also make it possible for environmental organizations to support EPA officials knowledgeably in instances when their enforcement work gives rise to unreasonable and misleading public criticism.

Environmental organizations have also been reluctant, in many instances, to involve themselves extensively in advocating budget increases for EPA. For example, of the twenty nongovernmental witnesses who testified with regard to EPA's budget in 1991 in hearings held by the HUD, VA and Independent Agencies Subcommittee of the Senate Appropriations Committee, only two were representatives of environmental organizations.[20] This lack of environmental organization involvement in EPA budget issues has been variously attributed to staff resource shortages[21] and to the fact that the appropriations process is difficult to influence because it involves internal congressional politics.[22] Despite these concerns, however, broader involvement in EPA budget matters by legislative lobbyists for national environmentalist organizations could be of great assistance to agency attempts to overcome EPA's chronic and debilitating resource shortfalls. In view of the critical importance of adequate budgetary allocations in the agency's vital enforcement work, such efforts would be most appropriate and well directed.

Finally, the citizens of the United States have a vital role to play in improving and sustaining the performance of EPA and other federal administrative agencies. When we elect representatives who delegate sensitive and important responsibilities to those agencies, provide them with conflicting and inadequate guidance, fail to allocate them adequate resources, and criticize them harshly and repeatedly when their decisions run contrary to our short-term preferences, we are likely to remain dissatisfied with the results of agency work. If, on the other hand, we make the effort to understand the complexity of the tasks assigned our executive agencies, equip them with the funds and people they need to carry out those tasks, and critique their efforts in informed, balanced, and measured terms, we are far more likely to endow them with the creativity and good judgment they must have to fulfill our collective needs.

NINE

Epilogue

EPA Enforcement in the Clinton Administration

At this writing (January 1995) it is far too early to evaluate the enforcement performance of EPA during the Clinton administration in an objective and meaningful way. Much of that administration's work remains undone. Moreover, the nature and impact of its relationship with the Republican-dominated Congress, which was elected in 1994, remain to be established. Nonetheless, at this stage it is possible to note at least some of the trends and developments that have characterized the first two years of enforcement at the Clinton EPA and to identify a set of as yet unanswerable questions whose responses may well have a crucial bearing on EPA enforcement in the coming months.

Before writing this epilogue, I reviewed a selection of internal EPA documents and secondary sources and had brief informal conversations and correspondence with a very small number of EPA enforcement officials whose identity I was asked to keep in confidence.

This methodology (which was necessitated by limitations of time and resources) differs from the approach I was able to take in the earlier chapters of this work, in which I relied quite extensively on the results of personal interviews.[1]

As the Clinton administration began, the selection and confirmation of a set of managers to fill EPA's highest positions proceeded very slowly. Although President-elect Clinton's choice for EPA administrator was named in December 1992, other high-level agency officials, including its deputy administrator and assistant administrator for enforcement, were not nominated until several months after the administration had taken power and were not confirmed by the Senate until May 1993. Still other EPA appointees were announced in July 1993 (midway through the first year of Clinton's term) and confirmed a few weeks later.

Notwithstanding these delays and the uncertainties they created for EPA's professional staff, environmental organizations, and regulated firms, the president's selections for EPA's top management jobs proved uncontroversial in most instances. During the 1992 presidential campaign, Bill Clinton and his running mate, Al Gore, had criticized the Bush administration's environmental positions and the seriousness of its commitment to environmental protection. It was thus unremarkable that their choice to head EPA, Carol M. Browner, was highly regarded by environmental organizations. Browner had served for two years as secretary of the Florida Department of Environmental Regulation. Prior to that she had been legislative director for then-Senator Al Gore (D-TN), general counsel for the Senate Committee on Energy and Natural Resources, and a legislative aide in the office of former Senator Lawton Chiles (D-FL).[2]

The administration's nominee for EPA deputy administrator was Robert Sussman, an expert in toxic substances law who had been a partner in a Washington law firm and an active participant in Democratic Party politics.[3] Sussman's tenure at EPA proved brief, however. He left the agency in October 1994 to assume another position within the administration.[4] Sussman's replacement as deputy administrator was Fred Hansen, director of the Oregon Department of Environmental Quality, who had previously served as a congressional aide, an executive officer in the Peace Corps, and deputy treasurer of the State of Oregon.[5]

For the position of assistant administrator for enforcement, President Clinton nominated Steven Herman, a veteran DOJ career attorney. Herman had been a VISTA volunteer in Little Rock, Arkansas, in the early 1970s, when he met and befriended the Clintons. The last position he had held at DOJ was assistant section chief in the Environment and Natural Resources Division. In that post he had specialized in the litigation of cases arising under the National Environmental Policy Act as well as other environmental matters.[6]

Soon after assuming office, EPA's new managers resolved to reorganize the unwieldy, inefficient structure of the agency's Office of Enforcement. Following a review by a thirty-five-member agency task force, headed by Associate Deputy Administrator Michael P. Vandenbergh, the administrator created an expanded headquarters Office of Enforcement and Compliance Assurance to include both headquarters enforcement attorneys and enforcement technical personnel who had previously been situated in media-specific program offices. The new office incorporated several previously existing entities, such as an Office of Criminal Enforcement, the Office of Federal Activities, and the National Enforcement Investigations Center. It also included a new Office of Site Remediation, with jurisdiction over Superfund matters, and two other entirely new organizational units: the Office of Regulatory Enforcement and the Office of Compliance Assurance. The Office of Regulatory Enforcement, which was given the lead role in supporting enforcement case development, was organized along traditional media-specific lines. It featured separate divisions devoted to enforcement of the Clean Air Act, the Clean Water Act, RCRA, and so on, along with a new Multi-Media Enforcement Division. In contrast, the Office of Compliance Assurance was given the lead in enforcement planning, inspection targeting, data management, compliance monitoring, and compliance assistance. Unlike the Office of Regulatory Enforcement, however, the Office of Compliance Assurance was organized by regulated sectors, including manufacturing, energy and transportation, and chemical, municipal, and commercial services. It also contained separate divisions for environmental planning, targeting, data analysis and management, and agriculture and ecosystems.[7]

After considerable deliberation Administrator Browner decided not to require EPA's regional offices to create separate enforcement divisions. Instead, she permitted the regions considerable flexibility in fashioning new enforcement structures. At a minimum, however, each region was required to appoint a single enforcement coordinator who reported directly to the deputy regional administrator and to create an identifiable, separate enforcement unit within each regional program division.[8]

At first blush, these changes appear to be a significant step in the direction of a streamlined EPA enforcement program. At least at the headquarters level, they eliminate duplications of function. They also further the integration of legal and technical staffs, which is crucial to an effective enforcement effort. Those benefits notwithstanding, the reorganization plan that Browner approved failed to delineate with sufficient precision the authority of the regulatory enforcement and compliance assurance components of the Office of Enforcement and Compliance Assurance. This ambiguity created a potential for conflict between those two offices—conflict which did, in fact, occur in the months following their creation.

More significantly, perhaps, in certain respects the enforcement reorganization effort of 1993/1994 appears to have failed to go far enough. By giving regional offices a free hand in restructuring their enforcement efforts, Browner and Herman and their colleagues have, in effect, allowed the regions to maintain an institutional separation of enforcement attorney and technical staffs that sometimes inhibits effective case development and, in many instances, presents obstacles to efficient multimedia enforcement. Although some EPA regional offices did choose to create unified enforcement divisions, others declined to do so.[9] In the months and years ahead, these inconsistencies among regional organizational arrangements may well diminish the overall benefits of EPA's enforcement restructuring.

Beyond reorganizing the agency's enforcement offices, EPA's national leadership has thus far continued the multimedia enforcement efforts that began to find favor within EPA in the mid-1980s.[10] It has also pursued (or planned) national enforcement initiatives with respect to illegal handling of hazardous waste, users and manufacturers of substances which deplete the stratospheric ozone layer, leakage of hazardous waste from industrial sewer lines, and improperly controlled hazardous waste combustion facilities.[11] In addition, the Clinton administration has placed renewed emphasis on improving the quality and accessibility of the agency's enforcement data and on "supplemental environmental projects" in which environmental law violators agree to undertake specific environmentally beneficial activities in return for reduced enforcement penalties.[12] The agency has also attempted to focus its enforcement efforts on facilities and areas that pose the greatest risk to large ecosystems (such as the Great Lakes and Chesapeake Bay) and to avoid patterns of enforcement actions that discriminate against members of minority groups and/or persons with low incomes.[13] Finally, the agency has begun a much-needed effort to redefine the ways in which it measures the successfulness of its enforcement programs.[14]

While this last project is still not complete at this writing, it appears that (at least as measured by the flawed gauges traditionally used to assess EPA enforcement success) the agency's enforcement efforts in 1993 and 1994 were indeed productive. In fiscal 1993, for example, EPA reportedly undertook 2,110 new enforcement actions, including 140 criminal cases, 338 civil judicial actions, 18 lawsuits to enforce existing Consent Decrees, and 1,614 administrative penalty actions. The agency also assessed $115.1 million in civil penalties that year, including a record $85.9 million in judicial fines and $29.2 million in administrative assessments.[15] Moreover, in fiscal 1994, even as EPA's enforcement program was in the midst of restructuring, the agency initiated the highest number of enforcement actions and collected the highest total dollar amount of enforcement penalties in EPA's history.[16]

At the start of the 103rd Congress (which convened in January 1993, shortly before the Clinton administration took office) many environmental organizations were hopeful that federal environmental law was about to be strengthened and expanded.[17] That optimism, however, proved to be ill-founded. After extensive consideration and debate, Congress declined to pass legislation reauthorizing the Clean

Water Act and the Safe Drinking Water Act. Efforts to elevate EPA to a cabinet-level agency were abandoned after the House of Representatives voted to allow debate on an amendment to the EPA cabinet bill that would have required EPA to conduct cost-benefit analyses and risk assessments before issuing any new regulations.[18] Moreover, notwithstanding the emergence of a remarkable consensus among industries, environmental organizations, and other interested parties, Congress failed to reauthorize the Superfund Act, whose taxing authority is scheduled to expire on December 31, 1995.[19]

In contrast with earlier periods, congressional criticism of EPA's enforcement performance diminished in the first two years of the Clinton administration. This trend may have been a reflection of greater congressional satisfaction with the new direction of the agency's enforcement efforts and the success of EPA's national leadership in convincing interested members of Congress and their staffs that EPA enforcement was, at last, on the right track. It may also have resulted from continuing congressional preoccupation with perceived problems at the DOJ environmental crimes unit, which was harshly criticized by Representatives Dingell (D-MI), Wolpe (D-MI), and Schumer (D-NY) toward the end of 1992.[20]

With respect to its budget, during the first two years of the Clinton administration EPA felt the impact of a continuing fiscal austerity that affected many components of the federal government at that time. In fiscal year 1994 the administration's budget proposal called for a $600 million decrease in funding for EPA.[21] The following year, the president's budget request did seek to restore most of the EPA funding that had been eliminated in the first year of Clinton's presidency. However, in fiscal year 1995, neither the administration nor Congress proposed (or provided) any meaningful increase in the funds that had been made available to EPA during the period preceding the 1992 presidential elections.[22]

The election of the 104th Congress, with Republican majorities in both the Senate and House of Representatives, may herald a new and dramatically different period in the history of EPA and its enforcement program. At this writing, though, the outcome of the 1994 election raises many more questions than it resolves.

Congress's current leadership has expressed a general preference for "rolling back federal regulations" and "getting Washington off our backs." Will Congress, then, enact into law those provisions of the House Republican "Contract with America" that require federal agencies to provide the subjects of agency enforcement investigations with extensive advance notifications?[23] Will congressional overseers now begin to criticize EPA enforcement as being abusive or heavy handed? Will Congress attempt to undercut EPA's enforcement efforts (and/or its other work) by cutting the agency's budget? Will Congress pass legislation that will make new EPA regulation difficult or impossible, as a practical matter, and require the agency to eliminate existing regulations?[24] Will Congress repeal or weaken the provisions of specific federal environmental statutes, including those which authorize federal enforcement actions?

Other questions arise with regard to the Democrats in Congress and the Clinton administration. To what extent will those elected and appointed officials oppose any or all of the kinds of initiatives and proposals referred to above? If so, what form will that opposition take and how effective will it be? Are there any instances in which the 104th Congress may appear willing to extend or supplement federal environmental legislation? If so, will the Clinton administration actively support congressional efforts to do so?

Finally, it remains to be seen what impact public and political debates regarding these matters will have on the morale of EPA's employees—in enforcement as well as other agency programs—and on the ability of the agency to carry out its current mission. It also remains to be seen what effect those same debates will have on the opinion of the public, which has, even recently, demonstrated strong support for effective environmental protection.[25]

For now those important questions remain unanswered. What the answers to them will be, and when those answers will come, is simply not clear. It does appear likely, however, that their resolution in the months, or perhaps years, ahead will have a wide-ranging impact on the quality of life in the United States.

APPENDIX A

Persons Interviewed

The information in this list was gathered during interviews conducted in 1984, 1986, 1991, and 1992. This list does not reflect any changes in the government position(s) of the interviewees which may have occurred after the time(s) that the individuals mentioned were interviewed. An asterisk indicates a non-EPA position.

Interviewee	Title(s) in Government Service (with Dates)	Date and Place of Interview(s)
Adamkus, Valdas	(1) Deputy Regional Administrator, Region V, January 1971–November 1981 (2) Regional Administrator, November 1981–interview date	May 2, 1986, Chicago, Ill.
Adams, Thomas	Assistant Administrator for Enforcement and Compliance Monitoring, 1986–1988	March 18, 1991, Washington, D.C.
Allen, Anne	(1) Staff Attorney, HWETF, 1979–1980 (2) Branch Chief, Waste Division, Office of Enforcement and Compliance Monitoring, 1981–1983 (3) RCRA Program Attorney, State of North Carolina, 1984–1986 (4) Branch Chief, Office of Enforcement and Compliance Monitoring, 1986–interview date	April 19, 1991, Washington, D.C.

Interviewee	Title(s) in Government Service (with Dates)	Date and Place of Interview(s)
Andrews, David	Legal Counsel and Special Assistant for Policy to the Deputy Administrator, 1977–January 1980	March 28, 1986, Washington, D.C.
Apostolou, Carrie	Professional Staff Member, Subcommittee on HUD, VA and Independent Agencies, Senate Appropriations Committee,* 1987–interview date	May 28, 1992, Washington, D.C.
Asbell, Anne	Senior Attorney (with RCRA and Superfund responsibility) and Associate Regional Counsel, Region IV, fall 1981–interview date	May 6, 1986, Atlanta, Ga.
Becker, Julie	(1) Attorney, National Projects Branch, Office of Enforcement and Compliance Monitoring, 1985–1986 (2) Special Assistant to Richard Mays, Jonathan Cannon, Edward Reich, and Thomas Adams, 1986–1988	April 18, 1991, Washington, D.C.
Bering, Charles	(1) Attorney, Enforcement Division, Region I, 1979–1981 (2) Attorney, Office of Regional Counsel, Region IV, 1982–interview date	July 28, 1984, Boston, Mass.
Biggs, Kirby	(1) Budget Officer, HWETF, 1980–1981 (2) Assistant to the Assistant Administrator for Solid Waste and Emergency Response, 1982–1983 (3) Budget Officer, Office of Emergency and Remedial Response, 1983–interview date	July 9, 1984, Washington, D.C.
Biros, Frank	(1) Various staff and supervisory positions in EPA headquarters hazardous waste	April 17, 1991, Washington, D.C.

Interviewee	Title(s) in Government Service (with Dates)	Date and Place of Interview(s)
	enforcement programs, 1979–1990 (2) Chief, Cost Recovery Branch, CERCLA Enforcement Division, Office of Solid Waste and Emergency Response, 1990–interview date	
Bloom, Jane	Attorney, Natural Resources Defense Council,* 1979–1990	May 27, 1992, New York, N.Y.
Boilen, Joan B.	(1) Staff Attorney, Law Branch, Office of Regional Counsel, Region IV, 1981–1982 (2) Acting Chief, Hazardous Law Branch, Office of Regional Counsel, Region IV, 1982 (3) Staff Attorney, Hazardous Law Branch, Office of Regional Counsel, Region IV, January–June 1983 (4) Chief, Air and Toxics Branch, Office of Regional Counsel, Region IV, June 1983–interview date	May 5, 1986, Atlanta, Ga.
Boxell, Phillip	(1) Attorney, Enforcement Division, Region I, 1979–1981 (2) Attorney, Office of Regional Counsel, Region I, 1981–interview date	October 12, 1984, Boston, Mass.
Brown, Michael	(1) Deputy General Counsel and Acting Enforcement Counsel, spring 1982–November 1982 (2) Enforcement Counsel, November–December 1982, February–October 1983 (3) Acting Assistant Administrator for Solid Waste and Emergency Response, January 1983	March 21, 1986, Washington, D.C.

(continued)

Interviewee	Title(s) in Government Service (with Dates)	Date and Place of Interview(s)
Bryan, Gerald	Director, Office of Compliance Analysis and Program Operations, January 1971–interview date	July 25, 1986, Washington, D.C.
Buente, David	Chief, Environmental Enforcement Section, Division of Lands and Natural Resources, DOJ,* spring 1984–November 1990	April 4, 1986, March 22, 1991, Washington, D.C.
Bunting, James D.	(1) Legal Advisor for National Managed Cases, HWETF, 1979–1981 (2) Acting Director, Legal Division, Office of Hazardous Waste Enforcement, February 1981–summer 1982	March 27, 1986, Washington, D.C.
Burkett, Michelle	Staff Assistant, Subcommittee on HUD, VA and Independent Agencies, House Appropriations Committee,* 1990–interview date	May 29, 1992, Washington, D.C.
Cannon, Jonathan	(1) Deputy General Counsel for Litigation and Regional Operations, Office of General Counsel, 1986–1987 (2) Deputy Assistant Administrator for Civil Enforcement, Office of Enforcement and Compliance Monitoring, 1987–1988 (3) Acting Director, Office of Waste Programs Enforcement, 1988 (4) Deputy Assistant Administrator, Office of Solid Waste and Emergency Response, 1988–1989 (5) Acting Assistant Administrator, Office of Solid Waste and Emergency Response, 1989	March 19, 1991, Washington, D.C.

Interviewee	Title(s) in Government Service (with Dates)	Date and Place of Interview(s)
Casto, Keith	(1) Staff Attorney (for Hazardous Waste), Enforcement Division, Region IV, August 1979–June 1981 (2) Staff Attorney, Office of Regional Counsel, Region IV, June 1981–May 1985	May 6, 1986, Atlanta, Ga.
Cintron, Maria	Attorney/Advisor, Office of Enforcement, 1988–interview date	April 19, 1991, Washington, D.C.
Clough, Stephanie	Professional Staff Member, Senate Committee on Environment and Public Works,* 1982–interview date	May 28, 1992, Washington, D.C.
Constantelos, William	Director, Hazardous Waste Division, Region V, 1982–interview date	May 1, 1986, Chicago, Ill.
Costle, Douglas	Administrator, EPA, 1977–1981	July 25, 1984, Washington, D.C.
Cummings, Phil	Attorney/Chief Counsel, Senate Committee on Environment and Public Works,* 1970–1988	March 22, 1991, Washington, D.C.
Deland, Michael	(1) Attorney, Enforcement Division, Region I, 1971–1972 (2) Chief, Legal Review Section, Enforcement Division, Region I, 1972–1973 (3) Chief, Enforcement Branch, Enforcement Division, Region I, 1973–1976 (4) Regional Administrator, Region I, 1984–interview date	July 28, 1984, Boston, Mass.
de Saillan, Charles	Staff Attorney, Office of Enforcement, September 1985–interview date	March 4, 1991, Washington, D.C.

(*continued*)

Interviewee	Title(s) in Government Service (with Dates)	Date and Place of Interview(s)
Drayton, William	(1) Assistant Administrator for Planning and Management, 1977–1981 (2) Director, Save the EPA Committee,* 1981–1984 (3) Director, Environmental Safety,* 1984–interview date	May 28, 1992, Washington, D.C.
Duffy, Richard F.	(1) Special Assistant to Edward Reich, 1980–1984 (2) Various staff and supervisory positions in the Office of Enforcement and Compliance Monitoring, 1984–1988 (3) Chief, Compliance Evaluation Branch, Office of Enforcement, 1989–interview date	April 17, 1991, Washington, D.C.
Elkus, Barbara	(1) Regional Coordinator, HWETF, October 1979–March 1981 (2) Chief, Technical Support Branch, Office of Waste Programs Enforcement, summer 1981–June 1983 (3) Chief, Compliance Branch, Office of Waste Programs Enforcement, June 1983–January 1985 (4) Acting Deputy Division Director, Office of Waste Programs Enforcement, January 1985–March 1985	April 1, 1986, Washington, D.C.
Farnsworth, Douglas B.	(1) Staff Attorney, Division of Stationary Source Enforcement, 1977–1978 (2) Supervisory Attorney, Steel Enforcement Task Force, 1978–1979 (3) Attorney, HWETF, 1980–1981 (4) Supervisory Attorney,	July 25, 1984, Washington, D.C.

Interviewee	Title(s) in Government Service (with Dates)	Date and Place of Interview(s)
	Office of Waste Programs Enforcement, 1982 (5) Attorney, Office of General Counsel 1983	
Fehrenbach, Marjorie P.	(1) Program Assistant, HWETF, 1979–1981 (2) Administrative Officer, Office of Solid Waste and Emergency Response, 1982 (3) Regional Liaison Specialist, Office of Waste Programs Enforcement, 1982–interview date	July 25, 1986, Washington, D.C.
Frandsen, Richard	(1) Vice Counsel, Subcommittee on Oversight and Investigation, House Committee on Energy and Commerce,* 1980–1988 (2) Counsel, House Committee on Energy and Commerce,* 1988–interview date	March 28, 1986, March 5, 1991 Washington, D.C.
Frey, Bertram	(1) Deputy Regional Counsel, Region V, 1989–1990 (2) Acting Regional Counsel, 1990–interview date	April 22, 1991, Chicago, Ill.
Fulton, Scott	(1) Trial Attorney, Environmental Enforcement Section, DOJ,* 1982–1985 (2) Senior Attorney, Environmental Enforcement Section, DOJ,* 1986 (3) Assistant Chief, Environmental Enforcement Section, DOJ,* 1987–1990 (4) Senior Enforcement Counsel, Office of Enforcement, 1990–1991 (5) Director, Office of Civil Enforcement, Office of Enforcement, 1991–interview date	April 18, 1991, Washington, D.C.

(*continued*)

Interviewee	Title(s) in Government Service (with Dates)	Date and Place of Interview(s)
Gallagher, Thomas	Director, National Enforcement Investigation Center, 1972–1989	April 18, 1986, March 15, 1991, Denver, Colo.
Gaynor, Kevin	Trial Attorney and Supervisor, Division of Land and Natural Resources, DOJ,* 1983–1984	March 4, 1991, Washington, D.C.
Gorsuch, Anne M.	Administrator, EPA, May 1981–March 1983	March 19, 1986, Washington, D.C.
Gray, Don	(1) Professional Staff Member and Investigator, House Committee on Government Operations,* 1983–1985 (2) Staff Director, Subcommittee on Environment, Energy and Natural Resources, House Committee on Government Operations,* 1985–1989 (3) Chief Investigator, Subcommittee on Environment, Energy and Natural Resources, House Committee on Government Operations,* 1989–interview date	March 20, 1991 Washington, D.C.
Guerci, Lloyd	(1) Assistant Chief, Hazardous Waste Section, DOJ,* 1979–1981 (2) Assistant Chief, Environmental Enforcement Section, DOJ,* 1981–1985 (3) Director, RCRA Enforcement Division, Office of Waste Programs Enforcement, 1985–1987 (4) Director, CERCLA Enforcement Division, Office of Solid Waste and Emergency Response, 1987–1990	April 28, 1986, March 8, 1991 Washington, D.C.
Harlow, George	Deputy Division Director, Waste Management Division,	May 5, 1986, Atlanta, Ga.

Interviewee	Title(s) in Government Service (with Dates)	Date and Place of Interview(s)
	Region IV, 1979–interview date	
Hedeman, William	Director, Office of Superfund EPA (Headquarters), October 1981–October 1985	March 27, 1986, Washington, D.C.
Hembra, Richard L.	(1) Various positions with the GAO involving environmental protection issues,* 1973–1988 (2) Director, Environmental Protection Issues, Resources, Community and Economic Development Division, GAO,* 1988–interview date	May 29, 1992, Washington, D.C.
Hohman, Merrill S.	(1) Director, Air and Hazardous Materials Division, Region I, 1979–1984 (2) Director, Waste Management Division, Region I, 1984–interview date	April 22, 1986, Boston, Mass.
Johnson, John	Chief, Hazardous Waste Branch, Office of Regional Counsel, Region IV, June 1983 interview date	May 5, 1986, Atlanta, Ga.
Kee, David	(1) Chief, Water Compliance Section, Enforcement Division, Region V, 1971–1972 (2) Chief, Air Compliance Section, Region V, 1972–1974 (3) Chief, Air Enforcement Branch, Region V, 1974–1979 (4) Director, Air and Hazardous Materials, Region V, 1979–1982 (5) Director, Air Management Division, Region V, 1982–interview date	June 19, 1984, Chicago, Ill.
Kelly, Peter	(1) Attorney, Enforcement Division, Region V, 1974–1981	June 29, 1984, Chicago, Ill.

(continued)

Interviewee	Title(s) in Government Service (with Dates)	Date and Place of Interview(s)
Kelly, Peter (continued)	(2) Senior Attorney, Office of Regional Counsel, Region V, 1982–1986	
Kilpatrick, Michael	(1) Chemical Engineer, RCRA Enforcement Program (Headquarters), 1978–1979 (2) Staff Engineer, HWETF, July 1979–December 1980 (3) Staff Engineer, Office of Waste Programs Enforcement, 1981–1983 (4) Chief, Compliance Section, Office of Waste Programs Enforcement, 1984–1985 (5) Senior Policy Coordinator, Office of Waste Programs Enforcement, 1986–interview date	April 1, 1986, Washington, D.C.
Kirk, Alan	Assistant Administrator for Enforcement, 1973–1974	July 9, 1984, Washington, D.C.
Kurent, Edward A.	(1) Chief Attorney, HWETF, July 1979–January 1981 (2) Director, Water Enforcement Division (Headquarters), January 1981–summer 1982 (3) Associate General Counsel for Waste Enforcement, summer 1982–February 1983	March 30, 1986, Washington, D.C.
Kyte, Lawrence	Assistant Regional Counsel, Region V, 1980–1987 Section Chief, Solid Waste and Emergency Response Branch, Office of Regional Counsel, Region V, 1987–interview date	May 2, 1986, April 22, 1991, Chicago, Ill.
Legro, Stanley	Assistant Administrator for Enforcement, 1975–1977	July 9, 1984, Washington, D.C.
Leifer, Steven	(1) Staff Attorney, Office of Pesticide and Toxic	March 6, 1991, Washington, D.C.

Interviewee	Title(s) in Government Service (with Dates)	Date and Place of Interview(s)
	Substances Enforcement, 1977–1981 (2) Staff Attorney, Office of Hazardous Waste Enforcement, 1981 (3) Chief, Guidance Development Branch, Office of Legal Enforcement Policy, 1981–1982 (4) Chief, National Projects Branch, Hazardous Waste Enforcement Division, 1983–1985 (5) Chief, Superfund Branch, Hazardous Waste Enforcement Division, 1985–1987 (6) Acting Director, Hazardous Waste Enforcement Division, 1988	
Lucero, Gene A.	(1) Deputy Director, Office of Emergency and Remedial Response, April 1982–July 1982 (2) Director, Office of Waste Programs Enforcement, July 1982–interview date	April 28, 1984, Washington, D.C.
MacMillan, Douglas	(1) Director, HWETF, August 1979–October 1980 (2) Acting Deputy Assistant Administrator for Hazardous Waste Enforcement, October 1981–October 1982	April 4, 1986, Washington, D.C.
Mays, Richard	(1) Staff Attorney, HWETF, 1981–1982 (2) Special Assistant to the Enforcement Counsel, 1982 (3) Senior Enforcement Counsel, 1982–interview date	March 20, 1986, Washington, D.C.
McDonald, James O.	Director, Enforcement Division, Region V, 1971–1979	June 26, 1984, San Diego, Calif.

(*continued*)

Interviewee	*Title(s) in Government Service (with Dates)*	*Date and Place of Interview(s)*
Miller, Jeffrey G.	Acting Assistant Administrator for Enforcement, fall 1979– March 1981	March 21, 1986, Washington, D.C.
Miller, W. Lamar	(1) Director, Enforcement Division, Region VII, 1978 (2) Deputy Director, Office of Water Standards and Regulations, early 1979 (3) Technical and Deputy Director, HWETF, 1979–1981 (4) Acting Director, Office of Waste Programs Enforcement, 1982	April 14, 1986, Gainesville, Fla.
Miner, William H.	Chief, Hazardous Waste Enforcement Branch, Region V, 1984–interview date	May 2, 1986, Chicago, Ill.
Moorman, James	Assistant Attorney General, Lands and Natural Resources Division, DOJ,* May 1977– January 1981	April 1, 1986, Washington, D.C.
Muno, William	(1) Staff Engineer, National Pollutant Discharge Elimination System Permit Program, Region V, 1973– 1975 (2) Unit Chief, Water and Hazardous Materials Enforcement Branch, Region V, 1976–1982 (3) Chief, RCRA Enforcement Section, Waste Management Division, Region V, 1982– 1991 (4) Associate Division Director, Waste Management Division, Region V, 1991– interview date	July 31, 1986, April 23, 1991, Chicago, Ill.
Nelson, T. Leverett	(1) Attorney, Solid Waste and Emergency Response Branch,	April 22, 1991, Chicago, Ill.

Interviewee	Title(s) in Government Service (with Dates)	Date and Place of Interview(s)
	Office of Regional Counsel, Region V, 1985–1989 (2) Section Chief, Solid Waste and Emergency Response Branch, Office of Regional Counsel, Region V, 1990–interview date	
Niedergang, Norman	(1) Environmental Engineer, Enforcement Division, Region V, 1979–1980 (2) Remedial Project Manager, Superfund Branch, Waste Management Division, Region V, 1981–1984 (3) Supervisor, Superfund Branch, Waste Management Division, Region V, 1985–1988 (4) Chief, Remedial Response Branch, Waste Management Division, Region V, 1988–1989 (5) Associate Division Director, Office of Superfund, Waste Management Division, Region V, 1989–interview date	April 22, 1991, Chicago, Ill.
Novick, Sheldon	(1) Special Assistant to Regional Administrator, Region III, fall 1978–March 1979 (2) Regional Counsel, Region III, March 1979–October 1984	March 7, 1986, Washington, D.C.
Olson, Erik	(1) Attorney, Office of General Counsel, 1984–1985 (2) Attorney, National Wildlife Federation, 1985–interview date	March 20, 1991, Washington, D.C.
Powell, Jimmie	(1) Staff Director, Subcommittee on Intergovernmental Relations,	March 22, 1991, Washington, D.C.

(*continued*)

Interviewee	Title(s) in Government Service (with Dates)	Date and Place of Interview(s)
Powell, Jimmie (*continued*)	Senate Committee on Government Affairs,* 1981–1983 (2) Legislative Director to Senator Durenberger,* 1983–1985 (3) Professional Staff Member, Senate Committee on Environment and Public Works,* 1985–interview date	
Prange, James	(1) Special Agent, Office of Criminal Investigations, Region X, 1982–1984 (2) Chief of Criminal Investigations, Criminal Enforcement Program, National Enforcement Investigations Center, 1984–interview date	April 18, 1986, Denver, Colo.
Price, Courtney	Assistant Administrator for Enforcement and Compliance Monitoring, 1983–1986	March 26, 1986, Washington, D.C.
Prothro, Martha	(1) Attorney, Division of Stationary Source Enforcement, 1973–1975 (2) Chief, Legal Branch, Division of Stationary Source Enforcement, 1976–1979 (3) Director, Noise and Radiation Enforcement Division, 1980–1981 (4) Director, Permits Division, Office of Water, 1981–interview date	July 9, 1984, Washington, D.C.
Raabe, Mark	(1) Chief Counsel and Staff Director, Subcommittee on Oversight and Investigation, House Committee on Energy and Commerce,* 1979–1980 (2) Counsel, House Committee on Energy and Commerce,* 1980–1983	March 28, 1986, Washington, D.C.

Interviewee	*Title(s) in Government Service (with Dates)*	*Date and Place of Interview(s)*
Ramsey, Steven	(1) Assistant Chief, Pollution Control Section, DOJ,* 1979–1980 (2) Chief, Pollution Control Section, DOJ,* 1980 (3) Chief, Environmental Enforcement Section, DOJ,* 1981–January 1985	May 2, 1986, Chicago, Ill.
Rechtschaffen, Joyce	(1) Senior Attorney, Environmental Enforcement Section, DOJ,* 1983–1989 (2) Environmental Counsel to Senator Joseph Lieberman,* 1989–interview date	March 7, 1991, Washington, D.C.
Reich, Edward	(1) Staff Attorney, Division of Stationary Source Enforcement, 1971–1972 (2) Chief, Air Enforcement Proceedings Branch, 1972–1974, 1975–1976 (3) Director, Division of Stationary Source Enforcement, 1976–1981 (4) Director, Stationary Source Compliance Division, 1984–1986 (5) Associate Enforcement Counsel for Waste Enforcement, 1986–1989 (6) Deputy Assistant Administrator for Civil Enforcement, 1988–1990 (7) Deputy Assistant Administrator, Office of Enforcement, 1990–interview date	July 9, 1984, March 7, 1991 Washington, D.C.
Reiter, Mark	(1) Various staff positions, Office of Water and Office of Congressional Relations, 1977–1987	March 22, 1991, Washington, D.C.

(*continued*)

Interviewee	Title(s) in Government Service (with Dates)	Date and Place of Interview(s)
Reiter, Mark (continued)	(2) Professional Staff Member, Senate Committee on Environment and Public Works,* 1987–interview date	
Roisman, Anthony	(1) Chief, Hazardous Waste Section, Lands and Natural Resources Division, DOJ,* October 1979–May 1981 (2) Special Litigator for Hazardous Waste, DOJ,* May 1981–June 1982	March 31, 1986, Washington, D.C.
Rothblatt, Steve	(1) Staff Engineer, Technical Section, Air Enforcement Branch, Region V, 1974–1976 (2) Chief, Technical Section, Air Enforcement Branch, 1977–1978 (3) Branch Chief and Deputy Division Director, Air Management Division, 1978–interview date	June 25, 1986, Chicago, Ill.
Sargent, Jay	Regional Counsel, Region IV, July 1980–interview date	May 6, 1986, Atlanta, Ga.
Schaffer, Amy	(1) Environmental Protection Specialist, RCRA Enforcement Program, 1977–1983 (2) Environmental Protection Specialist, Office of Solid Waste and Emergency Response, 1983–1985	April 29, 1986, Washington, D.C.
Schulteis, Jane	(1) Supervisor, Legal Section, Enforcement Division, RCRA and Superfund Enforcement Program, Region V, 1979–1981 (2) Interim Supervisor, Office of Regional Counsel, RCRA and Superfund Enforcement Program, Region V, 1981–1982	April 30, 1986, Chicago, Ill.

Interviewee	Title(s) in Government Service (with Dates)	Date and Place of Interview(s)
	(3) Associate Regional Counsel and Senior Attorney, RCRA and Superfund Enforcement Program, Region V, 1982–April 1984	
Skinner, John	Director, Office of Solid Waste (Headquarters), 1983– 1986	March 31, 1986, Washington, D.C.
Smith, Al J.	(1) Chief, Emergency and Remedial Response Branch, Waste Management Division, Region V, 1981–1986 (2) Deputy Director, Water Division, Region V, April 1986–present	May 6, 1986, Atlanta, Ga.
Smith, Arthur	(1) Attorney, Enforcement Division, Region V, 1976– 1978 (2) Senior Attorney, Enforcement Division, Region V, 1979 (3) Unit Chief, Enforcement Division, Region V, 1980– 1981 (4) Senior Attorney, Office of Regional Counsel, Region V, 1982–interview date	June 29, 1984, Chicago, Ill.
Smith, Bruce P.	Chief, Hazardous Waste Enforcement Branch, Region V, fall 1983–interview date	April 21, 1986, Philadelphia, Pa.
Smith, Michael G.	(1) Attorney, Enforcement Division, Region V, 1976– 1979 (2) Chief, Air Legal Section, Enforcement Division, Region V, 1979–1982 (3) Chief, Air Branch, Office of Regional Counsel, Region V, 1982–1984	August 1, 1984, April 22, 1991, Chicago, Ill.

(*continued*)

Interviewee	*Title(s) in Government Service (with Dates)*	*Date and Place of Interview(s)*
Smith, Michael G. (*continued*)	(4) Chief, Air, Water, Toxics and General Law Branch, Office of Regional Counsel, Region V, 1985–second interview date	
Smith, Richard	(1) Staff Attorney, HWETF, summer 1979–December 1980 (2) Special Assistant for Policy and Planning, January 1981–March 1982 (3) Acting Director, Office of Legal Enforcement Policy, spring 1982–July 1982	March 18, 1986, Washington, D.C.
Souzon, Jane	(1) Program Analyst, Office of Permit Programs, EPA (Headquarters), 1971–1975 (2) Attorney, Enforcement Division, Region V, 1979–1980 (3) Special Assistant to the Assistant Administrator for Enforcement, 1980 (4) Acting Chief, Special Projects and Policy Branch (Headquarters), 1981 (5) Special Assistant to the Assistant Administrator for Enforcement and Compliance Monitoring, 1982–interview date	July 26, 1984, Washington, D.C.
Stanley, Elaine G.	(1) Director, RCRA Enforcement Division, Office of Waste Programs Enforcement, 1988–1989 (2) Deputy Director, Office of Waste Programs Enforcement, 1989–1991	March 19, 1991, Washington, D.C.
Starr, Judson	Director, Environmental Crimes Unit, Lands and Natural Resources Division, DOJ, 1981–interview date	April 3, 1986, Washington, D.C.

Interviewee	*Title(s) in Government Service (with Dates)*	*Date and Place of Interview(s)*
Steinzor, Rena	Staff Counsel, House Subcommittee on Commerce, Transportation and Tourism (Florio Committee),* September 1983–interview date	March 31, 1986, Washington, D.C.
Stiehl, Frederick P.	(1) Attorney, HWETF, January 1980–spring 1981 (2) Chief, Litigation Branch, Office of Waste Programs Enforcement, spring 1981– summer 1982 (3) Deputy Associate Enforcement Counsel for Waste, 1982–1985 (4) Associate Enforcement Counsel for Waste, 1985– 1986	March 19, 1986, Washington, D.C.
Stonebraker, Jack	Deputy Chief, Emergency and Remedial Response Branch, Region IV, 1981–interview date	May 6, 1986, Atlanta, Ga.
Strickland, Ann	Staff Attorney, Office of Enforcement and Compliance Monitoring, 1979–interview date (on leave July 1983–October 1984)	March 17, 1986, Washington, D.C.
Sullivan, William A., Jr.	Enforcement Counsel and Deputy Associate Administrator for Enforcement, April 1981– April 1982	April 29, 1986, Washington, D.C.
Swofford, Anne	(1) Attorney, Enforcement Division, Region V, 1978– 1981 (2) Assistant Regional Counsel, Office of Regional Counsel, Region V, 1981– 1985	August 1, 1984, Chicago, Ill.

(*continued*)

Interviewee	*Title(s) in Government Service (with Dates)*	*Date and Place of Interview(s)*
Ullrich, David A.	(1) Enforcement Attorney, Enforcement Division, Region V, 1973–1976 (2) Chief, Air Legal Section, Enforcement Division, Region V, 1976–1979 (3) Chief, Air Enforcement Branch, Enforcement Division, Region V, 1979–1981 (4) Deputy Regional Counsel and Enforcement Coordinator, Region V, 1982–interview date	June 29, 1984, Chicago, Ill.
Voltaggio, Thomas C.	(1) Chief, Technical Support Group for Hazardous Waste Enforcement, Region III, January 1980–June 1980 (2) Acting Director, Enforcement Division, Region III, June 1980–June 1981 (3) Chief, Air and Hazardous Waste Enforcement Branch, Region III, July 1981–July 1983 (4) Chief, Superfund Branch, Region III, July 1983–interview date	April 21, 1986, Philadelphia, Pa.
Warren, Jacqueline	Senior Attorney, Natural Resources Defense Council,* 1973–1991	May 27, 1992, New York, N.Y.
Wasserman, Cheryl	(1) Chief, Legislative and Policy Analysis Branch, Office of Planning and Management, 1970–1981 (2) Chief, Program Integration Branch, Program Evaluation Division, 1981–1984 (3) Chief, Compliance, Policy and Planning Branch, Office of	March 21, 1991, Washington, D.C.

Interviewee	Title(s) in Government Service (with Dates)	Date and Place of Interview(s)
	Enforcement and Compliance Monitoring, 1984–interview date	
Wilson, Richard	(1) Special Assistant to the General Counsel, 1971 (2) Various enforcement management positions in EPA (Headquarters), 1972–1983 (3) Director, Office of Mobile Sources, 1983–interview date	July 26, 1984, Washington, D.C.
Wise, Neil	Chief, Hazardous Waste Enforcement Branch, Office of Regional Counsel, Region III, August 1982–interview date	April 21, 1983, Philadelphia, Pa.
Woitte, Deborah	(1) Staff Attorney, Offices of Legal Enforcement Counsel and Enforcement and Compliance Monitoring, 1981–1984 (2) Chief, RCRA Branch, Office of Enforcement and Compliance Monitoring, 1984–1986 (3) Trial Attorney, Environmental Crimes Section, DOJ,* 1986–interview date	March 18, 1991, Washington, D.C.
Wolf, Doug	(1) Environmental Fellow, Natural Resources Defense Council, New York,* 1986–1987 (2) Attorney, National Wildlife Federation,* 1989–interview date	March 5, 1991, Washington, D.C.

Appendix B

Standard Interview Questionnaire

I. Preliminary Questions of a General Nature
   A. What position (or positions) did you hold which involved EPA enforcement work?
   B. As you look back on each of the periods in the history of EPA's enforcement program in which you were personally involved (or were aware of), what do you consider the most significant events, developments, and trends?
   C. As to those same periods, what do you view as the most important achievements in EPA enforcement programs and the most significant problems which arose in those programs?

II. Questions Regarding the Management and Working Environment of EPA Enforcement Programs
   A. Please comment upon the following aspects of EPA enforcement programs:
      1. The adequacy of EPA's resources.
      2. The capability of EPA's professional staff.
      3. The quality and extent of supervision given to EPA's professional staff.
      4. The adequacy of the training given to EPA's professional staff.
      5. The physical conditions under which EPA's professional staff works (architecture, noise level, etc.).
      6. The adequacy of the clerical and secretarial support given EPA's professional staff.
      7. The adequacy of the agency's system for keeping records of enforcement activities.
      8. The opportunities for promotion and career development given to EPA's professional staff.
      9. The salary level of EPA's professional staff.

III. Questions Regarding Institutional Relationships in EPA Enforcement Work
   A. How would you characterize the following sets of institutional interrelationships among EPA enforcement personnel?

      1. EPA regional enforcement people and EPA headquarters enforcement people.

      2. EPA enforcement attorneys and EPA enforcement technical people.

  B. How would you describe the institutional interrelationships between EPA enforcement people and the following other government entities?

      1. State environmental protection agency personnel.

      2. Department of Justice attorneys and managers.

      3. U.S. attorneys and their professional staffs.

      4. Congress.

      5. Other federal agencies and departments.

      6. The White House.

IV. Question Regarding the Elements of an Effective Enforcement Program

  A. What elements do you feel are necessary for the creation of an effective and appropriate EPA enforcement program?

Notes

1. Introduction

1. U.S. General Accounting Office, *Creation of a Department of the Environment*, testimony of J. Dexter Peach, assistant comptroller general, Resources, Community and Economic Development Division, before the Senate Committee on Governmental Affairs, GAO/T-RCED-90-26 (February 8, 1990), 3.

2. Ibid.

3. The most significant of these are the Clean Air Act, 42 U.S.C. § 7401 et seq.; the Federal Water Pollution Control Act, 33 U.S.C. § 1251 et seq.; the Resource Conservation and Recovery Act, 42 U.S.C. § 6901 et seq.; the Comprehensive Environmental Response Compensation and Liability Act, 42 U.S.C. § 9602 et seq.; the Toxic Substances Control Act, 15 U.S.C. § 2601 et seq.; the Federal Insecticide, Fungicide and Rodenticide Act, 7 U.S.C. § 136 et seq.; the Safe Drinking Water Act, 40 U.S.C. § 300(f) et seq.; the Marine Protection, Research and Sanctuaries Act, 33 U.S.C. § 1401 et seq.; and the Emergency Planning and Community Right-to-Know Act, 42 U.S.C. § 11001 et seq.

4. The internal government debates that preceded EPA's establishment by executive order in 1970 have been chronicled in John Quarles, *Cleaning up America: An Insider's View of the Environmental Protection Agency* (New York: Houghton, Mifflin, 1976), 14–36.

5. For example, in April 1990, a survey conducted by the *New York Times* found that approximately three out of four people polled felt that protecting the environment was so important that continuing improvements must be made regardless of cost. Cited in U.S. General Accounting Office, *Observations on the Environmental Protection Agency's Budget Request for Fiscal Year 1992*, statement of Richard L. Hembra, director, Environmental Protection Issues, Resources, Community and Economic Development Division, before the Senate Committee on Environment and Public Works, GAO/T-RCED-91-14 (1991), 1–2.

6. Foreword, in Christopher H. Schroeder and Richard J. Lazarus, eds., "Assessing the Environmental Protection Agency after Twenty Years: Law, Politics and Economics," *Duke Journal of Law and Contemporary Problems* 54 (fall 1991): 1.

7. Cheryl E. Wasserman, "An Overview of Compliance and Enforcement in the United States: Philosophies, Strategies and Management Tools," in U.S. Environmental Protection Agency and Netherlands Ministry of Housing, Physical Planning and Environment, *International Enforcement Workshop Proceedings* (Utrecht, The Netherlands, May 8–10, 1990), 38.

8. U.S. General Accounting Office, *Alternative Enforcement Organizations for EPA,* GAO/RCED-92-107 (April 1992), 21.

9. Peter C. Yeager, *The Limits of Law: The Public Regulation of Private Pollution* (Cambridge: Cambridge University Press, 1990), 251.

10. Colin S. Diver, "A Theory of Regulatory Enforcement," *Public Policy* 28 (1980): 297.

11. Senate Committee on Environment and Public Works, statement of Senator Joseph I. Lieberman, *Oversight of the Environmental Protection Agency's Enforcement Program: Hearings before the Subcommittee on Toxic Substances, Environmental Oversight, Research and Development,* 101st Cong., 1st sess., S. Hrg. 101-503, November 15, 1989, 2.

12. See Appendix A for a list of the persons interviewed, their years in government service, and the positions they hold (or held) that involve or relate to EPA enforcement work.

13. See Appendix B for a list of the standard questions asked of interviewees in this study.

2. "Where the Rubber Hits the Road"

1. Interview with Douglas Farnsworth. Farnsworth's contributions to EPA's early enforcement efforts were both innovative and noteworthy. In the late 1970s he received a gold medal, the agency's highest award, for his extraordinary achievement as a supervisor with EPA's steel task force in negotiating "companywide" Consent Decrees that called for very significant commitments to air pollution control by much of the steel industry. Douglas Farnsworth's tragic death in January 1986 was a major loss to the entire community of individuals who have a continuing interest in the agency's work.

2. See, for example, Marver H. Bernstein, *Regulating Business by Independent Commission* (Princeton, N.J.: Princeton University Press, 1955), 75–76.

3. Latham, "The Group Basis of Politics: Notes for a Theory," *American Political Science Review* 46 (1952): 391.

4. Marc K. Landy, Marc J. Roberts, and Stephen R. Thomas, *The Environmental Protection Agency: Asking the Wrong Questions* (Oxford: Oxford University Press, 1990), 204.

5. Bernstein, *Regulating Business,* 224.

6. Diver, "A Theory of Regulatory Enforcement," 280.

7. Wasserman, "An Overview of Compliance and Enforcement," 16, 17–18, 40.

8. With respect to most violations of the Clean Air Act the EPA is *required* to commence its enforcement activities with such a notice. See Clean Air Act, § 113(a)(1), 42 U.S.C. § 7413(a)(1).

9. See Dale S. Bryson, "Practical Applications of an Enforcement Management System," in U.S. Environmental Protection Agency and Netherlands Ministry of Housing, Physical Planning and Environment, *International Enforcement Workshop Proceedings* (Utrecht, The Netherlands, May 8–10, 1990), 114.

10. Diver, "A Theory of Regulatory Enforcement," 287.

11. Bernstein, *Regulating Business*, 226.

12. This appears to be a persistent problem with respect to the enforcement of the Resource Conservation and Recovery Act (RCRA). In particular, as an EPA report openly admits, the agency's RCRA recycling regulations (40 CFR 261.2[e] and 261.6) and the miscellaneous exclusions discussed throughout 40 CFR 262.1 have proven "extremely difficult to understand and enforce due to their complexity." U.S. Environmental Protection Agency, *The Nation's Hazardous Waste Management Program at a Crossroads: The RCRA Implementation Study*, EPA/530-SW-90-069 (July 1990), 38.

13. Yeager, *The Limits of Law*, 251.

14. In many instances, DOJ has delegated responsibility for EPA enforcement matters to local U.S. attorneys and their staffs. For a cogent description of the role played by DOJ and U.S. attorneys' offices in regulatory enforcement, see Bernstein, *Regulating Business*, 240–242.

15. Landy, Roberts, and Thomas, *The Environmental Protection Agency*, 204–205.

16. Presentation of Vicki Masterman, attorney, Jones, Day, Reavis and Pogue, at ALI-ABA-ELI Course of Study on Environmental Law, Washington, D.C., February 15, 1992.

17. See Landy, Roberts, and Thomas, *The Environmental Protection Agency*, 205.

18. Presentation of Vicki Masterman.

19. This comment was made by an enforcement supervisor in EPA Region V in spring 1977 during internal discussions to decide the agency's negotiating strategy in a major case.

20. Bryson and Ullrich, "Legal and Technical Cooperation for Effective Environmental Enforcement," in U.S. Environmental Protection Agency and Netherlands Ministry of Housing, Physical Planning and Environment, *International Enforcement Workshop Proceedings* (Utrecht, The Netherlands, May 8–10, 1990), 145.

21. In the brief overview that follows, I am intellectually indebted to the thorough summaries found in Starfield, "The 1990 Contingency Plan—More Detail and More Structure but Still a Balancing Act," *Environmental Law Reporter* 20 (1990): 10222; and Environmental Law Institute, *Toward a More Effective Superfund Enforcement Program*, vol. 2, appendix 3 (Washington, D.C., March 1989).

22. See CERCLA § 105, 42 U.S.C. § 9605.

23. See CERCLA § 104, 42 U.S.C. § 9604.

24. See CERCLA § 111, 42 U.S.C. § 9611.

25. See CERCLA § 107, 42 U.S.C. § 9607. Liability under this provision has been generally held to be strict, joint, and several. The defenses avail-

able to PRPs are narrowly limited to acts of God, acts of war, and acts of third parties with whom the PRP did *not* contract regarding the hazardous wastes.

26. See CERCLA § 106, 42 U.S.C. § 9606.

27. See CERCLA § 107, 42 U.S.C. § 9607.

28. See CERCLA § 106, 42 U.S.C. § 9606.

29. In many instances, EPA will agree to permit PRPs to conduct necessary remedial measures at the site themselves at their own expense. From the PRPs' perspective, one major goal of negotiating with EPA is to arrive at the least costly cleanup program that is mutually agreeable.

30. If EPA and the PRPs have so agreed, this work can be carried out directly by PRPs with EPA oversight.

3. Heavy Seas before the Maelstrom

1. In fact, the Ash Council's staff had originally proposed a new cabinet-level Department of Natural Resources and the Environment to include the Department of the Interior as well as important components of the Departments of Commerce, Agriculture, and Health, Education and Welfare, the U.S. Army Corps of Engineers, and the Atomic Energy Commission. Though this plan was seriously considered, it was dropped after Walter Hickel, then secretary of the interior, fell from favor in the Nixon administration as a result of his well-publicized letter to the president sharply criticizing the attitudes of the White House toward young people protesting the Vietnam War. For a lively account of the birth of EPA, see Quarles, *Cleaning up America*, 14–36.

2. U.S. Environmenal Protection Agency, *The First Two Years: A Review of EPA's Enforcement Program* 2 (1970).

3. Ibid., 89. Armco Steel, Dupont, ITT, and Florida Power and Light Company were among EPA's enforcement targets during this time.

4. Ibid., 3.

5. Interview with James O. McDonald.

6. Interview with Richard Wilson.

7. Interviews with David Kee, Gerald Bryan, Thomas Gallagher, and James O. McDonald.

8. See generally Grad, "Intergovernmental Aspects of Environmental Controls," in Frank P. Grad, George W. Rathjens, and Albert J. Rosenthal, *Environmental Control: Priorities, Policies and the Law* (New York: Columbia University Press, 1971), 47, 117–129, for a discussion of problems faced by state and local enforcement authorities during this period.

9. Interview with Thomas Gallagher.

10. See House Committee on Government Operations, *Mercury Pollution and Enforcement of the Refuse Act of 1899: Hearings before the Subcommittee on Conservation and Natural Resources*, 92nd Cong., 1st and 2nd sess., 1971 and 1972, 1134–1228, 1281–1363; Senate Committee on Public Works, *Implementation of the Clean Air Acts Amendment of 1970, Part 1: Hearings before the Subcommittee on Air and Water Pollution*, 92nd

Cong., 2nd sess., 1972, 224–228, 236, 243; Joel D. Auerbach, *Keeping a Watchful Eye: The Politics of Congressional Oversight* (Washington, D.C.: Brookings Institution, 1990), 19; *Congressional Record*, 1973, 119: 41,127–41,129, 41,305, 41,728.

11. 33 U.S.C. § 1251(1).

12. 33 U.S.C. §§ 1401–1445.

13. 7 U.S.C. §§ 135–136.

14. U.S. Environmental Protection Agency, *EPA Enforcement: Two Years of Progress* (1975), iv.

15. Interviews with Edward Reich and James O. McDonald.

16. Interview with David Kee.

17. As of January 1, 1975, a total of nineteen states had secured EPA approval to operate their own NPDES permit program. U.S. Environmental Protection Agency, *EPA Enforcement*, 37.

18. This phrase was mentioned by both Edward Reich and James O. McDonald in interviews.

19. 42 U.S.C. § 7414.

20. Interviews with Richard Wilson and Edward Reich.

21. It should be noted that the SIPs in question did not specifically require the particular pollution control technology that gave rise to this controversy. The thrust of the Clean Air Act is that sources of air pollution must meet *performance* standards, rather than standards which require the application of specified technology. As a practical matter, however, many of the first sets of SIP standards for electric utilities, steel mills, and other industries could not be complied with by those sources unless expensive and relatively untried pollution controls were employed.

22. Interviews with Richard Wilson and James O. McDonald. I do not mean to suggest that during this period EPA's enforcement efforts were solely focused on stationary sources. Another development in this period was the initiation of enforcement efforts aimed at stemming air pollution from automobiles and other *mobile* sources.

23. Interview with James O. McDonald. Steve Rothblatt's remarks in an interview were to the same effect.

24. From January 1971 to March 1977 pollution control requirements were significant factors in decisions to close 107 U.S. plants, affecting 20,318 employees. In contrast, 677,900 people were employed directly for pollution abatement in calendar year 1974. U.S. Council on Environmental Quality, *Environmental Quality — 1977: The Eighth Annual Report of the Council on Environmental Quality*, 332. It should also be noted that many so-called environmental plant closures were strongly associated with other causes as well.

25. U.S. Environmental Protection Agency, *EPA Enforcement*, 5, 37.

26. Interviews with Peter Kelly and James O. McDonald.

27. Interview with Thomas Gallagher.

28. James L. Regens and Robert W. Rycroft, "Funding for Environmental Protection: Comparing Congressional and Executive Influences," *Social Science Journal* 26 (1989): 295.

29. Interviews with Thomas Gallagher, James O. McDonald, William Muno, and Marjorie Fehrenbach.

30. In fact, this agency policy closely paralleled the noncompliance penalty approach authorized by the 1977 Amendments to the Clean Air Act. Under § 120 of the act, EPA for the first time was permitted to assess civil penalties for certain violations of the act based upon the economic savings attained by the owners and operators of noncomplying sources (42 U.S.C. § 7420). No explicit parallel authority exists under the Water Pollution Control Act or other federal and environmental legislation.

31. Interviews with William Muno and James O. McDonald.

32. Interviews with Thomas Gallagher and James O. McDonald.

33. Interviews with Arthur Smith and David Ullrich.

34. Interview with James Moorman.

35. Interviews with James O. McDonald, David Ullrich, Jane Schulteis, Thomas Gallagher, and Peter Kelly.

36. Interview with Thomas Gallagher.

37. Ibid.

38. Judson W. Starr, "Turbulent Times at Justice and EPA: The Origins of Environmental Criminal Prosecutions and the Work that Remains," *George Washington Law Review* 59 (April 1991): 902–904. Moorman later reiterated that position in testimony before a U.S. Senate subcommittee. See Senate Committee on Environment and Public Works, *Enforcement of Environmental Regulations: Hearings before the Subcommittee on Environmental Pollution*, 96th Cong., 1st sess., 1979, 339.

39. Starr, "Turbulent Times at Justice and EPA," 904.

40. Barbara Blum, deputy administrator, EPA memorandum to regional administrators, director, National Enforcement Investigations Center, and acting assistant administrator for enforcement, January 5, 1981.

41. Starr, "Turbulent Times at Justice and EPA," 905–908.

42. House Committee on Public Works and Transportation, 97th Cong., 2nd sess., 1982, H. Rept. 97-968, 4–5.

43. Interview with Jeffrey Miller; telephone interview with Thomas Jorling.

44. Telephone interview with Thomas Jorling.

45. Interview with Lamar Miller.

46. U.S. Environmental Protection Agency, *Hazardous Waste Enforcement Activities: Chronology of Important Events* (1979), 2.

47. Interview with James Moorman.

48. In fact, the Superfund legislation Congress enacted was not the only funding available for the cleanup of chemical contamination. Under the authority of the Water Pollution Control Act, 33 U.S.C. § 1321, EPA developed a response program to deal with the spills of oil and hazardous materials to surface waters. The agency also utilized a twenty-million-dollar contingency fund to remedy chemical spill emergencies resulting from tanker truck accidents, train wrecks, and other sources. Interviews with Jack Stonebraker and Al J. Smith.

49. Barbara Blum, memorandum to regional administrators, "Managing EPA's Response to Inactive Hazardous Waste Sites," March 28, 1979.

50. Telephone interview with Barbara Blum; interview with James Moorman.

51. Barbara Blum, memorandum to assistant administrators, "Agency-wide Hazardous Waste Site Enforcement and Response System," June 2, 1979.

52. Interviews with David Andrews, Jeffrey Miller, Douglas MacMillan, and Edward Kurent.

53. Interviews with Lamar Miller, Jeffrey Miller, Edward Kurent, and Douglas MacMillan.

54. Interview with Lamar Miller.

55. Interview with Jane Schulteis.

56. Interview with Douglas MacMillan.

57. Ibid.

58. Ibid.

59. The data developed by this subcommittee came to be known as the Eckhardt List after Congressman Bob Eckhardt (D-TX), the subcommittee's chairman. House Committee on Interstate and Foreign Commerce, *Waste Disposal Site Survey*, 96th Cong., 1st sess., 1979, Committee Print, 33.

60. Interviews with Lamar Miller, Marjorie Fehrenbach, and Douglas MacMillan.

61. Interviews with Jeffrey Miller, Edward Kurent, Douglas MacMillan, Richard Smith, Frederick Stiehl, Richard Mays, Marjorie Fehrenbach, and Lamar Miller. This experience was not limited to headquarters personnel. It was also shared by some regional enforcement officials. Interviews with Thomas Voltaggio and Jane Schulteis.

62. Interview with James Bunting. Interestingly, this high level of morale was maintained despite extremely poor working conditions for the task force staff. These descriptions are instructively and amusingly portrayed in a 1980 EPA memorandum from Douglas MacMillan to Gerald Bryan entitled "Doom and Destruction."

63. Interviews with Douglas MacMillan, Jeffrey Miller, Lamar Miller, Frederick Stiehl, and Ann Strickland.

64. Interviews with James Bunting, Ann Strickland, Lloyd Guerco, Douglas MacMillan, Lamar Miller, and Frederick Stiehl; Steven Cohen and Marc Tipermas, "Superfund: Preimplementation Planning and Bureaucratic Politics," in James P. Lester and Ann O'M. Bowman, *The Politics of Hazardous Waste Management* (Durham, N.C.: Duke University Press, 1983), 43.

65. Interview with Edward Kurent.

66. Interviews with Neil Wise, Lawrence Kyte, and Frederick Stiehl.

67. Interview with Michael Kilpatrick.

68. 42 U.S.C. §§ 6934, 6973(b).

69. Interview with Douglas MacMillan.

70. This is not to suggest that an optimistic perspective was universally shared by *all* former members of the HWETF (which was formally renamed

the Office of Hazardous Waste Enforcement in the late autumn of 1980). Notations in a diary I kept from November 5, 1980, the day after President Reagan's election, until March 12, 1981, shortly before I left government service reveal that several rumors of deep cuts in EPA's work force began to circulate among the enforcement staff almost immediately following the election. The identity of the new administrator was a topic of intensely prolonged, guarded, and pessimistic speculation among EPA enforcement staffers. Many of the enforcement staff members at the agency were in what I perceived at the time to be a subdued, somber, philosophical mood.

71. Interview with Anthony Roisman.

4. Destruction, Confusion, Confrontation, and Disarray

1. Inasmuch as she went by that name for most of her term, I shall refer to EPA's fourth administrator as Anne M. Gorsuch, Anne Gorsuch, or Gorsuch. In fact, close to the end of her tenure, on February 20, 1983, EPA's administrator married Robert Burford and took his last name.

2. Subcommittee on Oversight and Investigations, House Committee on Energy and Commerce, *Report of the President's Claim of Executive Privilege over EPA Documents, Abuses in the Superfund Program, and Other Matters*, 98th Cong., 2nd sess., 1984, nn. 15, 16.

3. Interview with William Hedeman. For further evidence to the same effect, see Jonathan Lash, *A Season of Spoils: The Reagan Administration's Attack on the Environment* (New York: Pantheon, 1984), 10.

4. Interview with William Sullivan.

5. Interview with William Hedeman.

6. Interview with Anne Gorsuch.

7. Interview with William Sullivan.

8. Interview with Sheldon Novick.

9. "Decentralizing of Regulatory Programs Seen," *Washington Post*, March 13, 1981.

10. Interview with Valdas Adamkus. An incident recounted by William Sullivan also provides an indication of Gorsuch's personal attitude toward enforcement. Sullivan summarized a plan that he and his staff had devised for a special enforcement initiative with respect to plants that were discharging pollutants in the Niagara River Basin. He then described his attempt to brief Gorsuch regarding that proposal in these words: "I went in and made the presentation and Anne loved the part that concluded that the Niagara River Basin was not terribly dirty. . . . When we got to the enforcement section she said, 'Sullivan, you're getting too enforcement-minded' and walked out. So we had a program and no authority to go ahead with the key piece, which I think would have made it work." Interview with William Sullivan.

11. Interview with Edward Kurent. Several other present or former EPA officials share these impressions regarding the attitudes of the agency's top leadership at the outset of their terms. The following individuals also made comments regarding this matter: Jay Sargent ("The attitude from headquar-

ters, at least initially, was plug up the pipeline and stop those enforcement cases"); Richard Mays ("One perceived, over a period of months, that enforcement was something that was not in favor"); Ann Strickland ("There was no longer support for enforcement from the top. At best there was silence. At worst there was an effort to stop the cases and to prevent further cases in the area"); Michael Kilpatrick ("[T]here was a very clear attitude that enforcement was part of a program that should only speak when spoken to. I mean there was a real attitude that enforcement was a dirty word"); David Ullrich ("There was a perception in the regional offices that the administration had attempted to emasculate the enforcement program"); and Richard Wilson ("It was relatively clear for a while that they were seriously considering disbanding enforcement"). See also Landy, Roberts, and Thomas, *The Environmental Protection Agency*, 245–246, who suggest that, at the outset, the Reagan administration intentionally pursued a low visibility strategy to deregulate environmental protection quickly that included the appointment of loyalists to key EPA posts, budget restrictions, and internal EPA reorganizations.

12. Anne Burford, *Are You Tough Enough?* (New York: McGraw-Hill, 1986), 101.

13. Interview with Frederick Stiehl. Similar comments were also made by the following interviewees: Lawrence Kyte, Steve Rothblatt, Douglas MacMillan, Arthur Smith, and Richard Wilson.

14. Interview with William Sullivan.

15. Interview with David Ullrich.

16. Interview with Lawrence Kyte. EPA's strong preference for negotiation and "jawboning" as a means of encouraging voluntary compliance was also noted in interviews with John Skinner, William Sullivan, and David Ullrich. Valdas Adamkus recalled that he interpreted this policy as a direction to "negotiate until you are blue in the face." Interview with Valdas Adamkus.

17. Interview with Valdas Adamkus.

18. Interviews with John Skinner and David Ullrich. See also William Sullivan, memorandum to EPA regional administrators, "Enforcement Policies and Procedures," February 26, 1982.

19. Anne M. Gorsuch, memorandum, "Agency Re-organization," June 12, 1981. For Gorsuch's defense of her reasons for making this change, see Burford, *Are You Tough Enough?*, 57.

20. Subcommittee on Oversight and Investigations, House Committee on Energy and Commerce, *Hazardous Waste Enforcement*, 97th Cong., 2nd sess., 1982, Committee Print, 33.

21. Ibid.

22. For example, Douglas MacMillan, the former HWETF director, drafted a series of memorandums during late 1981 in which he outlined "serious programmatic problems" that might arise if various proposed reorganization schemes were implemented. See Douglas MacMillan, memorandum to William A. Sullivan, "Phase II Re-organization," June 25, 1981; Douglas MacMillan, memorandum to William Sullivan and Christopher Capper, "Resources for Technical Support for Superfund Program," September 17,

1981; and Douglas MacMillan, memorandum to Christopher Capper, "Location of Enforcement-Support Resources," November 17, 1981.

23. President Reagan, "Memorandum for the Heads of Executive Departments and Agencies," January 20, 1981.

24. Landy, Roberts, and Thomas, *The Environmental Protection Agency*, 250.

25. Regens and Rycroft, "Funding for Environmental Protection," 298.

26. Interview with Richard Wilson. Similar comments were made by Martha Prothro.

27. Interviews with Kirby Biggs, William Muno, and Keith Casto.

28. Staff turnover during the Gorsuch years was mentioned as a significant problem by several present or former EPA enforcement officials I interviewed, including Jane Schulteis, Keith Casto, John Skinner, and Richard Mays. One interviewee also stated that the attrition rate would have been higher, particularly among EPA's enforcement attorneys, if the job market for attorneys had not been unusually slow during the 1982 and 1983 recession. Interview with Keith Casto. Agencywide, between the beginning of 1981 and the end of 1982, more than 4,000 employees—close to 40 percent of EPA's workforce—resigned from government service. Landy, Roberts, and Thomas, *The Environmental Protection Agency*, 250.

29. Interviews with Douglas MacMillan, Richard Smith, and Keith Casto.

30. Interview with Richard Mays. The same views were expressed in interviews with Jane Souzon, Michael Brown.

31. Interview with Richard Mays. Douglas MacMillan had the impression that it had been Mr. Sullivan's intention "to put a politically loyal EPA attorney in each operating unit with the function of reporting deviant behavior back to the central committee." Interview with Douglas MacMillan.

32. Interviews with James Bunting, Keith Casto, Ann Strickland, Frederick Stiehl; telephone interviews with James Dragna and Charles Hungerford.

33. Interview with Thomas Gallagher. Similar views were expressed in interviews with William Hedeman, Ann Strickland, and Keith Casto. In discussing Broccoletti's work, William Sullivan stated, "Broccoletti never had a light touch [with the staff]. I think he went out of the way to offend them." Interview with William Sullivan. Anne Gorsuch stated in an interview with me that she would "not know [Broccoletti] if he walked in the door. Generally speaking, I don't manage below my management." Interview with Anne Gorsuch. In contrast, however, in her memoir of her tenure as EPA administrator Gorsuch wrote: "I knew my agency cold, down to the smallest local levels." Burford, *Are You Tough Enough?*, 76.

34. Telephone interview with Peter Broccoletti.

35. Interview with James Bunting.

36. Interview with William Hedeman.

37. Interviews with James Bunting and Douglas MacMillan; Subcommittee on Oversight and Investigations, House Committee on Energy and Commerce, *Hazardous Waste Enforcement*, 97th Cong., 2nd sess., 1982, Committee Print, 36–37.

38. Interviews with Gene Lucero and Anthony Roisman.

39. Interview with Frederick Stiehl.

40. Interviews with Keith Casto and James Bunting.
41. Interview with Douglas MacMillan.
42. Interview with Ann Strickland. Similar views were stated during my interviews with Keith Casto, James Bunting, and Douglas Farnsworth.
43. Interview with Michael Kilpatrick.
44. Interview with Barbara Elkus.
45. Interview with William Hedeman. In Anne Gorsuch (Burford)'s memoirs, Hedeman was quoted to a similar effect: "[T]here was a lack of cohesiveness unlike anything I had ever seen in government, and, essentially, a trial period in which each individual was attempting to establish their own notoriety and their own recognition within the agency, perhaps at the expense of their peers." Burford, *Are You Tough Enough?*, ix.
46. Interview with William Hedeman.
47. Interview with Anne Gorsuch.
48. Interview with Michael Brown.
49. Interviews with Anne Bollen, John Johnson, and Jane Schulteis.
50. Interview with William Hedeman.
51. Interviews with Barbara Elkus, William Hedeman, Michael Kilpatrick, and Gene Lucero.
52. "A Conversation with Superfund Chief Bill Hedeman," *Environmental Forum* 2 (August 1983): 7.
53. Interview with Keith Casto.
54. Ibid.
55. See *Federal Register* 47 (1982): 214–215.
56. Christopher J. Capper, acting assistant administrator for solid waste and emergency response, memorandum to regional administrators, January 19, 1982; Rita M. Lavelle, assistant administrator for solid waste and emergency response, memorandum to regional administrators, January 28, 1983.
57. Interviews with Joan Bollen, Keith Casto, William Constantelos, William Hedeman, Gene Lucero, Steve Rothblatt, and Neil Wise. See memorandum from enforcement counsel to regional administrators, "Enforcement Policies and Procedures," February 26, 1982, 3, 7; Robert M. Perry, associate administrator for legal and enforcement counsel and general counsel, memorandum to associate administrator for policy and resource management, assistant administrator, regional administrators and office directors, "General Operating Procedures for the Civil Enforcement Program," July 6, 1982.
58. Interview with Michael Brown.
59. Interview with Gene Lucero.
60. Interviews with Kirby Biggs, Gene Lucero, William Constantelos, and John Skinner.
61. Subcommittee on Oversight and Investigations, House Committee on Energy and Commerce, *Hazardous Waste Enforcement*, 30.
62. Interview with William Sullivan. Similar comments were made in my interviews with Jane Schulteis, Michael Smith, Al Smith, and Fred Stiehl.
63. Interviews with Mel Hohman, Steve Rothblatt, David Kee, and Keith Casto.

64. Interviews with Frederick Stiehl, Richard Mays, Ann Strickland, Richard Smith, Michael Smith, David Ullrich, Neil Wise, Douglas MacMillan, Lamar Miller, and Jane Schulteis.

65. Interviews with Lawrence Kyte, Peter Kelly, and Jane Schulteis.

66. Interviews with Joan Boilen, James Bunting, Keith Casto, Barbara Elkus, John Skinner, Michael Smith, Anne Swofford, Jane Souzon, and Neil Wise; Burford, *Are You Tough Enough?*, 125.

67. Interview with William Muno.

68. Interview with Martha Prothro.

69. Interview with Richard Smith.

70. Jones and Smith [pseuds.], "Critics of EPA Are Right," *New York Times*, September 1, 1982, 23. This article is an anonymously written employee criticism of EPA enforcement in a public forum.

71. Interview with Steve Rothblatt.

72. Ibid.

73. Interviews with Jeffrey Miller, Edward Kurent, Michael Brown, James Bunting, and Keith Casto.

74. Interview with Barbara Elkus.

75. Interview with Gene Lucero.

76. Interviews with Jane Schulteis, Richard Mays, and Gene Lucero.

77. Interview with Richard Frandsen. Similar information was also supplied to the legal staff of the Senate Environment and Public Works Committee, some of it on an anonymous basis. Telephone interview with Kathy Cudlipp.

78. Interview with Richard Frandsen.

79. Trudeau, *Doonesbury*, January 25, 1982. The Ted Simpson cartoons also prompted attempts at humor by the agency's staff, which noted their publication with considerable interest.

80. Train, "The Destruction of EPA," *Washington Post*, February 2, 1982, A15.

81. See Shabecoff, "EPA Wants to Allow Burial of Barrels of Liquid Wastes," *New York Times*, March 1, 1982, A1; *Federal Register* 47 (1982): 8307 (proposed February 25, 1982).

82. See Shabecoff, "U.S. Reversing Stand on Burial of Toxic Liquids," *New York Times*, March 18, 1982, A1; *Federal Register* 47 (1982): 10,059 (correction March 6, 1982).

83. As Sullivan later recalled: "At one point I testified seven times in five days. I was being offered up for cannon fodder." Interview with William Sullivan. In addition to appearing before the Dingell Committee, Sullivan also was called to testify at hearings of the Senate Environment and Public Works Committee, as well as other congressional panels. Interview with Kathy Cudlipp.

84. Subcommittee on Oversight and Investigations, House Committee on Energy and Commerce, *Hazardous Waste Enforcement*.

85. Interviews with Keith Casto and Frederick Stiehl.

86. Interview with Edward Kurent.

87. Interview with Gene Lucero.

88. Interviews with Neil Wise and Lawrence Kyte.

89. Interview with Lloyd Guerci. Similar comments were made during my interview with Steven Ramsey. In fact, on September 30, 1982, the last day of fiscal year 1982, EPA referred eight Superfund enforcement cases to the DOJ. The Superfund referrals on this day were nearly *three times* the total number of Superfund actions the EPA had referred to DOJ over the previous *fifteen months*. Subcommittee on Oversight and Investigations, House Committee on Energy and Commerce, *Hazardous Waste Enforcement*, 30.

90. Starr, "Turbulent Times at Justice and EPA," 910.

91. Congressmen John Dingell and James Florio, letter to Anne M. Gorsuch, June 15, 1982.

92. Interviews with Jane Souzon, Edward Kurent, Joan Boilen, and Michael Kilpatrick.

93. Congressmen John Dingell and James Florio, letter to Anne M. Gorsuch, August 31, 1982.

94. Subcommittee on Investigations and Oversight, House Committee on Public Works and Transportation, *Hazardous Waste Contamination of Water Resources (Access to EPA Superfund Records)*, 97th Cong., 2nd sess., 1982, Committee Print.

95. House Judiciary Committee, *Investigation of the Role of the Department of Justice in the Withholding of Environmental Protection Agency Documents from Congress in 1982–83*, 99th Cong., 1st sess., 1985, H. Rept. 435, pt. 1, vol. 1, 10.

96. Subcommittee on Investigations and Oversight, House Committee on Public Works and Transportation, *Hazardous Waste Contamination*, 7–8.

97. House Committee on Public Works and Transportation, *Relating to the Contempt Citation of Anne M. (Gorsuch) Burford*, 98th Cong., 1st sess., 1983, H. Rept. 323, 8–9.

98. Subcommittee on Oversight and Investigations, House Committee on Energy and Commerce, *Report on the President's Claim of Executive Privilege over EPA Documents Abuses in the Superfund Program and Other Matters*, 1984, Committee Print, 1, 20.

99. Ibid., 21.

100. House, *Relating to the Contempt Citation*, 10.

101. The extent of press interest is illustrated by the fact that from September 1982 through March 1983 at least 156 articles regarding EPA appeared in the *New York Times* and that from February 1983 through March 1983 the *Washington Post* published 131 such articles.

102. Interview with Thomas Gallagher. Similar views were expressed by Michael Brown.

103. Interviews with Douglas Farnsworth, Thomas Gallagher, Amy Schaffer, Ann Boilen, Michael Kilpatrick, Edward Kurent, Richard Smith, and Neil Wise.

104. Interview with Mark Raabe.

105. Interviews with Barbara Elkus and Amy Schaffer.

106. House, *Relating to the Contempt Citation*, 11–12; see *United States v. House of Representatives of the United States*, 556 F. Supp. 150, 153 (D.D.C. 1983).

107. Subcommittee on Oversight and Investigations, House Committee on Energy and Commerce, *Report on the President's Claim of Executive Privilege*, 23–24.

108. House, *Relating to the Contempt Citation*, 114. Approximately one month earlier, the DOJ and Congressman Levitas signed a memorandum of understanding which reflected a partial settlement of the dispute.

109. With respect to the circumstances of her departure, see Burford, *Are You Tough Enough?*, 6.

110. Subcommittee on Oversight and Investigations, House Committee on Energy and Commerce, *Report on the President's Claim of Executive Privilege over EPA Documents Abuses in the Superfund Program and Other Matters*, 6.

111. Ibid., 262–263.

112. Ibid., 295. The Dingell Committee report's Republican minority views are, in fact, replete with similar criticisms of Gorsuch and her colleagues. See 297, 298, 309, 317–318.

113. As we have seen and will examine further, congressional influence on EPA enforcement approaches has not, by any means, been limited to the dramatic events of the Gorsuch era.

5. "Away from the Brink" — But Not Out of the Woods

1. David Andrews, "What Would You Do if You Were Running EPA?," *Environmental Law Reporter* 18 (July 1988): 10,243.

2. See EPA press release, "Ruckelshaus Takes Steps to Improve Flow of Agency Information," May 19, 1983, 1. In order to carry out this "openness policy," Ruckelshaus and his top assistants made an attempt to meet with interested parties before specifically deciding how to change the agency's approach to Superfund and other programs. Interviews with Keith Casto and William Hedeman. Unilateral contacts with representatives of regulated industry were discontinued with the exception of a few unique situations. Interview with Courtney Price. A recusal system was also established to prevent the reality or appearance of conflicts of interest by EPA officials.

3. Interview with Barbara Elkus.

4. Interview with Keith Casto.

5. Interviews with William Hedeman, Courtney Price, and Frederick Stiehl.

6. Interviews with William Constantelos, Barbara Elkus, John Johnson, Courtney Price, Jay Sargent, Amy Schaffer, John Skinner, Al Smith, and Neil Wise.

7. Interview with Keith Casto.

8. In lieu of taking those steps, Ruckelshaus and Alm created a new headquarters Office of Enforcement and Compliance Monitoring.

9. Telephone conversation with Alvin Alm.

10. Interview with Richard Mays.

11. See "Transcript of William D. Ruckelshaus' Remarks, EPA National Compliance, and Enforcement Conference," *Environmental Forum* (April 1984): 14–15.

12. Starr, "Turbulent Times at Justice and EPA," 911–912.

13. See House Committee on Energy and Commerce, *EPA's Law Enforcement Authority, 1983: Hearings before the Subcommittee on Oversight and Investigations*, 98th Cong., 1st sess., 1983, 102.

14. Starr, "Turbulent Times at Justice and EPA," 912. In 1988 Congress formally granted full police powers to EPA criminal investigators when it passed the Medical Waste Tracking Act of 1988, Pub. L. No. 100-588, 102 Stat. 2950, 18 U.S.C. § 3063.

15. See U.S. General Accounting Office, *Environmental Protection Agency. Protecting Human Health and the Environment through Improved Management*, GAO/RCED-88-01 (August 1988), 161

16. Alvin L. Alm, deputy administrator, memorandum to assistant administrators, regional administrators, et al., "Implementing the State/Federal Partnership and State/Federal Enforcement Agreements," June 26, 1984. This document was revised and expanded by the agency in the summer of 1986. See A. James Barnes, deputy administrator, memorandum, "Revised Policy Framework for Implementing State/EPA Enforcement Agreements," August 26, 1986.

17. *Policy on Civil Penalties*, EPA General Enforcement Policy GM-21, February 16, 1984.

18. Interview with Michael Kilpatrick. To the same effect were interview comments by Keith Casto, Barbara Elkus, William Hedeman, Richard Mays, and Frederick Stiehl.

19. Interviews with Barbara Elkus, William Hedeman, Richard Mays, and Gene Lucero.

20. Interviews with William Hedeman and Richard Mays. Along with this preference was an acknowledgment that the Superfund trust fund would need to be renewed and expanded following its formal expiration in September 1985. Interviews with Barbara Elkus, William Hedeman, and Gene Lucero.

21. Interviews with Gene Lucero, Michael Kilpatrick, and Frederick Stiehl.

22. Interview with Mel Hohman.

23. Interviews with Steven Leifer, Scott Fulton, and Kevin Gaynor.

24. Interviews with Keith Casto, William Hedeman, and Al Smith.

25. Interview with Mel Hohman.

26. Interview with Gene Lucero.

27. In order to expedite the preparation of RI/FSs, the requirement that states furnish a 10 percent share of RI/FS costs was abandoned.

28. See "Hazardous Waste Enforcement Policy," *Federal Register* 50 (1985): 5034; Lee M. Thomas and Courtney M. Price, memorandum to regional administrators, "Participation of Potentially Responsible Parties in Development of Remedial Investigations and Feasibility Studies under CER-

CLA," March 20, 1984; Gene A. Lucero, memorandum to directors, waste management divisions, "Procedures for Issuing Notice Letters," October 12, 1984; Lee M. Thomas and Courtney M. Price, memorandum to regional administrators, "Guidance Memorandum on Use and Issuance of Administrative Orders under § 106(a) of CERCLA," December 21, 1983; Courtney M. Price and Lee M. Thomas, memorandum to enforcement counsel, "Guidance on Pursuing Cost Recovery Actions under CERCLA," August 26, 1983.

29. Interviews with William Hedeman, Jack Stonebraker, and John Johnson. These planning mechanisms were referred to as the Superfund Comprehensive Accomplishment Plan (SCAP) and the Strategic Planning and Management Systems (SPMS). See Lee M. Thomas, memorandum to regional administrators, "FY 1986 Superfund Comprehensive Accomplishments Plan," December 24, 1986.

30. Interviews with John Johnson, Neil Wise, Michael Brown, Richard Mays, Sheldon Novick, and Amy Schaffer.

31. This point should not be overstated, however. During 1984 EPA headquarters did issue at least two important policy guidance memorandums. See Courtney M. Price and Lee M. Thomas, memorandum, "Final RCRA Civil Penalty Policy," May 8, 1984; and Lee M. Thomas, memorandum to regional administrators, "Enforcement Response Policy," December 21, 1984.

32. Mugdan and Adler, "The 1984 RCRA Amendments: Congress as a Regulatory Agency," *Columbia Journal of Environmental Law* 10 (1985): 217.

33. For a summary of the Dingell Committee's findings, see Subcommittee on Oversight and Investigation, House Committee on Energy and Commerce, *Groundwater Monitoring Survey* (Comm. Print. 1985).

34. See Subcommittee on Oversight and Investigations, House Committee on Energy and Commerce, *Ground Water Monitoring*, 1985, Committee Print, 8–9.

35. "Dingell Challenges EPA Enforcement of RCRA, Oversight of the States," *Hazardous Waste Report*, May 13, 1985.

36. Interviews with Lloyd Guerci and William Muno. For an evaluation of this EPA enforcement initiative by the GAO, see U.S. General Accounting Office, *Hazardous Waste Enforcement of Certification Requirements for Land Disposal Facilities*, GAO/RCED-87-60-BR (January 1987).

37. See "Thomas Pledges Tough Enforcement Effort, New Emphasis on Bringing Criminal Actions," *BNA Environment Reporter*, February 22, 1985, 1764.

38. See U.S. General Accounting Office, *Environmental Protection Agency: Protecting Human Health and the Environment through Improved Management*, GAO/RCED-88-101 (August 1988), 37–39.

39. "Adams Confirmed by Senate for EPA Post, Wants to 'Get Things Moving' on Superfund," *BNA Environment Reporter*, August 15, 1986, 562, 563.

40. Interview with Michael G. Smith.

41. Interview with Thomas Gallagher.

42. "Multi-Media Inspections and Enforcement Planned," *Hazardous Waste Report*, April 29, 1985, 15.

43. Interview with Thomas Gallagher.

44. U.S. Environmental Protection Agency, Office of Enforcement and Compliance Monitoring, *Summary of Enforcement Accomplishments: Fiscal Year 1985* (April 1986), 4–5.

45. U.S. Environmental Protection Agency, Office of Enforcement and Compliance Monitoring, *Summary of Enforcement Accomplishments: Fiscal Year 1986* (April 1987), 9–11.

46. Ibid., 10.

47. *Fiscal Year 1985 Enforcement Accomplishments Report*, 15.

48. *Fiscal Year 1986 Enforcement Accomplishments Report*, i.

49. U.S. Environmental Protection Agency, Office of Enforcement and Compliance Monitoring, *Summary of Enforcement Accomplishments: Fiscal Year 1987* (April 1988), i.

50. Interviews with Julie Becker, Phil Cummings, Kevin Gaynor, Cheryl Wasserman, David Buente, and Thomas Gallagher

51. Interview with Phil Cummings.

52. Wasserman, "Oversight of State Enforcement," in Novick et al., *Law of Environmental Protection* (Environmental Law Institute, 1986), § 8.02, 8-119–8-120.

53. Ibid., 8-122; interview with Richard Duffy.

54. Interviews with Julie Becker, Richard Frandsen, Steven Leifer, Thomas Adams, and Edward Reich.

55. "EPA Picks 18 Issues as 'Critical Delegations' to Regions under New Superfund," *Inside EPA*, March 13, 1987, 5.

56. Thomas L. Adams, Jr., assistant administrator, memorandum to regional administrators, deputy regional administrators, regional counsel, assistant administrators, associate enforcement counsel, and Office of Enforcement and Compliance Monitoring office directors, "Expansion of Direct Referral of Cases to the Department of Justice," January 14, 1988.

57. Thomas L. Adams Jr., assistant administrator, memorandum to regional administrators, "Responsibilities for Assuring Effective Civil Judicial Enforcement," February 8, 1988.

58. Thomas L. Adams Jr., assistant administrator, memorandum to regional administrators, deputy regional administrators, and regional counsel, "Criteria for Active OECM Attorney Involvement in Cases," May 2, 1988.

59. Thomas L. Adams Jr., assistant administrator, Office of Enforcement and Compliance Monitoring, and J. Winston Porter, assistant administrator, Office of Solid Waste and Emergency Response, memorandum to regional administrators, "Revision of CERCLA Civil Judicial Settlement Authorities under Delegations 14-13-B and 14-14-E," June 17, 1988.

60. Presentation of Raymond L. Ludwiszewski, acting general counsel, U.S. Environmental Protection Agency, at ALI-ABA-ELI Course of Study on Environmental Law, Washington, D.C., February 13, 1992.

61. Interviews with Rett Nelson, Norman Niedergang, Scott Fulton, David Buente, Frank Biros, Joyce Rechtschaffen, and Jonathan Cannon.

62. Interviews with Jonathan Cannon, Richard Frandsen, Edward Reich, and Norman Niedergang.

63. Interviews with Rett Nelson and Lawrence Kyte.

64. Interviews with Rett Nelson, Lawrence Kyte, Lloyd Guerci, and Joyce Rechtschaffen.

65. Interview with Frank Biros.

66. Presentation of Raymond Ludwisczewski.

67. Interview with David Buente.

68. "President Requests 4% Increase in Operating Costs, 45% Superfund Jump," *BNA Environment Reporter*, February 8, 1985, 1627.

69. Senate Committee on Appropriations, *Hearings on Departments of Veterans Affairs and Housing and Urban Development and Independent Agencies Appropriations for Fiscal Year 1992*, 102nd Cong., 1st sess., 1991, Senate Hearing 102-113, pt. 1, 497–507.

70. R. Mays, "Superfund Enforcement in the Dump: What's Wrong with the Superfund Enforcement Program?," *National Environmental Enforcement Journal* (February 1989): 3, 4.

71. Interviews with Charles de Saillan, Maria Cintron, Anne Allen, Steven Leifer, Erik Olson, and Thomas Gallagher.

72. Interview with Steven Leifer. Similar views were expressed by Erik Olson.

73. Environmental Law Institute, *Toward a More Effective Superfund Enforcement Program* (Washington, D.C., March 1989), 152–153. The ELI also observed: "[I]t is frequently unclear which office has jurisdiction. There appears to be overlapping jurisdiction on some matters. Regional [EPA] personnel complain that they receive conflicting and inconsistent advice from the different [headquarters] offices. This organizational structure results in inefficiency, uncertainty and duplication. Ultimately, it reduces the accountability of each office for Superfund enforcement" (153).

74. Interviews with Deborah Woitte, Don Gray, Stephanie Clough, Steven Leifer, Mark Reiter, Phil Cummings, Joyce Rechtschaffen, and Thomas Gallagher.

75. Interviews with Lloyd Guerci, William Muno, Richard Frandsen, Rett Nelson, Deborah Woitte, Thomas Gallagher, Judson Starr, Norm Niedergan, Steven Leifer, and Frank Biros; see also U.S. Environmental Protection Agency, *The Nation's Hazardous Waste Management Program at a Crossroads*, 66–67; and U.S. General Accounting Office, *Environmental Protection Agency*, 36.

76. U.S. General Accounting Office, *Superfund: Improvements Needed in Workforce Management*, GAO/RCED 88-1 (October 1987), 4.

77. In fiscal years 1985 and 1986, the "quit rate" for Superfund employees increased from 2.9 to 7.2 percent. Several critical Superfund occupations had quit rates that were two to six times higher than the average for similar jobs in other parts of the federal government. Ibid.

78. Interview with Don Gray. Enforcement staff turnover was also identified as a problem by the following interviewees: Rett Nelson, Deborah Woitte, Richard Frandsen, Jonathan Cannon, Phil Cummings, Thomas Gallagher, Anne Allen, and Steven Leifer.

79. Telephone interview with Bill Gillespie. This was also a problem for

EPA in its efforts to hire experienced law enforcement personnel as criminal investigators. FBI background checks and other safeguards frequently delayed their retention by as much as six months.

80. Interviews with Julie Becker, Erik Olson, Don Gray, Kevin Gaynor, Thomas Gallagher, Richard Frandsen, David Buente, and Deborah Woitte.

81. Alfred A. Marcus, *EPA's Organizational Structure*, in Schroeder and Lazarus, eds., *Assessing the Environmental Protection Agency*, 33.

82. Hearing before the Subcommittee on Toxic Substances, Environmental Oversight and Research and Development of the Senate Committee on Environment and Public Works, *Oversight of the Environmental Protection Agency's Enforcement Program*, 101st Cong., 1st sess., 1989, Senate Hearing 101-503; testimony of John C. Martin, inspector general, U.S. Environmental Protection Agency, 29. A number of the present and former federal officials I interviewed agreed with Martin's conclusion regarding the existence of inconsistencies among state governmental attitudes and approaches to environmental enforcement. Interviews with Rett Nelson, Lloyd Guerci, Bill Muno, Scott Fulton, Steve Leifer, and Thomas Adams. The GAO has criticized the agency for poor oversight of inadequate state enforcement efforts. U.S. General Accounting Office, *Hazardous Waste: Many Enforcement Actions Do Not Meet EPA Standards*, GAO/RCED 88-140 (June 1988), 2–3.

83. Interview with Rett Nelson.

84. Interview with Maria Cintron.

85. Interviews with Deborah Woitte, Steven Leifer, Thomas Gallagher and Judson Starr; Judson W. Starr, "Too Many Cooks," *Environmental Forum* (January/February 1989): 9, 13.

86. See U.S. Environmental Protection Agency, Office of the Inspector General, *Capping Report on the Computation, Negotiation, Mitigation and Assessment of Penalties under EPA Programs*, EPA/IG/EIG 8E 9-05-0087-9100485 (September 27, 1989); and U.S. General Accounting Office, *Environmental Enforcement: Penalties May Not Recover Economic Benefits Gained by Violators*, GAO/RCED 91-166 (June 1991).

87. American Management Systems, Inc., *Improving Information Support for EPA Compliance Monitoring and Enforcement* (Arlington, Va., April 21, 1986), 4–5.

88. Ibid. Telephone interview with Charlene Swibas. Regrettably, the agency's subsequent attempts to remedy these problems have been unsuccessful.

89. K. Gaynor, "Too Many Cooks," *Environmental Forum* (January/February 1989): 11.

90. Environmental Law Institute, *Toward a More Effective Superfund Enforcement Program*, 157.

91. Interviews with Steven Leifer, Michael Smith, Rett Nelson, Norm Niedergang, and Lawrence Kyte.

92. Interview with Rett Nelson.

93. Interviews with Thomas Adams, Anne Allen, Julie Becker, Frank Biros, Michael Brown, James Bunting, Jonathan Cannon, Maria Cintron, Phil Cummings, Charles de Saillan, Rick Duffy, Douglas Farnsworth, Scott Fulton, Anne Gorsuch, Edward Kurent, Steven Leifer, Douglas MacMillan, Erik

Olson, Joyce Rechtschaffen, Amy Schaeffer, Richard Smith, Jane Souzon, Ann Strickland, Anne Swofford, and Doug Wolf.

94. Interviews with Anne Allen, Julie Becker, Scott Fulton, Frank Biros, Charles DeSaillan, Maria Cintron, Richard Frandsen, Erik Olson, and Phil Cummings.

95. Interview with Scott Fulton.

96. Gaynor, "Too Many Cooks," 11–12.

97. Interview with Thomas Adams.

98. Interview with Frederick Stiehl.

99. Letter from Representative John D. Dingell to Lee M. Thomas, October 6, 1986.

100. Letter from EPA Administrator Lee M. Thomas to Representative John D. Dingell, December 9, 1986.

101. "New Criminal Enforcement Branch, Policy Shop Seen in OECM Overhaul," *Inside EPA*, September 19, 1986, 8.

102. Interviews with Charles de Saillan, Steven Leifer, and Thomas Gallagher. The morale of Superfund attorneys at EPA headquarters plummeted further in the spring and summer of 1988, when their role in Superfund cases was drastically reduced. See "EPA Gives Settlement Powers to Regions, Precludes Headquarters Concurrence," *Inside EPA*, July 1, 1988, 1, 8. Deborah Woitte, Charles de Saillan, Richard Frandsen, Thomas Gallagher, and Scott Fulton expressed similar views.

103. See *PCB Disposal: Is EPA Doing Its Job?*, hearing before a Subcommittee of the House Committee on Government Operations, no. 73-657, April 6, 1987; *Implementation of the Toxic Substances Control Act, the PCB Rule and Federal Hazardous Substance Laws: Concerning the Performance of the Environmental Protection Agency in the Matter of Texas Eastern Gas Pipeline Company*, Report from the Subcommittee on Superfund and Environmental Oversight to the Senate Committee on Environment and Public Works, 100th Cong., 2nd sess., no. 81-135, February 1988; *Laundering Waste: EPA's Efforts to Prevent Criminal Activity in PCB Disposal*, Hearing before a Subcommittee of the House Committee on Government Operations, 100th Cong., 2nd sess., no. 93-980, August 19, 1988; House Committee on Government Operations, *PCB's: EPA Must Strengthen Regulations, Improve Enforcement and Prevent Criminal Activity*, 101st Cong., 1st sess., H. Rept. 101-118, June 29, 1989; *Sham Recycling*, Hearing before the Subcommittee on Hazardous Wastes and Toxic Substances, Senate Committee on Environment and Public Works, 100th Cong., 2nd sess., Senate Hearing 100-663, April 13, 1988; Hearing Record, Subcommittee on Oversight and Investigations, House Committee on Energy and Commerce, *Progress of the Superfund Program*, 100th Cong., 2nd sess., no. 100-203, June 20, 1988; and Hearing Record, Subcommittee on Energy, Environment and Natural Resources, House Committee on Government Operations, *Superfund Implementation*, 100th Cong., 2nd sess., no. 88-559, April 11, 1988; *Delays and Weaknesses in EPA's Program to Ensure Proper Closure of Hazardous Waste Sites*, Hearing before a Subcommittee of the House Committee on Government Operations, 100th Cong., 1st sess., no. 87-569, December 15, 1987; *En-*

vironmental Compliance by Federal Agencies, Hearing before the Subcommittee on Oversight and Investigations of the House Committee on Energy and Commerce, 100th Cong., 1st sess., no. 100-39, April 28, 1987; *Review of DOE's Compliance with Environmental Laws in Managing Its Hazardous and Mixed Radioactive-Hazardous Wastes,* Hearing before a Subcommittee of the House Committee on Government Operations, 99th Cong., 2nd sess., no. 64-6890, July 11, 1986; and *Hazardous Waste Problems at Department of Defense Facilities,* Hearing before a Subcommittee of the House Committee on Government Operations, 100th Cong., 2nd sess., no. 86-073, November 5, 1987.

104. See U.S. General Accounting Office, *Superfund: Interim Assessment of EPA's Enforcement Program,* GAD/RCED 89-40BR (October 1988); U.S. General Accounting Office, *Hazardous Waste: Enforcement of Certification Requirements for Land Disposal Facilities,* GAO/RCED-87-60-BR (January 1987); U.S. General Accounting Office, *Superfund: Improvements Needed in Workforce Management,* GAO/RCED 88 1 (October 1987), U.S. General Accounting Office, *Hazardous Waste Facility Inspections Are Not Thorough and Complete,* GAO/RCED-88-20 (November 1987); and U.S. General Accounting Office, *Hazardous Waste: Many Enforcement Actions Do Not Meet EPA Standards,* GAO/RCED-88-140 (June 1988).

105. See "RCRA Compliance Suffers from Lack of Staff, Lenient Attitudes of States, EPA Reports Say," *BNA Environment Reporter,* April 12, 1985, 2179–2180; U.S. Environmental Protection Agency, Office of the Inspector General, *Capping Report on the Computation, Negotiation, Mitigation and Assessment of Penalties under EPA Programs,* EPA/IG/EIG 8E 9-05-0087-9100485, September 27, 1989.

106. Hearing Record, Subcommittee on Energy, Environment and Natural Resources, House Committee on Government Operations, *Superfund Implementation,* 100th Cong., 2nd sess., no. 88-559, April 11, 1988, 2.

107. Hearing Record, Subcommittee on Oversight and Investigations, House Committee on Energy and Commerce, *Progress of the Superfund Program,* 100th Cong., 2nd sess., no. 100-203, June 20, 1988, 1–2.

108. *Right Train, Wrong Track: Failed Leadership in the Superfund Cleanup Program,* June 20, 1988.

109. Ibid., 1.

110. U.S. Congress, Office of Technology Assessment, *Are We Cleaning Up?: 10 Superfund Case Studies,* OTA-ITE-362 (Washington, D.C.: U.S. Government Printing Office, June 1988).

111. Ibid., 1–4.

112. P. Shabecoff, "Congress Report Faults U.S. Drive on Waste Cleanup," *N.Y. Times,* June 18, 1988, A1.

113. "EPA Officials Defend Against Attacks in Two Reports Criticizing Superfund Cleanups," *BNA Environment Reporter,* June 24, 1988, 260.

114. "Superfund Officials Confront Critics, Call Negative Reports Unfair, Misleading," *BNA Environment Reporter,* July 29, 1988, 419–420. Kovalick also stated that EPA's definition of "performance" with respect to Superfund site remedies does not agree with OTA's. OTA calls for total destruction of

all contaminants. On the other hand, Kovalick indicated, EPA believes that "permanent remedies are a spectrum of remedies that can range from total destruction, like thermal incineration, through fixation or consolidating the waste on site."

6. Modest Progress and Renewed Suspicion

1. Environmental Law Institute, *Toward a More Effective Superfund Enforcement Program.*

2. Ibid., E-1, 50−51, 54−55, 152−155, 159, 192−197.

3. Ibid., 210.

4. Senate Subcommittee on Superfund, Ocean and Water Protection, *Lautenberg-Durenberger Report on Superfund Implementation: Cleaning Up the Nation's Cleanup Program,* May 1989.

5. Ibid., 8−12.

6. Ibid., 8.

7. *Nomination of William K. Reilly,* Hearing before the Senate Committee on Environment and Public Works, 101st Cong., 1st sess., January 31, 1989, 23.

8. Hearing before the Subcommittee on Toxic Substances, Environmental Oversight, Research and Development of the Senate Committee on Environment and Public Works, *Oversight of the EPA's Enforcement Program,* 101st Cong., 1st sess., Senate Hearing 101-503, November 15, 1989, 4.

9. See U.S. Environmental Protection Agency, *A Management Review of Superfund,* administrator's preface, June 1989.

10. "EPA Superfund Review Aims for Cease Fire with Critics, Changes Recommended," *Hazardous Waste Report,* May 22, 1989, 1.

11. Interviews with Jonathan Cannon, Joyce Rechtschaffen, Elaine Stanley, and Thomas Adams.

12. U.S. Environmental Protection Agency, *A Management Review of Superfund,* 2.

13. "Reilly Shelves Controversial Deferral Policy until Reauthorization, to Surprise of EPA Staff," *BNA Environment Reporter,* June 23, 1989, 460.

14. In fact, Congress's response to the Ninety Day Study and Reilly's recommendations led to approximately a five-hundred-person increase in the size of the EPA staff devoted to Superfund implementation on a full-time basis. Interviews with Norm Niedergang and Jonathan Cannon.

15. Interview with Mark Reiter; Hearing before the Subcommittee on Toxic Substances, Environmental Oversight, Research and Development of the Senate Committee on Environment and Public Works, *Oversight of the EPA's Enforcement Program,* 101st Cong., 1st sess., Senate Hearing 101-503, November 15, 1989, 2.

16. "EPA Superfund Review Aims for Cease Fire," 1.

17. U.S. Environmental Protection Agency, "Strock Nominated as EPA Assistant Administrator," *Environmental News,* August 7, 1989.

18. Interview with Mark Reiter.

19. "Enforcement: Reorganization Nears Approval Despite Discontent in Regions," *Inside EPA*, April 13, 1990, 4.

20. Interview with Charles de Saillan. Similar views were expressed by William Muno.

21. James M. Strock, "EPA's Environmental Enforcement in the 1990's," *Environmental Law Reporter* 20 (August 1990): 10,330.

22. Ibid., 10,239.

23. Ibid.

24. H. Henry Habicht II, deputy administrator, EPA memorandum to assistant administrators, general counsel, inspector general, associate administrators, and regional administrators, "Implementation of the Administrator's Multi-Media Enforcement Goal," February 19, 1991, 1, 3–4.

25. See U.S. General Accounting Office, *EPA's Management of Cross-Media Information*, GAO-IMTEC-92-14 (April 1992).

26. Strock, "EPA's Environmental Enforcement," 10,331.

27. Ibid., 10,327–10,328, 10,330, 10,332.

28. James M. Strock, "Environmental Criminal Enforcement Priorities for the 1990's," *George Washington Law Review* 50, no. 4 (April 1991): 917, 937.

29. U.S. Environmental Protection Agency, *Enforcement in the 1990's Project: Recommendation of the Analytical Workgroups* (October 1991), iii.

30. U.S. Environmental Protection Agency, Office of Enforcement and Compliance Monitoring, *Enforcement Accomplishments Report for Fiscal Year 1989* (February 1990), 1.

31. Ibid., 15, 16, 64. In fiscal 1989 EPA reached 218 Superfund settlements with PRPs. The estimated total work value of these settlements exceeded $1 billion. In addition, the agency referred 153 Superfund civil judicial actions to DOJ that year. Most of those cases sought injunctive relief for hazardous waste cleanup by responsible parties, recovery of public money spent on site cleanup, or site access to perform investigations or cleanup work. Moreover, in the same time period, $34.9 million in civil penalties were assessed, including $21.3 million in civil judicial penalties and $13.6 million in administrative penalties.

32. Hearing before the Subcommittee on Toxic Substances, Environmental Oversight, Research and Development, *Oversight of the EPA's Enforcement Program*, 9.

33. "Environmental Crimes Enforcement Increases during Fiscal 1989, Justice Department Reports," *BNA Environment Reporter*, January 5, 1990, 1510.

34. "1990 Record Year for Criminal Enforcement of Environmental Violators, Justice Announces," *BNA Environment Reporter*, November 23, 1990, 1397.

35. "Lieberman Crafts Bill to Strengthen EPA's Enforcement Activities," *Inside EPA*, March 2, 1990, 6.

36. See "Corporations Face Increased Penalties under Revised RCRA Civil Enforcement Policy," *BNA Environment Reporter*, November 2, 1990, 1245.

37. Interviews with Edward Reich and Joyce Rechtschaffen.

38. Interviews with Norman Niedergang, Rett Nelson, Scott Fulton, Erik Olson, and Jimmie Powell.

39. Interview with William Frank.

40. "Enforcement Chief Vies for Major EPA Shift to Centralize Enforcement Decisions," *Inside EPA*, January 11, 1991, 1.

41. Ibid., 6.

42. See "Reilly Vetoes Enforcement Chief's Plan for Major Reorganization," *Inside EPA*, February 1, 1991, 1, 5.

43. "Enforcement Chief Expects Successor to Carry on with New Initiatives," *Inside EPA*, February 22, 1991, 12.

44. "EPA Picks New Jersey County Prosecutor for Top Enforcement Post," *Inside EPA*, June 28, 1991.

45. See U.S. General Accounting Office, *Alternative Enforcement Organizations for EPA*, GAO/RCED-92-107 (April 1992).

46. U.S. General Accounting Office, *EPA's Management of Cross-Media Information*, GAO/IMTEC-92-14 (April 1992), 7–8, 12.

47. Ibid., 12.

48. Interview with Charles de Saillan.

49. Interviews with Bertram Frey and Michael G. Smith.

50. U.S. Environmental Protection Agency, *The Nation's Hazardous Waste Management Program at a Crossroads*, 60. A similar view was expressed by William Muno in an interview.

51. See U.S. General Accounting Office, *Hazardous Waste*.

52. Interviews with Mark Reiter, Jimmie Powell, Richard Frandsen, Anne Allen, Rett Nelson, Scott Fulton, Don Gray, Elaine Stanley, Joyce Rechtschaffen, Deborah Woitte, and Phil Cummings.

53. Subcommittee on Oversight and Investigations, House Committee on Energy and Commerce, *Activities of EPA's Office of Inspector General*, June 1991, Committee Print 102-E, 2–4, 7.

54. "Reilly Considers Major Program Changes to Accelerate Site Cleanups, Define Risks," *BNA Environment Reporter*, August 30, 1991, 1187.

55. Ibid.

56. See "Study Finds Unjustified Expenditures: EPA to Standardize Limits on PRP's," *BNA Environment Reporter*, October 4, 1991, 1406.

57. "Reilly Considers Major Program Changes," 1187.

58. "Study Finds Unjustified Expenditures," 1406; "New Superfund Head, Trouble-Shooter Staff Named to Review Contracts, Speed Cleanups," *BNA Environment Reporter*, October 4, 1991, 1405.

59. "Lautenberg, Dingell Blast Superfund Studies; Reilly Focuses on Accomplishments of the Program," *BNA Environment Reporter*, October 11, 1991, 1531.

60. Ibid.

61. See U.S. General Accounting Office, *Inland Oil Spills: Stronger Regulation and Enforcement Needed to Avoid Future Incidents*, GAO/RCED-89-65 (February 1989); U.S. General Accounting Office, *Water Pollution: Improved Monitoring and Enforcement Needed for Toxic Pollutants Entering Sewers*, GAO/RCED-89-101 (April 1989); U.S. General Accounting Office,

Air Pollution: Improvements Needed in Detecting and Preventing Violations, GAO/RCED-90-155 (September 1990); and Statement of Richard L. Hembra, director, Environmental Protection Issues, Resources, Community and Economic Development Division, U.S. General Accounting Office, before the Subcommittee on Water Resources, House Committee on Public Works and Transportation, *Observations on EPA and State Enforcement under the Clean Water Act*, GAO/T-RCED-91-53 (May 1991).

62. U.S. General Accounting Office, *Environmental Enforcement: Penalties May Not Recover Economic Benefits Gained by Violators*, GAO/RCED-91-166 (June 1991).

63. Ibid., 1, 4–5. EPA officials took issue with those portions of GAO's conclusions that pertained to RCRA enforcement cases. See "EPA Clash over Report Finding Fault with EPA Assessments," *Inside EPA*, June 21, 1991, 16; and U.S. General Accounting Office, *Environmental Enforcement*, 6–9.

64. Keith Schneider, "Environment Laws Are Eased by Bush as Election Nears," *New York Times*, May 20, 1992, A1; Keith Schneider, "White House Snubs U.S. Envoy's Plea to Sign Rio Treaty," *New York Times*, June 5, 1992, A1; Keith Schneider, "Industries Gaining Broad Flexibility on Air Pollution," *New York Times*, June 26, 1992, A1; and John H. Cushman, Jr., "Quayle, in Last Push for Landowners, Seeks to Relax Wetland Protections," *New York Times*, November 12, 1992, A16.

65. Interview with Michael Smith.

7. Lessons Learned

1. Beyond the selected works summarized and discussed below, the regulatory activities of EPA have also been considered in Landy, Roberts, and Thomas, *The Environmental Protection Agency*; Peter Yeager, *The Limits of Law*; Bruce Ackerman and William Hassler, *Clean Coal/Dirty Air* (New Haven, Conn.: Yale, 1981); Alfred Marcus, "The Environmental Protection Agency," in James Q. Wilson, ed., *The Politics of Regulation* (New York: Basic Books, 1980); Alfred Marcus, *Promise and Performance: Choosing and Implementing an Environmental Policy* (Westport Conn.: Greenwood, 1981); Christopher T. Bosso, *Pesticides and Politics: The Life Cycle of a Public Issue* (Pittsburgh: University of Pittsburgh Press, 1987); Richard A. Harris and Sidney M. Milkis, *The Politics of Regulatory Change: A Tale of Two Agencies* (Oxford: Oxford University Press, 1989); David Doniger, *The Law and Policy of Toxic Substances Control* (Baltimore: Johns Hopkins University Press, 1978); R. Shep Melnick, *Regulations and the Courts: The Case of the Clean Air Act* (Washington, D.C.: Brookings Institution, 1983); Rosemary O'Leary, "The Impact of Federal Court Decisions on the Policies and Administration of the U.S. Environmental Protection Agency," *Administrative Law Review* 41 (1989): 549; Walter A. Rosenbaum, "Environmental Politics and Policy," 2nd ed., *Congressional Quarterly* (1991); and B. Dan Wood, "Principals, Bureaucrats and Responsiveness in Clean Air Act Enforcements," *American Political Science Review* 82, no. 1 (March 1988); as well as in other writings.

2. Keith Hawkins and John M. Thomas, eds., *Enforcing Regulation* (Boston: Kluwer Nijhoff, 1984).

3. Keith Hawkins and John M. Thomas, "The Enforcement Process in Regulatory Bureaucracies," in ibid., 13–15.

4. U.S. Environmental Protection Agency, *The Nation's Hazardous Work Management Program at a Crossroads,* 56.

5. See Wasserman, "An Overview of Compliance and Enforcement," 26.

6. Personal communication with two EPA regional attorneys who preferred not to be identified.

7. Robert A. Kagan and John T. Scholz, "The 'Criminology of the Corporation' and Regulatory Enforcement Strategies," in Hawkins and Thomas, eds., *Enforcing Regulation,* 67–68, 84–86.

8. Ibid., 86.

9. Ibid., 84.

10. Spitzer, "Beyond Enforcement," *Environmental Forum* 9, no. 5 (October 1992): 19.

11. Wasserman, "An Overview of Compliance and Enforcement," 14.

12. Steven Shimberg, "Checks and Balances: Limitations on the Power of Congressional Oversight," in Schroeder and Lazarus, eds., "Assessing the Environmental Protection Agency," 247.

13. Auerbach, *Keeping a Watchful Eye,* 195.

14. See Richard J. Lazarus, "The Tragedy of Distrust in the Implementation of Federal Environmental Law," and Richard J. Lazarus, "The Neglected Question of Congressional Oversight of EPA: Quis Custodiet Ipsos Custodes (Who Shall Watch the Watchers Themselves?)," in Schroeder and Lazarus, eds., "Assessing the Environmental Protection Agency," 311–374.

15. Auerbach, *Keeping a Watchful Eye,* 198.

16. Steven A. Cohen, "EPA: A Qualified Success," in Sheldon Kaminiecki, Robert O'Brien, and Michael Clarke, eds., *Controversies in Environmental Policy* (Albany, N.Y.: SUNY Press, 1986), 174.

17. Donald E. Mann, "Democratic Politics and Environmental Policy," in ibid., 4.

18. U.S. General Accounting Office, *Environmental Protection Agency: Protecting Human Health and the Environment through Improved Management,* GAO/RCED-88-101 (August 1988), 216.

19. Gaynor, "Too Many Cooks," 9, 10.

20. Interview with David Buente.

21. Interviews with Julie Becker, Phil Cummings, and Thomas Gallagher.

22. Lazarus, "The Neglected Question," 228.

23. Ibid., 229.

24. Interviews with Thomas Adams and Julie Becker. Somewhat surprisingly, in his reply to Lazarus Steven Shimberg appears to concede Lazarus's point. See Shimberg, "Checks and Balances," 244 ("Congressional oversight *does* divert valuable, scarce Agency resources" [emphasis in original]). My own research, however, does not indicate that such a diversion has created serious obstacles for EPA enforcement efforts.

25. Interviews with Anne Allen, Scott Fulton, Thomas Gallagher, Norm Niedergang, and Elaine Stanley.

26. See Lazarus, "The Neglected Question," 212–213, 232–234.

27. Ibid., 230.

28. Shimberg, "Checks and Balances," 244.

29. Lazarus, "The Neglected Question," 227.

30. See e.g. Matthew D. McCubbins and Thomas Schwartz, "Congressional Oversight Overlooked: Police Patrols and Fire Alarms," *American Journal of Political Science* 28 (February 1984): 165; and Auerbach, *Keeping a Watchful Eye*, 121.

31. My research has not always revealed this to be true. For example, Phil Cummings, formerly chief counsel to the Senate Committee on Environment and Public Works, candidly told me: "I was involved for so long in the business of putting pressure on [EPA] to do more that it's hard for me mentally to give them credit for doing anything." Interview with Phil Cummings. Another congressional staff member, who asked not to be identified by name, stated: "[In overseeing EPA enforcement] it's the sore thumbs that get attention. You don't really ever have a feeling of what else is out there."

32. Lazarus, "The Neglected Question," 230.

33. Interview with Lloyd Guerci.

34. Interview with Steven Leifer. Thomas Adams and Julie Becker were also largely critical in their assessments of Congress's oversight performance.

35. Interviews with Thomas Gallagher, Elaine Stanley, Norm Niedergang, Anne Allen, and Scott Fulton. One of Fulton's comments was reasonably typical of their views: "By and large [congressional oversight of the agency] is constructive, even though it's been a pain to deal with . . . At times, oversight has helped us focus and to identify where our weaknesses are so we can respond to them. Sometimes, when you're in the middle of it, you don't see your weaknesses as readily as someone more objective."

36. Lazarus, "The Neglected Question," 231.

37. Some observers have opined that statutory fragmentation has limited EPA's abilities to deal comprehensively with broad, cross-program environmental challenges. See e.g. Alfred A. Marcus, "EPA's Organizational Structure," in Schroeder and Lazarus, eds. "Assessing the Environmental Protection Agency," 39. ("[M]icro-management by Congress severely constrains EPA from balancing the costs and benefits of its many activities and from coming up with a rational calculus of what it should and should not do.")

38. Jeffrey G. Miller, "Federal Enforcement," in Sheldon Novick, ed., 1 *Law of Environmental Protection* § 8.01 (1990), 8-6.

39. Lazarus, "The Neglected Question," 230.

40. This quotation appears in Cohen, "EPA: A Qualified Success," in Kaminiecki, O'Brien, and Clarke, eds., *Controversies in Environmental Policy*, 179.

41. *Observations on the Environmental Protection Agency's Budget Request for Fiscal Year 1992*, Statement of Richard L. Hembra before the Senate Committee on Environment and Public Works, GAO/T-RCED-91-14, March 7, 1991. Hembra's testimony is consistent with a careful, scholarly study of the agency's budget: Regens and Rycroft, "Funding for Environmental Protection," 289–301.

42. Interview with Scott Fulton.

43. Interviews with Rett Nelson, Elaine Stanley, and Thomas Gallagher.
44. Interview with Thomas Gallagher.
45. As Keith Hawkins and John M. Thomas have incisively observed in the context of regulatory enforcement generally: "Bargaining . . . suffers a loss of legitimacy if it occurs by default as a response to resource constraints." Keith Hawkins and John M. Thomas, "The Enforcement Process in Regulatory Bureaucracies," in Hawkins and Thomas, eds., *Enforcing Regulation*, 16.
46. Interviews with Norm Niedergang and Rick Duffy. See also Nancy Firestone, "Regulating Solid and Hazardous Wastes: Has Federal Regulation Lived Up to Its Mandate or Can the States Do a Better Job?," *Environmental Law Reporter* 22 (January 1992): 10,039 (describing problems caused by budget shortages for implementation of the RCRA) and Environmental Law Institute, *Toward a More Effective Superfund Enforcement Program*, 69.
47. Interviews with Thomas Adams, Julie Becker, David Buente, Maria Cintron, Scott Fulton, Steven Leifer, Rett Nelson, Eric Olson, Joyce Rechtschaffen, and Deborah Woitte.
48. For a detailed description of this process within EPA, see Environmental Law Institute, *Toward a More Effective Superfund Enforcement Program*, 178–181.
49. Interview with Carrie Apostolou.
50. Interview with Michelle Burkett.
51. Ibid.
52. Interview with Stephanie Clough.
53. U.S. Senate Committee on Appropriations, *Department of Veterans Affairs and Housing and Urban Development and Independent Agencies Appropriations Bill*, 1991, no. 101-474, September 1990, 84–98.
54. See Environment and Energy Study Institute, *Statutory Deadlines in Environmental Legislation: Necessary but Need Improvement* (Washington, D.C., September 1985), 62–63, for a similar recommendation advanced in the context of an independent assessment of deadlines in federal environmental laws.

8. The Future of Environmental Enforcement

1. Gaynor, "Too Many Cooks," 9, 10; comments to the same effect were made in interviews, by Maria Cintron and Thomas Adams; see also the statement of Senator Harry Reid (D-NV) in Hearing before the Subcommittee on Toxic Substances, Environmental Oversight, Research and Development, *Oversight of the EPA's Enforcement Program*, 2.
2. I have referred to this question as "how strong is strong?," by which I mean, What practical, working definition can be assigned to the commonly invoked EPA goal of "strong enforcement"?
3. Although this issue has been extensively discussed by EPA enforcement officials and congressional committee staff members, little of that discourse has been reduced to writing. The question *has* been perceptively addressed, however, in published work by one EPA headquarters enforcement

manager. See Wasserman, "An Overview of Compliance and Enforcement," 27–31; and U.S. Environmental Protection Agency, *Principles of Environmental Enforcement* (February 1992), 9-2, 10-11. This book is one of three documents, principally written by Cheryl E. Wasserman, chief, Compliance Policy and Planning Branch, EPA Office of Enforcement, for use in a training course prepared by the agency in response to a request by Poland's Ministry of Environmental Protection, Natural Resources and Forestry. Ibid., iii. Though I do not necessarily agree with her discussion in every particular, I do here wish to acknowledge my intellectual debt to Wasserman's writings in some portions of the analysis that follows.

4. Hearing before the Subcommittee on Toxic Substances, Environmental Oversight, Research and Development, *Oversight of the EPA's Enforcement Program*, 89.

5. Interview with William Muno.

6. The latter deficiency can probably be corrected over time if a decision is made that the benefits of a change in the government's methodology for gathering data on environmental quality, to take account of the impacts of individual sources and completed enforcement cases, would justify the effort and expense such a change would entail.

7. Interview with William Muno.

8. Interview with Edward Reich.

9. Interview with Rick Duffy.

10. Interviews with William Muno and Rick Duffy.

11. Interviews with Jonathan Cannon, Edward Reich, Steven Leifer, Elaine Stanley, Eric Olson, Julie Becker, Lawrence Kyte, Bert Frey, Scott Fulton, Anne Allen, Richard Hembra, William Muno, and Jacqueline Warren. See also Landy, Roberts, and Thomas, *The Environmental Protection Agency*, 9 ("Our interviews and observations of [EPA's] public officials have, for the most part, impressed us with their dedication to public service and their desire to do a superior job to the public's will"), and National Academy of Public Administration, *Steps toward a Stable Future: An Assessment of the Budget and Personnel Processes of the Environmental Protection Agency* (May 1984), 3 ("Since its creation and in part because of broad public support for its programs, EPA has attracted a bright, aggressive, talented and committed workforce, many of whose members are also intellectually and emotionally involved with the cause of environmental protection. . . . The strong overall commitment of EPA's career employees to its mission has been of critical importance to an agency whose members are intellectually and emotionally involved with the cause of environmental protection").

12. For sensible and balanced proposals to deal with these problems, see National Academy of Public Administration, *Steps toward a Stable Future*.

13. As noted previously, these techniques were employed with relatively sanguine results in the early part of the Bush administration.

14. Notably, the National Aeronautics and Space Administration has only three positions that are filled by presidential appointees. The Federal Aviation Administration has two. National Academy of Public Administration, *Steps toward a Stable Future*, 4.

15. Interview with Erik Olson. The paucity of systematic attention paid by national environmental organizations to EPA enforcement work was confirmed in in-person and telephone interviews with other present and former environmentalist lawyers, including David Lennett, Jacqueline Warren, Jane Bloom, and James Simon.

16. Telephone interviews with David Lennett and James Simon.

17. Interview with Jacqueline Warren.

18. Interview with Erik Olson.

19. As noted earlier, several environmental organizations did precisely that in preparing an evaluation of EPA's remedy selection process in the Superfund program. Similar efforts would be useful in other areas.

20. Senate Committee on Appropriations, *Hearings on Departments of Veterans Affairs and Housing and Urban Development and Independent Agencies: Appropriations for Fiscal Year 1992*, 1991, Senate Hearing 102-113, pt. 3. Neither of the two environmental organization representatives who testified made any mention of the enforcement aspects of EPA's budget. The fact that most major environmental organizations do not devote many resources to EPA budget issues was noted in telephone and in-person interviews with James Simon, David Lennett, and Jane Bloom.

21. Telephone interviews with David Lennett and James Simon.

22. Telephone interview with David Lennett. As Lennett described it: "Appropriations committees march to different drummers."

9. Epilogue

1. I suspect that this epilogue is therefore less comprehensive than my analysis of EPA's earlier enforcement history, although not less accurate.

2. "Browner Portrayed as Hard-Working, Results-Oriented," *BNA Environment Reporter*, December 18, 1992, 2086.

3. "White House Nominations for Some EPA Posts Draw Varied Reactions," *Inside EPA*, March 5, 1993, 11.

4. "EPA Deputy Administrator Nominee Receives Broad Support," *Inside EPA*, September 30, 1994, 4.

5. Ibid.

6. "White House Nominations," 12.

7. "Browner Splits Enforcement Office by Function and Sector," *Inside EPA*, October 15, 1993, 11, 12; "Compliance, Regulatory Offices Created under Reorganization of EPA Enforcement," *BNA Environment Reporter*, October 15, 1993, 1137.

8. "Browner Calls for Limited Enforcement Reorganization in Regions," *Inside EPA*, June 24, 1994, 1, 10.

9. "Several EPA Regions Likely to Consolidate Enforcement Offices," *Inside EPA*, September 23, 1994, 2, 3; "Two EPA Regional Offices Plan Major Restructuring of Operations," *Inside EPA*, October 14, 1994, 1, 13, 14.

10. "Maximum Fines Sought in 24 Cases under RCRA, EPCRA, Water Act, Air Act, Agency Announces," *BNA Environment Reporter*, July 23,

1993, 508; "Enforcement Office Asks Regions to Set New Goals in Array of Areas," *Inside EPA*, September 30, 1994, 1, 6.

11. "Illegal Operators Enforcement Initiative Involves 32 Civil, 11 Criminal Cases under RCRA," *BNA Environment Reporter*, July 9, 1993, 412; "Enforcement Action Promised by Agency against Users of Ozone-Depleting Substances," *BNA Environment Reporter*, October 28, 1994, 1274; "EPA Enforcement of Sewer Leaks May Lead to Major New Industry Costs," *Inside EPA*, October 21, 1994, 1, 10; "10 Hazardous Waste Burners Targeted in Second Cluster Enforcement Action," *BNA Environment Reporter*, March 4, 1994, 1885, 1886.

12. "Move toward Supplemental Projects Envisioned While Multimedia Enforcement Expands, EPA Says," *BNA Environment Reporter*, March 4, 1994, 1896; "Updated Enforcement Policy Would Mean Wider Use of Supplemental Projects, EPA Says," *BNA Environment Reporter*, October 21, 1994, 1220, 1221.

13. "EPA Drafts Plan for Boosting Ecosystem Focus in Enforcement," *Inside EPA*, December 2, 1994, 5; "Region I Sets Environmental Justice Plan; More Inspections Eyed in Low Income Areas," *BNA Environment Reporter*, May 13, 1994, 62. The latter initiative was actually begun at the end of the Bush administration, after a well-publicized study in the *National Law Journal* concluded that penalties for violating environmental laws were lower in minority communities and that Superfund site cleanups proceeded more slowly in those areas. "Study Indicating EPA Discrimination Came As Surprise, Agency Official Says," *BNA Environment Reporter*, September 25, 1992, 1475.

14. "EPA Plans New Measures of Enforcement Success to Begin in FY95," *Inside EPA*, September 9, 1994, 1, 6, 7; "EPA Plans Test Run of New Enforcement Success Measures," *Inside EPA*, December 2, 1994, 14. For information regarding some further trends and developments in EPA enforcement during the first half of the Clinton administration, see "Guidance Soon As Help for Agency in Deciding on Criminal Investigations," *BNA Environment Reporter*, January 21, 1994, 1644; "EPA Enforcement Office Weights No-Penalty Compliance Inspections," *Inside EPA*, April 22, 1994, 1; "More Use of 'Compliance Assistance' Planned by Enforcement Office, EPA Says," *BNA Environment Reporter*, April 22, 1994, 2194; "Comprehensive Program Being Developed to Assist Industry in Compliance, EPA Says," *BNA Environment Reporter*, May 6, 1994, 13; "EPA to Revamp Hazardous Waste Enforcement Guidelines for Regions," *Inside EPA*, November 11, 1994, 3.

15. "Criminal Cases, Fine Collections Rise in 1993, EPA Says in Report on Enforcement," *BNA Environment Reporter*, December 17, 1993, 1516, 1517; "Greater Use of Administrative Authority Documented in Enforcement Report for 1993," *BNA Environment Reporter*, August 5, 1994, 624.

16. "New Records for Actions, Fines Set by EPA despite Restructuring of Program," *BNA Environment Reporter*, December 2, 1994, 1501. In fiscal year 1994 EPA initiated a total of 2,249 enforcement actions to redress violations of environmental laws. It collected $165.2 million in penalties, in-

cluding $128.4 million in civil penalties and $36.8 million in criminal fines (ibid.).

17. See "Transition to Clinton Administration Raises Expectations As Environmental Professionals Assume Policy Responsibility," *BNA Environment Reporter*, January 22, 1993, 2514.

18. "General Policy: Future of EPA Cabinet Bill Uncertain Following House Vote on Amendment Rule," *BNA Environment Reporter*, February 4, 1994, 1719; John H. Cushman Jr., "EPA Critics Get Boost in Congress," *New York Times*, February 7, 1994, A1.

19. For a thoughtful, well-written analysis of the 103rd Congress's deliberations regarding Superfund, see Rena I. Steinzor, "The Reauthorization of Superfund: Can the Deal of the Century Be Saved?," *Environmental Law Reporter* 25 (January 1995): 10,016.

20. See *Summary Report on the Department of Justice Undercutting the Environmental Protection Agency's Criminal Enforcement Program*, 102nd Cong., 2nd sess., September 9, 1992; Subcommittee on Investigations and Oversight of the House Committee on Science, Space and Technology, *Report on the Prosecution of Environmental Crimes at the Department of Energy's Rocky Flats Facility*, 102nd Cong., 2nd sess., 1993; and Environmental Crimes Project, National Law Center of George Washington University, *Preliminary Report on Criminal Environmental Prosecution by the U.S. Department of Justice* (1992). This castigation of DOJ criminal enforcement was highly controversial. "Congressional Adjournment Will Not End Investigation of DOJ Record, Staffers Say," *BNA Environment Reporter*, October 16, 1992, 1588; "DOJ Attacks Project's Critical Report Alleging 'Improprieties' by Law School," *BNA Environment Reporter*, January 22, 1993, 2496; "Bar Association Proposes Block on Oversight of DOJ Environmental Cases," *Inside EPA*, July 15, 1994, 6. For a detailed criticism of the methodology employed by DOJ's congressional and academic critics, see William T. Hassler, "Congressional Oversight of Federal Environmental Prosecutions: The Trashing of Environmental Crimes," *Environmental Law Reporter* 24 (February 1994): 10,074.

21. "Special Report: The President's 1994 Budget Request for EPA," *Inside EPA*, April 9, 1993, 1. Congress ultimately decided to cut the agency's budget by $300 million. "Senate Passes $6.7 Billion EPA Budget, Extends Funding for White House Council," *BNA Environment Reporter*, September 24, 1993, 899.

22. "Special Report: The President's 1995 Budget Request for EPA," *Inside EPA*, February 7, 1994, 1; "Clinton Proposes 8% Hike for Agency, Shift of Superfund Contractors to Agency," *BNA Environment Reporter*, February 11, 1994, 1747; "Big Boost in Water Funds Leads to Senate Funding Increase for EPA," *Inside EPA*, July 22, 1994, 8.

23. Specifically, the contract proposes a Job Creation and Wage Enhancement Act, which, among other things, grants individuals being inspected or investigated by a federal agency the right to remain silent, refuse a warrantless search, be warned that statements may be used against them, have an attorney or accountant present, be present at the time of the agency inspec-

tion or investigation, and be reimbursed for "unreasonable damages." The proposed legislation also permits individuals to take legal action against a federal agency which has threatened them with a "prohibited regulatory practice," which is defined as "an inconsistent application of any law, rule or regulation causing mismanagement of agency resources by any agency or employee of the agency." *Contract with America* (Times Books, 1994), 134.

24. It might be argued that some proposals contained in the House Republican Contract with America would have such an impact. See e.g. those aspects of the Job Creation and Wage Enhancement Act that would require risk assessment and cost-benefit analysis, a "regulatory budget," paperwork reduction, regulatory flexibility, regulatory impact analysis, and compensation for owners of private property which is subject to regulation. Ibid., 24–25, 131–135. However, because earlier chapters of this book have focused on the enforcement aspects of EPA's work (rather than the agency's rule-making activities) and since the precise provisions of House and Senate Republican proposals in this area may very well change in the months ahead, I will not attempt to analyze the legislative proposals in this epilogue.

25. A poll conducted in summer 1992 by the Wirthlin Group found that the public favored environmental protection by a 2 to 1 margin if asked to choose between economic growth and a clean environment. Moreover, 80 percent of those questioned agreed with the notion that "protecting the environment is so important that requirements and standards cannot be made too high, and continuing environmental improvement must be made regardless of cost." See "Poll Shows Four out of Five Americans Support the Environment, Even over Economy," *BNA Environment Reporter*, August 7, 1992, 1155. Similarly, a poll conducted by the Roper Organization, during approximately the same time period, found that 63 percent of the 1,200 individuals polled felt that environmental laws and regulations have not gone far enough, and 64 percent of those surveyed would choose environmental protection over economic development if they had to choose between the two. Brad Knickerbocker, "Voters Rank Importance of Environment," *Christian Science Monitor*, October 1, 1992, 10.

Index